THE SMILE REVOLUTION IN
EIGHTEENTH CENTURY PARIS

THE SMILE
REVOLUTION
IN
EIGHTEENTH
CENTURY PARIS

COLIN JONES

OXFORD
UNIVERSITY PRESS

OXFORD
UNIVERSITY PRESS

Great Clarendon Street, Oxford, OX2 6DP,
United Kingdom

Oxford University Press is a department of the University of Oxford.
It furthers the University's objective of excellence in research, scholarship,
and education by publishing worldwide. Oxford is a registered trade mark of
Oxford University Press in the UK and in certain other countries

Published in the United States of America by Oxford University Press
198 Madison Avenue, New York, NY 10016, United States of America

British Library Cataloguing in Publication Data
Data available

Library of Congress Control Number: 2013957963

ISBN 978–0–19–871581–8

Printed in Great Britain by
Clays Ltd, St Ives plc

Links to third party websites are provided by Oxford in good faith and
for information only. Oxford disclaims any responsibility for the materials
contained in any third party website referenced in this work.

For Alec, Ethan, Jonah, Milo, Greta, and Rosa.
You make me smile.

Acknowledgements

I have been working on this topic for some years, and sometimes had the impression that the book at the end of the project was like the smile of Lewis Carroll's famous Cheshire cat, endlessly receding in and out of focus at the end of the trail. The advantage of working on such a topic over a lengthy period, however, is that I have constantly been able to add anecdotes, stories, and perspectives along the way, as relevant references cropped up in dispersed and often unlikely sources. Audiences at lectures, seminars, and around many dinner-tables and in numerous cafés and bars have invariably been drawn into the intrinsic interest of the topic and I thank them warmly for their numerous, fertile, and helpful suggestions. (Occasionally in return I have learnt more about a listener's dental problems than I would strictly have liked to hear—this is one of the oddities and indeed the charms of my subject.) As well as the assistance of friends and colleagues I would like to acknowledge the unfailingly kind and helpful staff of numerous archives, libraries, museums, and galleries consulted. So numerous have the individuals been who have helped in some way that I am simply unable to list them all. Let this be a token of thanks to those not mentioned here: I hope they realize how grateful I am.

The idea behind the book sprang out of an exchange with Richard Wrigley, who told me about the painted smile of Madame Vigée Le Brun just as I had been working on Parisian tooth-pullers. I immediately glimpsed the makings of a topic. I thank Richard warmly for his inspiration and his continued encouragement over the years. In the two universities which have employed me while I researched this topic I was fortunate to enjoy the company of scholars who, quite possibly without realizing it, offered more intellectual stimulation, inspiration, and camaraderie than any academic has a right to expect. In particular I thank Maxine Berg, Margot Finn, Sarah Hodges, Gwynne Lewis, Roger Magraw, Hilary Marland, Carolyn Steedman, Claudia Stein, Mathew Thomson, and Stephane Van Damme from Warwick University days; and at Queen Mary University of London,

Richard Bourke, Thomas Dixon, Rhodri Hayward, Julian Jackson, Miri Rubin, Quentin Skinner, Amanda Vickery, and the 'History of the Emotions' group. In Paris, Daniel Roche and Jean-Jacques Courtine have offered unfailing inspiration and support. I also wish to acknowledge the Leverhulme Trust for a research network grant to explore the history of physiognomy and facial expression. My fellow organizers on the project— Nadeije Laneyrie-Dagen, Lina Bolzoni, Thomas Kirchner and Martial Guedron—comprised a brilliant group within which to develop my ideas.

I am also particularly grateful to those friends and colleagues—Emma Barker, Thomas Dixon, Roger King, Melissa Percival, Richard Taws, Charles Walton—who kindly read an earlier version of the manuscript and offered insightful suggestions for improvements. So did my friend Michael Sonenscher: for the last forty years, I now realize, he has helped me with his advice whenever I needed a steadying intellectual hand. My debt to him is very great. I am also very fortunate in having the inimitable Felicity Bryan as my agent, and the help and encouragement that she and her team, particularly Michele Topham and Jackie Head, provide. I also thank the staff at Oxford University Press for their help throughout the publishing process and my copy-editor Jeremy Langworthy.

I am a mildly obsessive writer and rewriter. I am aware that, though since transformed, some of the ideas in the book overlap with earlier writings published elsewhere. These include 'French Dentists and English Teeth in the Long Eighteenth Century', in John Pickstone et al. (eds.), *Medicine, Madness and Social History: Essays in Memory of Roy Porter* (Basingstoke, 2007), pp. 73–89, 247–50; 'Bouche et dents dans l'*Encyclopédie*: une perspective sur l'anatomie et la chirurgie des Lumières', in R. Morrissey and P. Roger (eds.), *L'Encyclopédie: du réseau au livre et du livre au réseau* (Paris, 2001), pp. 73–91; 'Pulling Teeth in Eighteenth-century Paris', *Past and Present*, 166 (2000), pp. 100–45; and 'The King's Two Teeth', *History Workshop Journal*, 65 (2008), pp. 79–95. The topic is also touched on lightly in my Presidential Lectures for the Royal Historical Society, in particular 'French Crossings II: Laughing over Boundaries', *Transactions of the Royal Historical Society*, 21 (2011), pp. 3–38, and 'French Crossings III: The Smile of the Tiger', *Transactions of the Royal Historical Society*, 22 (2012), pp. 3–35.

Towards the end of completing the manuscript, I accepted a kind invitation from Simon Chaplin and Quentin Skinner to give a paper recapitulating some of my arguments as the Roy Porter Lecture at the Wellcome Library in London in 2012. I have always felt that the book would be written with the spirit of Roy Porter hovering over it and I am sad he is not around to read it.

Finally, my greatest debt is to my wife Josephine McDonagh for just about everything in the making of this book. She has been by my side or in my thoughts throughout the researching and writing. The book is dedicated with much love and indeed many smiles to our grandchildren.

Contents

List of Illustrations

Introduction

In the autumn of 1787, the celebrated painter Madame Élisabeth-Louise Vigée Le Brun displayed a self-portrait at the Paris Salon, the biennial art exhibition held in the Louvre which was renowned for setting the standards of Parisian and European taste. She portrayed herself dandling her daughter on her lap, and with her own mouth set into a pleasing smile, her lips parting to reveal white teeth (Fig. 0.1).

In our own day, a white-tooth smile like this is the most banal and unremarkable of social gestures. It stares out at us from our television screens and dominates advertising hoardings and campaign posters. Yet this smile from 1787 provoked a scandal. 'An affectation which artists, connoisseurs and people of good taste are unanimous in condemning', noted a journalist, 'and of which no example is found in Antiquity, is that in smiling Madame Vigée Le Brun shows her teeth.' Her evidently surprising smile, which was held to mock civilized conventions dating back to ancient times, seemed in its way quite as revolutionary as the political events which soon, in 1789, became the first modern-day revolution.

The Vigée Le Brun smile was part of a larger Smile Revolution occurring in eighteenth-century Paris which is the subject of this book, and which overlapped in important ways with the great 1789 French Revolution. It took the form of a radical transformation in the cultural significance of the smile. The 1787 painted smile was merely the tip of a very sizeable and well-formed iceberg that already extended into literature and the arts and a wide range of other cultural domains. It had assumed added significance in social and political life as well, and, as we shall see, had come to constitute an overt critique of the *Ancien Régime* monarchy and aristocracy.

The white-tooth smile would have been unthinkable without major new developments taking place at the same time in dentistry, surgery, and medicine. Late eighteenth-century Parisian dentistry was the envy of the

Fig. 0.1 Madame Vigée Le Brun, *Self-portrait* (1786)

world. The city had generated new ways of thinking about teeth, and new ways of presenting them to the world. This shift in social practices and in sensibilities involved the emergence of the perception, common in our own day, that the smile offered a key to individual identity. In late eighteenth-century Paris, the smile came to be viewed as symbol of an individual's innermost and most authentic self. In a way that was perceived as both novel and modern, it was held to reveal the character of the person within.

But can the smile be said even to have a history, let alone a revolution? It is a valid question, and the smile is certainly not the easiest or most straightforward of historical subjects. The list of books devoted to its history is extremely short. What has been written is either very general or highly specific, often boiling down to the analysis of one particular smile (the *Mona Lisa* smile, in particular). *The Smile Revolution in Eighteenth Century Paris* differs in its approach. Here, the aim is to view the smile as a cultural product of a particular time and place, namely, eighteenth-century Paris, and to explore it in diverse social, economic, political, cultural, and medical contexts.

The smile is also a problematic topic in that there is no self-evident and universally accepted way of delimiting it from the laugh. A very high proportion of historical and scientific literature tends to view the laugh as a more accentuated smile and even to conflate the two gestures. The French word for laugh is *rire* or *ris*, while the smile is a *sourire* or *souris*. The latter terms come from '*sous-rire*', indicating 'sub-laugh' or 'little laugh'. This blurring of the two categories was very evident in the eighteenth century. The great *Encyclopédie*, the Bible of the French Enlightenment, in 1771 defined '*ris*' as 'a slight laugh in which the corners of the mouth move apart without the lips opening'. The description seems better to fit a smile than a laugh in fact. There was, as we shall see, a growing sense of differentiation between the two in this period.

The smile is also a difficult subject to grasp in that, as we all know from personal experience, it is invariably transient, slippery, and short-lived. It is and seemingly always has been notoriously difficult to hold: smirking, simpering, laughing, grimacing, and awkward facial rictus are just a split second away. Where smiles occur in literary sources, moreover, they are invariably not described attentively, often not at all, and frequently in a rather clichéd fashion. It is as if it is not worth taking time to define, portray, or describe a smile in any detail, since everyone recognizes when they see one. Visual images of the smile are problematic and unreliable too. The technical difficulty of successfully capturing a sitter's smile deterred artists from the Renaissance onwards from seeking to try. Even where they did try, moreover, doubt remained about a portrait's truthfulness to life, especially as all sorts of other cultural factors complicated the issue. There was a spirited and long-running artistic debate, for example, over whether the best portrait was the most life-like or else the one that best captured the idealized likeness or underlying character of the sitter. Very rarely did the case for truth-to-life and warts and all (including smiles) carry the day.

As the psychologist Paul Ekman has shown in our own day, the smile is the easiest facial expression for fellow-humans to recognize. (It shares this quality with surprise.) It requires a shorter glance than other expressions to register its existence. And, more than is the case with the other expressions, a smile can be regularly and easily identified at 100 yards' remove (though admittedly it can be confused with weeping). In terms of facial physiology, moreover, the smile is very simple and straightforward. Only one muscle—the zygomatic major on the cheek which raises the corner of the mouth—is needed to produce the smiling effect. It seems that when this combines with movement of the orbicularis oculi muscle around the eye the cheeks rise and wrinkles form round the eyes, giving a highly positive, joyful, and sincere effect.

This 'sincere', 'true', and 'felt' smile is often now called the 'Duchenne smile'. This is in homage to the mid nineteenth-century French experimental physiologist Guillaume Duchenne de Boulogne who first localized the muscular reactions involved. He did this by attaching electrodes to different parts of the face of a man suffering a disease which made his face insensible to feeling (Fig. 0.2). When electricity was passed through them it triggered a range of facial expressions which Duchenne analysed in terms of both the set of muscles involved and also the emotions associated with them. He photographed his results. Many of these images are included in his research monograph on facial physiology, *Le Mécanisme de la physiologie humaine* (1862), which established the enormous potential of this new visual technology for medicine. Duchenne realized that the smile may become much more complex and expansive, and can involve up to around a score of muscles. But in essence, the fact remains that a sincere, joyful 'Duchenne smile' only requires the involvement of two muscles maximum. All other expressions of emotions (those associated with fear, anger, distress, and so on) need between three and five.

Present-day studies of smiling and laughing in early infant development highlight the overlap between them. The muscles to make a smile and a laugh assemble in the womb, and are ready for action at birth. Some sources claim that babies can smile hours after delivery; more usually they do so after three or four weeks. Laughter follows, usually at between four and six months, by which time babies are often becoming discriminating in their

Fig. 0.2 'Natural laughter', from Duchenne de Boulogne, *Mécanisme de la physiognomie humaine* (1862)

smiles, reserving them for carers. Although a baby's smile and laugh are identical in terms of the facial muscles used, the laugh often involves noise, greater facial distortion, altered breathing patterns, and bodily agitation. The same is usually held to be true of adult laughs and smiles too. The beaming Duchenne smile can involve a good deal of action outside the face. Spontaneous laughter is often a major face-and-body event.

The joyful, instinctive and acoustic aspects of human baby smiling and laughter appear to link these gestures to the play-face of a number of great apes, including chimpanzees, particularly when they are expressing pleasure in being tickled. Charles Darwin noted this convergence in his pioneering work on *The Expression of the Emotions in Man and Animals* in 1872, thereby overturning a Western belief, held to have derived from Aristotle and reaffirmed in the Renaissance by Rabelais, that smiling and laughing were what distinguished humans from animals. After studying his and others' pets (and also Duchenne's photographs), Darwin concluded that dogs could smile. He also provided an image to show a great ape smile

136   SPECIAL EXPRESSIONS: CHAP. V.

Fig. 16. *Cynopithecus niger*, in a placid condition. Drawn from life by Mr. Wolf.

Fig. 17. The same, when pleased by being caressed.

Fig. 0.3 Charles Darwin, 'Smiling ape', from *The Expression of the Emotions in Man and Animals* (1872)

(Fig. 0.3). (The latter image, with its clumsily conspicuous retouching, must stand as one of the least convincing illustrations ever displayed in a revered scientific text.)

On the basis of this kind of inferential evidence, evolutionary scientists predicate a common point of origin for laughter in a prehuman ape species dating back at least 6 million years. Yet understanding the origins of smiles and laughs (as well as their original meanings) is not easy. Some scientists maintain that human laughter and the 'Duchenne smile' relate, not to the apes' play-face, but rather to their baring of the teeth to denote aggression.

It is also possible that this negative, joyless, malign smile (on which Darwin also commented) is a later evolutionary development. Certainly the lack of instinctiveness and spontaneity in a 'non-Duchenne', aggressive smile suggests a form of competence involving greater and more sophisticated mental cognitive functioning. So it could well (but need not) have post-dated the play-face from which the 'Duchenne smile' emerged.

On the basis of this inevitably blurry evolutionary story, we can conclude that smiling and laughing are deeply ingrained forms of human communication that predated the acquisition of language. But it cannot be established whether the story demonstrates that humans are fundamentally aggressive or else essentially benign. What further complicates the issue is the extraordinarily wide range of emotions with which smiles and laughs are associated (and presumably have been for millions of years). Evolutionary, psychological, and social scientists have indicated the presence of smiling and laughing in association with just about every emotion between the two benign ('play-face') and malign ('teeth-baring') poles. This is a characteristic that they share with no other facial expression (apart arguably from weeping). Paul Ekman, for example, has patiently established a smile taxonomy that extends to scores of what he acknowledges must be an even larger list of smiles. The range covers sensory pleasure and delight, cheerfulness, amusement, contentment and satisfaction, affection, flirtatiousness, relief from pain or pressure, embarrassment, sadness, nervousness, shame, superiority, aggression, fear, contempt, and much besides. The smile may thus well be, for Ekman, 'the most underrated facial expression'. It is certainly one of the most versatile and the most widely used.

The extremely wide range of emotions to which smiling and laughing relate is reflected in the many functions that smiling and laughing perform in social situations. On the more negative, malign side, smiles and laughs may threaten and deliver warnings, delineate the boundaries between insiders and outsiders to a group, and they may also serve as a defence mechanism. Working from the other, benign end of the scale, smiles promote socialization, lubricate social interaction, curtail negative emotions and stress, ease tensions, and coordinate group fellow-feeling. Smiling and laughing are thus particularly social, collective phenomena. The positive benefits they deliver are not only individual and subjective but also social and collective.

Furthermore, like some forms of laughter, the smile often sets up a kind of behavioural feedback loop. Even an artificial, 'non-Duchenne' smile may have a positive impact on the smiled-at. It appears to be rather difficult to greet a smile without smiling in return. The other's smile is mirrored back to the original smiler, who by the same token receives positive and confirmatory affect. The smile becomes contagious. This starts in the relationship between babies and their carers, and may continue throughout life.

This feedback loop shows that the smile and the laugh may function in a way that is similar to what the historian, William Reddy, has labelled 'emotives'. The idea behind the latter is derived from the philosopher J. L. Austin's theory of performative utterances, according to which certain spoken words do not simply describe or reflect reality ('the cat sat on the mat'), but may change that reality ('Sit on the mat!'). In a similar way, we could think of the smile as a non-verbal 'performative utterance'. It may enact, express, or reflect any number of underlying feelings. Given the existence of the smiling feedback circuit, it also has the potential to change the mood of a social encounter. The cliché 'smile and the world smiles with you' thus seems more than a weak commonplace from the world of Hollywood-style motivational pop psychology and management sales-speak. It can be extended to the whole of the human past, dating back to before the advent of language.

The belief of evolutionary psychologists that smiling and laughing are hard-wired into the human brain is understandable. After all, as we have suggested, laughter may date back as much as 6 million years. However, there is also more than enough evidence to indicate that many of the limitless forms that the smile takes are learned rather than biologically determined behaviour. With the smile, we can never rule out social and cultural influence. In this respect, the gesture is rather like the wink, as discussed by the American anthropologist Clifford Geertz. Purely in terms of the facial action involved, the wink is indistinguishable from the blink, an involuntary twitch reaction that is completely physiological in character. But in a given social encounter, a wink has meaning, and that meaning relates to the intentions of the winker, the complicity or collusion of the winked at, and the cultural messages that are encoded in winks in the wider society. A simply physiological explanation, in other words, risks missing the point completely. As Geertz points out, one needs to enter into and to understand the cultural context in which the wink took place.

By the same logic, we can only comprehend the growing prevalence of the smile in eighteenth-century French culture by scrutinizing the broader context in which it was performed or represented. Biology can only take us part of the way. At some point, body and mind, instinct and learned response blur. I may be hard-wired to smile, but when confronted by a camera and asked to pose, setting my mouth in a cheesy grin owes less to biology than to the cultural norms of our own society. A history of the smile is thus about a lot more than biological hardwiring. And this is where historians can make a contribution. For time, context, and meaning are entities in which we deal.

The Smile Revolution in Eighteenth Century Paris will show that the form and the meaning of the smile changed in the eighteenth-century city in ways that can be understood historically and that illuminate many aspects of the social, political, and cultural history of the period. At the start of the century, a particular facial regime held sway, which interpreted smiles as hierarchical, disdainful, and sometimes aggressive. Of course peoples smiled other types of smiles as well. Given the polyvalence and multifunctionality of the smile that we have noted, we would be unwise to assume anything else. (And indeed common sense tells us that lovers have always smiled, and poets celebrated the fact.) Yet *c*.1700 a snooty, aggressive, closed-mouth smile was the norm in French public life, meaning that there were cultural as well as biological constraints on smiling in other ways. Towards the end of the eighteenth century, however, this kind of facial regime was in retreat before another, which featured as its leading feature the open-mouth, white-tooth smile with which Madame Vigée Le Brun caused such a fuss in 1787. This had been developing over the course of the century not only in painting but also in a wide gamut of social and cultural contexts. A new and more recognizably modern kind of smile was on the horizon of public life. A Smile Revolution was in the offing.

In some ways, the existence of the Smile Revolution at this time was counterintuitive, for the teeth of the inhabitants of major European cities were particularly bad in the late eighteenth century. Sugar harvested from the wider world had become a staple of elite diet in the course of the sixteenth and seventeenth centuries. The eighteenth century saw its entry into the diet of the popular classes, particularly in the cities. It took the form of sugared foodstuffs, chocolate, tea, coffee, lemonade, and so on. Archaeological evidence derived from urban cemeteries suggests that teeth had rarely or indeed ever been worse in the whole prior history of humanity. This makes unravelling the mystery of the emergence of the white-tooth smile in this period all the more intriguing.

As we shall see in Chapter 1, care of the mouth was not high on the agenda in an 'Old Regime of Teeth' adjusting to the mass advent of sugar, while care offered by the medical community was pitifully meagre. The ghastly dental trials of Louis XIV showed that a king of France was well nigh as medically unprotected against tooth loss and mouth disease as the poorest of his subjects. Yet if the closed mouth thus had something to do with bad teeth, it also was linked to broader cultural values. Conduct books drawing on the counsels of Antiquity and replicating advice on civility from the Renaissance onwards had established the firmly shut mouth as the default model for anyone with pretensions to gentility. Cultural disapproval of open lips was based on the feeling that the gaping and toothless or gap-filled mouth was ugly and indecorous and indeed often quite disgusting. It was not good form to open the mouth.

This facial regime in public life altered over the course of the eighteenth century in a way that allowed and encouraged the display of an open-mouth and charming Vigée Le Brun smile, even several generations before her self-portrait was exhibited. Particularly significant in this respect, as I shall show in Chapter 2, were changing conceptions of the emotions and associated developments regarding the expression of feeling. The rise of the cult of sensibility, at first evident at the theatre, then powerfully relayed by the novel and subsequently in painting, led to a complete re-evaluation of what was deemed appropriate facial behaviour. The fixed and immobile visage still favoured in the royal court at Versailles began to crack under emotional pressure. Crying, laughing, and smiling now became acceptable public gestures among the Parisian elite and middling classes, who seemed to have been infected by the emotionality of imaginative literature. This kind of benign behaviour was often judged to be an instinctive response to inequities of the human condition. It also appeared emblematic of a person's essential humanity and identity. The Enlightenment, the cultural and intel-lectual movement aimed at individual and collective social improvement, gave its imprimatur to these enhanced levels of emotion. Furthermore, the social infrastructure of Enlightenment Paris—salons, coffee-houses, prom-enades, and the like—provided an accommodating framework for face-to-face encounters in which a smiling demeanour prevailed. The smile could thus operate, in ways we have described, as an emotive, triggering, smiling contagion.

If the emergence of the cult of sensibility in Enlightenment Paris was crucial to changes in the facial regime, so too was the rise of what was effectively modern dentistry, which I shall consider in Chapter 3. Where tooth care was as minimal and sketchy as it was in the Old Regime of Teeth, mouth disease and toothache were never far away, and the standard response to them was the extraction of guilty teeth, often by colourful tooth-pulling itinerant charlatans. In eighteenth-century Paris, in contrast, and really for the first time in the history of the West, the tooth-puller of yore was replaced by a professionalized grouping which came to offer a range of mouth-care services oriented around the preservation rather than the removal of teeth. The pioneer and model here was the practitioner Pierre Fauchard, a key player in our story. His *Le Chirurgien-Dentiste* (1728) coined the term *dentiste* and effectively founded dentistry as a branch of scientific surgery. This meant that at least those Parisians who could afford the services of Fauchard and his like could live without the social embarrassment deriving from deficient teeth, bad breath and, *in extremis*, a ghastly black hole. They could open their lips, display the teeth, and smile to an approving world.

In Chapter 4, I shall go on to show how the new science of dental surgery and this new vocation of dentistry established themselves within the city from the middle decades of the century onwards. Using the rhetoric of Enlightenment improvement, and displaying an impressive range of entrepreneurial skills, dentists established a comfortable niche for themselves within the professional landscape, under the aegis of Paris's powerful group of surgeons. They responded to but also helped to expand the demand for good, healthy white teeth and cared-for mouths. Such issues were at a premium in elite social life within Paris, which was increasingly in thrall to the dictates of fashionable appearance. The glittering prestige that Enlightenment Paris enjoyed throughout Europe meant that the city's dentists also started to enjoy international acclaim.

Significantly, the new smile seemed more beautiful, more natural, and more virtuous than anything that the royal court had to offer. At least in the city, if not at the royal court, it eclipsed the long-established tight-lipped smile which insinuated social hierarchy and moral worth. Throughout the century, the royal court stuck rigidly by the stern ceremonial rituals of Louis XIV, including the tradition of facial immobility. The monarchy thereby cut itself off from cultural norms that it formerly had dictated. The Parisian public sphere bade to overtake the Versailles court as the legitimate arbitrator of social value—a development with potential political consequences.

By the eve of the political revolution of 1789, the seal seemed to be set on the displacement of the Versailles mask of fixity by the Parisian smile of sensibility. As we have seen, the exhibition of the Vigée Le Brun portrait in

1787 marked the apotheosis of the new smile. In the same year, moreover, the Parisian dentist Nicolas Dubois de Chémant invented porcelain white dentures. These permitted the triumphant white-toothed smile to be displayed even by the toothless. (This number included himself, in fact, and he wore his own dentures—but did not care to show them in his portrait (Fig. 0.4).) These developments, that I shall examine in Chapter 5, suggest that the city was on the brink of a Smile Revolution. The smiles and tears of joy that greeted the Parisian political revolution of 1789 appeared to be a ringing endorsement for the concomitant Smile Revolution.

Fig. 0.4 Nicolas Dubois de Chémant

Radical transformation was not, however, to come to pass. The Smile Revolution was to prove as slippery and transient as the smile itself. Despite these promising beginnings, post-1789 revolutionary political culture would in the event reject the emergent white-tooth smile just as radically as it had rejected the disdainful fixity of the Versailles facial regime. Political passions were soon so strong that smiles seemed too anodyne to have any purchase, especially with the advent of the Terror (1792–4). The political mood was not right for smiling. Full-throated mocking and aggressive laughter characterized the political extremes, from aristocratic counter-revolutionaries through to *sans-culotte* popular radicals. People were well advised to keep their heads and smiles beneath the parapet and out of public view in a political landscape in which even the word 'moderation' became an object of suspicion. Moreover, revolutionary politicians tended to prefer to set their faces in the elevated mode of ancient stoicism that had been establishing itself in the previous decades, influenced by neo-classical tastes. Antagonism towards the smile in revolutionary culture was further exacerbated by the smile of resistance with which many of the opponents of the regime went to the guillotine during the Terror.

The open mouth that many would now come to associate with the Revolution was not the white-tooth smile; but rather the gaping, gothic mouth set in a scream of violence. Parisians were no longer viewed as the smiling avatars of social gaiety and human perfectibility. On the contrary, particularly outside France, popular political cartoonists like James Gillray portrayed Parisians as the savage, sharp-toothed, cannibalistic 'dangerous classes' who posed a perennial threat to civilized values (Fig. 0.5).

The Smile Revolution and the French Revolution of 1789 had initially seemed to be pointing in the same benign, civilized direction. But in the event, the course of politics had put paid to the possibility of a Smile Revolution along the lines that had been shaping up in the late 1780s. The end of the Terror softened the perception of the smile as a counter-revolutionary gesture, but it did not resurrect it as an approved cultural norm. Smiling had lost its contagious edge and its iconic status in public life. From the late 1790s, the influential physiognomic theories of Johann-Caspar Lavater downplayed the assumption that facial expression revealed character. So, from a different perspective, did the neo-classical dramatic firmness of feature endorsed in the Napoleonic era (1799–1815). Napoleon and his successors would feel more comfortable with Louis XIV's facial

Fig. 0.5 James Gillray, *Un petit souper à la parisienne* (1792)

immobility than with the world that Madame Vigée Le Brun had seemed to be opening up.

The transient Smile Revolution of late eighteenth-century had been a co-production. Cultural impulses associated with the taste for sensibility had worked in tandem with the emergence of scientific dentistry to produce real change. Yet, as we shall see in Chapter 6, from the 1790s onwards a further barrier was set against the re-emergence of the smile as a cultural norm by the collapse of professional dentistry in France. Revolutionary legislation ended the productive niche which dentists had occupied within the *Ancien Régime* medical system, and no proper training was established for a career in dental surgery. Dentists found themselves back in a situation where they were competing with the tooth-pulling charlatans of old. The Old Regime of Teeth would have a long afterlife in nineteenth- and twentieth-century France.

The Parisian Smile Revolution was thus to prove almost as evanescent as the smile itself. In a way, the smile went into hibernation as a public gesture for over a century. As we will see in the Postscript, it was only really in the twentieth century that it re-emerged, under the influence of a range of factors, including new, highly visual advertising practices, Hollywood media presentation, and the final re-emergence of decent, high-class dentistry. The twentieth century would experience its own Smile Revolution completely unaware of the eighteenth-century precursor. The subject of this book is that smile that we have lost.

I

The Old Regime of Teeth

Hyacinthe Rigaud's famous state portrait of Louis XIV in full regalia presents the king at the height of his powers, framed in an ostentatiously theatrical setting (Fig. 1.1). Painted in 1701 and displayed at the Paris

Fig. 1.1 Hyacinthe Rigaud, *Louis XIV* (1701)

Salon in 1704, the work dazzles the viewer with sumptuous ceremonial display. Crown, sceptre, great sword of state, and heavy, fleur-de-lys ermine robes evoke the putatively timeless nature of the French monarchy, then at the zenith of its power.

The king's posture is unfazed, mildly if swaggeringly disdainful. Strongly featured are his sculpted legs, which the court chronicler, the duc de Saint-Simon, a far from sycophantic observer of court society at Versailles, adjudged the finest he ever saw. They painstakingly replicate the pose which Louis, as a young man, had adopted when dancing as Apollo in court ballets as his own Premier Dancer. The king's lofty and impassive gaze, dictating reverential obeisance from the humble spectator, emerges from a body polished, primped, puffed up, and more than a little prettified for the occasion. Such a portrait had not been designed to be naturalistic but rather to improve on nature, which it did. The calf-muscles portrayed are scarcely those of a sixty-year-old. The red-heeled courtier shoes lift the ruler well above his unimpressive 5 foot 4 inches. The copious curls of a towering black wig obscure Louis's baldness. And the unruffled forehead suggests a ruler with scarcely a care in the world—even though when it was painted he was embarking on what would be his last, ruinous war, the War of Spanish Succession (1701–14). In this mythologizing, mendacious portrait, with its aspiration to erase the passage, even the existence, of time, one feature does, however, stand out for its realism: hollow cheeks and wrinkled mouth reveal a ruler with not a tooth in his head.

Louis XIV's non-smile

This shard of oral realism in Rigaud's painting surprises for its rarity value in portraits of the king, and indeed in paintings depicting other European rulers of the time, and we can only speculate why Rigaud should have chosen to represent the royal mouth in this way. We know that his royal subject did not disavow his toothlessness. Saint-Simon records that the king, chatting frankly with the octogenarian Cardinal d'Estrées in 1714, for example, 'complained of the inconvenience caused by no longer having any teeth'. 'Teeth, Sire?', replied the Cardinal, 'Ah! Who does have any?' Such a reply may have caused courtiers to snigger behind their hands, since, as Saint-Simon noted, 'what was striking in this response was the fact that at his age he [d'Estrées] had had fine white teeth'.

Empty mouths were a fact of adult life in Europe's Old Regime of Teeth, for the most powerful kings and the humblest of subjects alike. Tooth loss after a certain age was the norm. The process usually began before one's forties and proceeded at a steady, unrelenting pace towards complete toothlessness. 'Individuals who keep all their teeth healthy until an advanced age are extremely rare', concluded an expert source in the early eighteenth century. 'Some owe this advantage to a fortunate temperament, others to particular care. But the great majority of individuals have rotten teeth from the earliest age, and lose their teeth long before due time.' The situation was also sporadically worsened by the demographic crises and other disasters which struck early modern Europe. When combined with the interlocked impact of warfare and epidemics, harvest failures in the last two decades of Louis XIV's reign caused millions of deaths across France. In the appalling winter of 1693–4, for example, there were between 1,400 and 1,500 deaths a day in Paris, a city of half a million souls, while the years 1709–10 were if anything worse. Besides high mortality, these crises brought in their train severe under-nourishment and malnutrition for huge numbers, impacting damagingly on teeth and gums. This was probably most detrimental for small children: even in normal times, teething—and particularly the conse-quences of dehydration associated with teething fevers—were a significant cause of infant mortality. The fragility of the lives (and mouths) of the very young was even more pronounced when times were hard for all.

With teeth vanished good looks, posing a conundrum for portrait-paint-ers. Capacity for speech suffered too, for talking could transmute into an affair of grunts and whistles. Discomfort, inconvenience, problems with chewing food, chronic indigestion, and facial disfigurement caused by the bad state of the mouth were the substance of everyday middle-aged life. Lack of effective pain relief could drive a sane man mad, or straight into the hands of the tooth-puller. The surgeon Jacques Guillemeau noted in 1612 that 'often toothache is so bad that the suffering individual runs through the streets and seems to lose his reason. Reasoning that no remedy suffices to lessen the pain, he prefers to have the tooth pulled out.'

Against this stark background, a flashing smile became as out of the question for the humblest peasant or urban worker as for an absolute monarch. From highest to lowest, from prince to pauper, from château to cottage, Louis XIV and his subjects were collectively locked tight in an unforgiving Old Regime of Teeth. Louis XIV's rotten teeth, which even the glamour of his court regalia could not hide, highlight the nature and deficiencies of mouth care within his kingdom in general, and his capital city in particular.

Louis XIV's compressed, toothless, and unsmiling mouth was biology's revenge on a ruler who had always had himself portrayed in the accoutrements of timelessness. At one time, indeed, it had been his teeth which had marked him out to become 'Louis the Great'. Fortune-tellers and soothsayers had had a field day at his birth in 1638, for he was discovered to have two teeth already present in his mouth. This precocious dentition was thought to confirm the hand of God in a conception which had already been widely saluted as miraculous—the lateness of the pregnancy of his mother Anne of Austria (in her late thirties) had been a source of pan-European wonder. To the somewhat sadistic amusement of the royal court the two infant teeth wreaked havoc on a long line of wet-nurse nipples. To contemporaries, these prodigious, gluttonous, voracious teeth seemed to presage the wonders which an all-devouring prince, hungry for glory, would effect on the map of Europe in the fullness of time. At first, Louis lived up to the expectations of rapacity on the international stage, greatly expanding France's frontiers. Yet he bit off more than he could chew, and from the 1680s the victories started to dry up. It was with sarcasm rather than wonder, that Dutch anti-French pamphleteers would evoke the king's power during the War of Spanish Succession (1701–14). Louis the Great had transmuted into Louis the Toothless.

Long before they lost their metaphorical symbolism, Louis XIV's teeth lost their physical bite. In the late 1670s, the detailed health journals kept by royal physicians noted that 'the king's teeth are poor by nature'. The royal mouth, another witness observed, 'became toothless when nearly all [the king's] teeth fell out around his fortieth year'—thus maybe from the late 1670s. His mouth required increasing intervention.

It was not that Louis ever lacked for medical attention—unlike the vast majority of his subjects. Indeed, he had the best levels of dental care that any individual could possibly have had at this time. The royal household contained a subgrouping of medical practitioners, hand-picked for excellence. In 1649, there had been around forty such individuals—physicians, surgeons, apothecaries, and others—serving the king's health needs, under the king's Premier Physician (the *premier médecin du roi*). The size of this grouping more than doubled over the course of his reign, although its structure remained the same. The Premier Physician's duties covered surveillance of all aspects of the ruler's health and well-being. He was present, for example, at the formal ceremonies surrounding the king's waking and retiring (the *Lever* and the *Coucher*), and he inspected the royal body should the king not feel himself. He oversaw all aspects of the royal regimen, including advising the king on mouth-cleansing: washing the mouth out with water and rubbing the teeth and gums with a cloth was about as far as this went. At mealtimes, he ensured that the Master of the Goblet (*Chef du Gobelet*) tested the king's bread, salt, and wine—there were some, not unjustified, worries about court poisoning—and proffered to his ruler the regal knife, spoon, and toothpick. The latter was fashioned from a sprig of rosemary or some other aromatic plant. Were the king to have toothache, the Premier Physician summoned court apothecaries to supply remedies in order to keep pain at bay. Thyme and distilled cloves were particularly favoured, and might be washed down with honey.

We are dwelling on the dental history of Louis XIV, which is particularly well-documented, in order to give a sense of the very best that money could buy in terms of mouth care at the time—and to highlight its general inefficacity. Significantly, Premier Physicians and the royal medical household seem to have shrugged off tooth loss as an inescapable epiphenomenon of the ageing process that little concerned them. Their *Journal de santé du Roi* contained very precise details about the vast number of bloodlettings, purges, and enemas which physicians inflicted on the royal body, but surprisingly few references to the king's everyday tooth problems. Only major mouth problems stirred the doctors to rise above dull fatalism. Medical men offered little or nothing by way of prevention. Their view of tooth problems drew on the Galenic theory of the bodily humours, which downplayed local, mechanistic causation. Diseases of any kind arose when the body suffered an excess of the secretions of one of the vital organs, often the consequence of the body becoming overheated. It was one of Louis's courtiers—not his medical team—who saw the cause of Louis's bad teeth in 'the large quantity of confitures which he ate at the end of meals and in his snacks'. His physicians, in contrast, did not monitor his sugar intake. As good Galenists, they saw health in holistic terms and would not have given a moment's thought to the notion that ingesting a single, otherwise anodyne, food substance could cause severe tooth problems.

Largely disarmed in regard to prevention, physicians had next to nothing to offer in terms of hands-on treatment either. Since the Middle Ages, they had always shunned manual operations of any sort. University-educated, they regarded themselves as the eye and the brain of medical intervention, while the surgeon, operating under their strict instructions, provided the hand. For any problems which required manual expertise, the Premier Physician thus looked to the king's Premier Surgeon. Yet by the late seventeenth century, most elite surgeons were also tending to disdain manual operations upon the teeth. One reason for this, according to the royal surgeon Pierre Dionis, writing in 1708, was that the kind of intense wrist pressure needed to extract teeth risked upsetting a surgeon's subsequent capacity for delicate and speedy operational procedures. He also noted that the pulling of teeth was best left to inferiors, since it 'smacks of the charlatan and the mountebank'. Surgeons consequently tended to leave tooth care in the hands of the semi-artisanal grouping of tooth-pullers known as 'operators for the teeth', whose presence within the royal medical household was attested from 1649.

It was to one such rather lowly individual—the Parisian surgeon, Charles Dubois, 'operator for the king's teeth'—that Premier Physician Antoine Daquin turned in 1685 to pull out all the remaining teeth on the upper right side of Louis's jaw, an operation necessitated by the growing intolerability of the king's few remaining teeth. Unfortunately, the operator also accidentally took out much of the jaw itself. The consequent perforation of the king's palate left a gaping hole in his oral cavity. As a result, according to Daquin, 'every time that the king drank or gargled, the liquid came up through his nose, from where it issued forth like a fountain'. The fountains of the château of Versailles were becoming of course world-famous, but this was one fountain the king could do without, especially in his public displays of eating. Worryingly, moreover, the hole became nauseously infected. Realizing that there was simply no other way, Premier Surgeon Charles-François Félix, determined to undertake a full-blown operation on the royal mouth. In two fearful sessions, with Daquin looking anxiously on, Félix cauterized the king's palate, sealing it off from the maxillary sinus. The red-hot iron which the surgeon deployed—which will have caused Louis quite extraordinary levels of pain—managed to block up the hole, after an extensive period of healing. The fountain dried up: Louis could henceforth eat normally again.

The ageing mouth in Rigaud's 1701 swagger portrait was thus a site of royal heroism quite as impressive in its way as the king's experiences on the field of battle and a chastening reminder of biological destiny. 'Get on with it', the king had told his surgeons as they readied themselves for the blood-curdling operation, 'and don't treat me as a king; I want to be cured as though I were a peasant.' The phrase was a meaningful royal nod towards the classless nature of mouth problems in the Old Regime of Teeth. The gruesomeness of the case also underlines the limitations that the greatest monarch of his day had to accept in regard to matters of the mouth. We may salute Félix's cool and intrepid surgery (available only to very few). Yet equally we should not forget that it had been made necessary by the manifest incompetence of a hand-picked 'operator'.

One can thus understand why, outside the rarified atmosphere of the royal court and the court elite, individuals suffering toothache or serious mouth ailments would normally put up with pain until it went away or else became unbearable. It was not uncommon to pull out one's own teeth, especially if they had been loosened by old age or gum disease. Otherwise, individuals might find solace in prayer. The intercession of Saint Apollonia was particularly sought after: a third-century Christian martyr she had been tortured by having all her teeth pulled out prior to her death, so clearly was an appropriate cult figure. Otherwise, an individual in pain would seek out aid from family and neighbours, or else turn for advice to popular medical writings. These offered little succour. In 1582, in the earliest French surgical work specifically devoted to the teeth, Urbain Hémard recommended for toothache a mixture of chicken fat, hare's brain, and honey. The famous, much-published popular recipe book of Madame Fouquet, which had first appeared in 1673, recommended holding a hot shovel, for the time it took to recite two *Misereres*, as closely above the pate of the head as the victim could bear. Alternatively, it was held, the back leg of a toad, dried and crushed, should be placed next to the painful tooth. Where extraction was needed, and strong wrists might be required, village blacksmiths and neighbourhood barbers fitted the bill. But for more complicated matters, with trained physicians and surgeons increasingly uninterested in dental treatment, the field was clear for the emergence of more specialized tooth-pullers or tooth-drawers (*arracheurs de dents*), increasingly known as *opérateurs pour les dents* ('operators for the teeth'), who formed the core of what passed as specialized mouth care for the majority of the population.

In Paris, the professional street-cry of the often itinerant tooth-puller had long formed part of a distinctive soundscape made up of the *cris de Paris* (as they were called) of street-based salesmen, petty traders, and operators offering water, milk, fish, wood, chestnuts, flowers, brooms, pots and pans, and the like. An engraving from 1582 of one such tooth-puller (Fig. 1.2) was accompanied by the motto:

A tirer   la den

Quand ie tire à quelqu'vn la dent, & la douleur,
Il piffe en fa chemife & change de couleur:
Les plus mauuais ie fais tenir par trois ou quatre,
Car en leur faifant mal, ils me pourroient bien batre.   12.

Fig. 1.2 *Cris de Paris*; tooth-puller, 1582

When I pull out the pain and the tooth
A man changes colour and pisses his shirt
The worst need men to hold them down
And I risk being beaten, for doing them hurt.

Such figures also criss-crossed the French provinces, travelling from fair to fair, marketplace to urban street corner, practising their craft in a way that combined tooth-pulling heroics with theatrical representations of various kinds. Actor-charlatans composed a milieu well-known to the great sixteenth-century writer, François Rabelais. His Gargantua, for example, had been 'to see jugglers, mountebanks and quacksalvers, and . . . considered their miming, their shifts, their somersaults and smooth tongue'. The mouth, which was the centre of tooth-pulling charlatanism, was also in many senses a quintessentially Rabelaisian orifice. Like the anus, on which so much of Rabelais's humour focused, the aching, gormlessly gaping mouth was the source of intense pain as well as a trigger for spontaneous hilarity in everyone save the sufferer. In the world of Rabelais, pain in the mouth was as funny (and as malodorous) as pain in the arse—and indeed for comic purposes the two were often interchangeable.

The most colourful and striking of such tooth-pullers were the Italian troupes of players who spread throughout France from the Wars of Religion onwards. Although they themselves preferred to be known as *opérateurs pour les dents*, they were widely known as 'charlatans', a term that derived from the Italian, either from *circolare* ('to circulate, to wander about') or from *ciarlare* ('to chatter': a nice way of evoking their sales patter). They won a substantial popular following by infusing the age-old business of tooth-pulling with a new razzmatazz. One such individual was known for extracting a tooth with one hand while firing a pistol in the air with the other, and with his head in a sack. Others performed the act of extraction while seated on a horse: from the saddle, they placed the tip of a sword blade on the base of the throbbing tooth; a flick of the wrist was enough to achieve the desired result. The wonderment that such tooth-pulling stunts created was magnified by virtuosos passing them off as trade secrets.

It may indeed be more accurate to think of such tooth-pulling characters less as 'operators for the teeth' than as strolling *commedia dell'arte* players, who brought into France innovative theatrical repertoire and staging techniques, and did some tooth-pulling on the side. From makeshift trestle stages, such Italian players offered other forms of street-theatre too such as acrobatics, singing, tightrope walking, the display of exotic animals, and comedy routines. They were also famous for simultaneously retailing allegedly miraculous snake-bite remedies, such as theriac, mithridate, and, from the early seventeenth century, orviétan (named after Orvieto, its alleged birth-place). Their penchant for hyperbole, outrageous claims and tall tales ensured that the phrase 'to lie like a tooth-puller' passed uncontested into the French language.

As time went on, the medical landscape within Paris came to be increasingly strictly policed by the Paris Medical Faculty and especially, after 1667, by the Lieutenant-Général de Police, a powerful Crown appointee with wide-ranging powers over public order. Yet it was still possible throughout the seventeenth century for such actor/tooth-pullers to break into the Parisian market, licitly as well as illicitly. Under a convention whose origins were lodged in the misty past, any practitioner who served the reigning monarch had the right to practice in the capital city without needing to pass through the normal procedures of training and certification. This meant that physicians who had acquired an office as a *médecin du roi* (royal physician), for example, could avoid the lengthy and expensive training in the Medical Faculty which was the normal route into Parisian practice. Court surgeons (*chirurgiens du roi*) similarly side-stepped the requirements of Paris's surgical college. The same principle obtained for the numerous tradespeople known as *artisans suivant la cour* ('artisans following the court'). As their name suggests, in the past these artisans had followed the royal court in its bouts of itineracy around the provinces. The court was more sedentary in the seventeenth century, at first in Paris, and after 1683 in Versailles, and this changed the nature of their practice. *Artisans suivant la cour*, who collectively fell within the jurisdiction of a royal household officer, the *prévôt de l'hôtel du roi*, were initially based at court. But many also ran a shop within the capital, circumventing Parisian guild requirements and trading publicly 'by Royal Authority'. By the late seventeenth century, there were ninety-seven authorized trades, including a couple of 'operators', alongside glove-makers, vintners, wig-makers, and others of that ilk.

Another route open to 'operators for the teeth' wishing to practise in Paris was through a royal grant of the privilege of retailing approved medical treatments, again under the jurisdiction of the *prévôté de l'hôtel du roi*. Thus in 1678, the Montpellier apothecary Sébastien Matte La Faveur was given the right to sell and distribute throughout France his wound salve, or 'styptic water' (which could be used on the lips or inside the mouth). Towards the end of the seventeenth century, what had been an occasional practice developed into a complex system of regulation, particularly for the sale of the snake-bite remedy orviétan. The wonder-drug, whose exact composition was a jealously held trade secret, had arrived in Paris in the first decade of the seventeenth century in the hands of the once-itinerant Roman mountebank and tooth-puller, Hieronymus Ferranti. It was to retain its close association with tooth-pulling well into the nineteenth century. The theatricality of the tooth-pulling performances with which Ferranti accompanied his sales patter was the stuff of legend. In particular, he practised the seemingly miraculous feat of extracting the toughest molars with the sole use of thumb and fore-finger. The gesture was made all the more dramatic by his colourful costume and the violinists, veiled slave-girls and ancillary actors who accompanied him.

Ferranti set up his trestle stage in the courtyard of the law courts (the *Palais de Justice*) on the Île de la Cité. It was this general area, through to the Place Dauphine and on to the Pont-Neuf, that other such player/tooth-pullers frequented. Paris's 'new bridge', which had opened in 1606, was the first in the city's history to span from the Left to the Right Bank (taking in the tip of the Ile de la Cité), and the first major bridge not to be covered with houses. Open to the elements, it had a marketplace, piazza-style ambiance. The choice pitch for tooth-pullers was at the bridge's centre next to the famous equestrian statue of Henri IV, the *cheval de bronze* ('the bronze horse'). One late seventeenth-century visitor noted the presence of such figures among the colourful motley of street tradesmen, thieves, recruiting sergeants, old clothes merchants, street performers, and tricksters to be found on this 'rendezvous of charlatans':

> A host of people give out handbills. Some individuals are replacing lost teeth, others offer glass eyes, while others heal incurable ailments. One individual claims to have discovered the secret virtue of some powdered gem to whiten and beautify the face. Another will assure you that he rejuvenates the aged, while others will drive wrinkles away from your forehead and eyes, or else make you a wooden leg to repair the violence done by battlefield bombs.

A characteristic figure of this teeming street culture centred on the Pont-Neuf was Tabarin who, with his theatrical foil Mondor, dominated the bridge's tooth-pulling culture in the 1620s (Fig. 1.3). The medical services of the pair were accompanied by highly popular (and very crude) stand-up comedy dialogues of the Rabelaisian kind: why do dogs lift their legs in pissing; which was created first, man or beard; why do women have larger buttocks than men; which month is best for copulation; why does one fart while pissing; what is the difference between a nose and an arse? Tooth care was offered on the side, their publicity proclaiming:

> If your teeth are rotten
> Pomades take—and often.
> Rosemary and opium,
> Tabarin supplies of 'em.

A charlatan of much the same stripe as Hieronymus Ferranti and Tabarin was Christophe Contugi, a naturalized Roman, who married Ferranti's widow, inherited his troupe of players, and also acquired a royal franchise for the nationwide sale of orviétan. It was characteristic of such figures that they became subsumed within the wider Parisian culture, both elite and popular. Individuals from their troupes passed back and forth promiscuously between the Pont-Neuf and the more respectable theatre setting of the Hôtel de Bourgogne, where Molière had fallen in love with the stage. As with Rabelaisian laughter, which gloried in both 'high' scholastic wit and

Fig. 1.3 Tabarin and Mondor on stage, after early seventeenth-century engraving

'low' belly-laughs, Pont-Neuf humour could be enjoyed by the whole spectrum of urban society. The demotic street-corner patter of charlatans delighted passers-by of whatever rank, and some ended up in print, as was the case with Tabarin's ditties and dialogues. Charlatans became figures of literary and visual reference. Engravings of the bridge invariably highlighted the colourful activities of tooth-pulling showmen. Tabarin had numerous satires penned in his name, while Contugi was a character in one of Molière's plays. Barry, a later practitioner on the bridge, had a whole comedy written about him. Contugi and other Pont-Neuf operators also appeared as fictional commentators on current events in the 'Mazarinades', the polemical pamphlets of the civil wars known as the Fronde (1648–52). A fanciful poem-pamphlet describing a turbulent moment in August 1648, for example, evoked Carmelina, who throughout the 1640s and 1650s contested pride of place on the Pont-Neuf with Contugi. Sabre at his side, Carmelina was depicted presiding over the building of a huge barricade on the bridge using anything to hand, including medical chests, herniary trusses, suppositories, tooth-pulling instruments, false teeth, and ostrich eggs. The creation was topped with two stuffed crocodiles to repel all boarders ('True they were not alive but dead / Yet no one knew so no one said').

In the Old Regime of Teeth that we have described thus far, tooth loss and mouth pain were everyday realities, and, as we have seen, the level of medicalized mouth care was poor, and personal concern with mouth hygiene pretty primitive. There may have been some differences between rich and poor, but they hardly affected this general picture. By the same token, the appeal of Pont-Neuf charlatans was universal in tooth-pulling as in humour. Moreover, it is also worth noting that sugar had not yet entered the popular diet in any quantity, so that the poor may have been saved from saccharine-derived dental caries which did for Louis XIV's teeth and doubtless those of others in his court. Surgeon Bernardin Martin, writing in 1679, reckoned that for dietary reasons the state of a courtier's mouth was often far worse than that of a peasant. Yet there were other reasons than bad or missing teeth causing Louis XIV and his courtiers to keep their mouths shut as they smiled.

Smiles under strict control

Under the Old Regime of Teeth, the low level of oral health and hygiene across the social spectrum helped to determine the way in which the mouth and certain forms of mouth behaviour were regarded. The facial regime that held sway dictated that in public life smiles were rare and kept under control, so as to avoid the display of oral infirmities and deformities. As we have seen, Louis XIV kept his mouth shut for Rigaud's portrait partly at least because of his lack of teeth. Yet the closed, unsmiling royal mouth was a response to cultural as well as biological imperatives. Some of these related to artistic conventions about depicting the passions that we shall discuss in the following chapter. In addition, codes of courtly comportment emerging from the sixteenth century sought to moderate the uproarious mirth of the Rabelaisian tradition—and, in so doing, to close the gaping mouth. The most eloquent and influential text in this regard was Baldassare Castiglione's *Il Libro del cortegiano* ('The Book of the Courtier'), which took the form of gently jovial imagined conversations between courtiers. Published in 1528 at the behest of the French monarch, Francis I, and translated into French as *Le Livre du courtisan* in 1537, the work became the *vade mecum* of the denizens of Europe's courts for the next two centuries or more, and the ur-text of European manners.

The *Book of the Courtier* showed much concern with the mouth and its uses. A point of particular discussion was the laughing mouth. Castiglione categorically resisted jesting that was relentless, boorish, and unseemly. It was only the popular classes, he noted, who laughed 'after the fashion of fools, drunken men, the silly, the inept or buffoons', in those great, open-mouthed gusts of laughter that Rabelais had exemplified. Castiglione sought to set parameters around what was deemed laughable, to define the physical manner in which the courteous should actually laugh, and to identify the appropriate targets of laughter. If laughter was at the expense of others, it derived much of its convivial character from the fact that one laughed at life's follies in company with like-minded individuals, whose values one respected. However, mocking an out-group, it was held, should always be done with human decency, avoiding the impression of savaging like wild dogs. Rather, as one of Castiglione's disciples put it, such criticism should resemble the nibbling of a sheep.

The *Book of the Courtier* was a quintessential Renaissance humanist text. To a considerable extent, its injunctions on the laughing mouth revived and relayed the classical tradition regarding laughter, derived from Aristotle, Cicero, and Quintilian. Although some vestiges of medieval chivalry were also evident, little concerning humour and laughter in Castiglione's text could not be found in the second book of Cicero's rhetorical text, *De Oratore* (55 BCE). Aristotle had defined the comic as the perception of 'deformity without pain', and for Cicero, in essence, one laughed at individuals who were either indulging in ridiculous behaviour or else not observing norms of good decency. Such mocking laughter served the social function of reproving vice.

These perspectives on the causes, character, and consequences of laughter, endorsed by Castiglione, were elaborated in many contemporary philosophical, moral, and medical explorations of laughter in light of the classical heritage. It is important to note the assumption that runs through all these debates that the smile was essentially subsumed within the laugh. Commentators pointed out the etymology of '*sourire*' or '*souris*', the words used to denote a smile. They derived directly from 'sous-rire' or 'sous-ris' ('surrisus' or 'subrisus' in Latin ; 'sorisa' or 'soureír' in Spanish). Effectively, a smile was a 'sub-laugh'. Historically, the term 'ris' (little used in our own day) covered most of the ground from mild smile through to open-throated laughter. Conceptually, then, *sourire* signified a subset of the act of laughing (*rire*). Latin and French grammar endorsed the subordinate place of the smile in early modern culture.

The lesser status of the smile was evident in one of the most influential of related writings in France, namely, the *Traité du ris* ('Treatise on Laughter' (1579)) written by the Montpellier-trained physician Laurent Joubert. Like nearly all similar writings, Joubert's was a deeply unhumorous scholastic text, whose high seriousness would only too easily be satirized by future generations. It sought avidly to affirm laughter's mission to attack vice, which Joubert defined as everything that was 'ugly, deformed, unseemly, indecent, malicious and indecorous'. Joubert also followed Castiglione in seeking to rescue laughter from the hands of jesters and jokers, and to give it moral purpose.

In the dedication of his volume to Henri IV's queen, Marguerite de Valois, Joubert painted a rather delightful picture of the laughing face. He depicted it in humane and tolerant terms (which derived largely in fact from a description in Ovid) as 'an encounter of much grace, amidst salutations, caresses and greetings':

> Certainly there is nothing that gives more pleasure and recreation than a laughing face, with its wide, shining, clear and serene forehead, eyes shining, resplendent from any vantage point, and casting fire as do diamonds; cheeks vermillion and incarnate, mouth flush with the face, lips handsomely drawn back (from which are formed the small dimples called gelasins, in the very middle of the cheeks), chin drawn in, widened and a bit recessed. All this is in the smallest laugh and in the smile favouring an encounter of much grace, amidst salutations, caresses and greetings . . .

Reading the text carefully one can see that Joubert is in fact describing a smile rather than a laugh—a point that highlights the frequent blurring of the two gestures. There is no evocation of the visibility of teeth in this description, however. The polite laughing face was smiling with mouth shut.

Joubert went on to describe a much bleaker and scarier picture of the laugh too, a kind of dark avatar to the benign gesture he had just described. He evoked

> the great opening of the mouth, the notable drawing back of the lips, the broken and trembling voice, the redness of the face, the sweat that sometimes comes out of the entire body, the sparkling of the eyes with the effusion of tears, the rising of the veins in the forehead and throat, the coughing, the expelling of what was in the mouth and nose, the shaking of the chest, shoulders, arms, thighs, legs and the whole body, like a convulsion, the great pain in the ribs, sides and abdomen, the emptying of the bowels and the bladder, the weakness of the heart for want of breath, and some other effects.

The ungraceful facial distortions involved in such bursts of laughter deformed the face and risked turbulent explosions from every orifice.

Implicit in these definitions was a social taxonomy of laughter which highlighted decorous courtesy and strongly condemned Rabelaisian uproar. Hearty, rumbustious, open-mouthed, side-splitting, thigh-slapping, trouser-wetting Rabelaisian laughter of the sort that was instigated by strolling players might be enjoyed and indulged in by the popular classes. But it should not, it was held, penetrate beneath the carapace of gentlemanly courtesy. For a gentleman to laugh like Rabelais put him on the same level as plebeians and buffoons, and animals too. Joubert was not alone in expressing alarm at how immoderate, Rabelaisian laughter could transform men into beasts. He disapprovingly depicted a whole cacophonous medley of undignified farmyard noises which laughter produced. It could sound like geese hissing, pigs grunting, dogs yapping, owls hooting, donkeys braying, and so on. Such laughter was also, it seemed, medically ill-advised. Physicians followed laughter-theorist Joubert's lead in highlighting the dangers to health caused by excessive mirth: according to Marin Cureau de La Chambre, writing in the middle of the seventeenth century, besides pains caused by bodily shaking, the immoderate laugh risked dislocating the limbs, and causing faints, syncopes, and even death. Laughing could be extremely bad for the health.

The *Book of the Courtier* and its derivative texts were written for gentlemen. 'What makes a soldier or a villager laugh', one author noted, for example, 'is very different from what tickles a man of letters'. The art theorist André

Félibien similarly noted that 'laughter varies according to social rank'. Queens should thus show their feelings in different ways from peasant girls. Félibien was reflecting in the aesthetic realm a sense of decorum that was fundamental to the literature of courtesy and laughter. Avoidance of the nightmare of plebeian laughter was particularly enjoined on women. Adrien de Montluc de Cramail's *Discours académique du ris* ('Academic Discourse on Laughter') in 1630 stated that one needed proper judgement in order to know when to laugh. He thought such judgement was likely to be in short supply among 'little boys, the people and women'. Given the subjacent misogyny in elite and popular culture at this time, women were thought to need particular attention, since their weak constitutions, impulsiveness, and lack of intellect made them more prone to unseemly behaviour. Laughing to show off good teeth was thought to betray their inherent lasciviousness too. This had added dangers in the light of the age-old equation between a woman's open mouth and her vagina. Neither should be flaunted in public. Even in the Middle Ages, the *Roman de la rose*, the classic of the literature of courtly love, had loftily declared that 'women should laugh with a shut mouth', and this was to be an endless refrain throughout the early modern period. Women might laugh at jokes, some authors generously conceded, but certainly not tell them. Writing in 1587, Henri Estienne had even ingeniously recommended that women should be allowed to pronounce 'e' in a closed manner that did not necessitate them opening their lips in ways that could be perceived as indecent.

The more these Renaissance debates on laughter developed in the late sixteenth and seventeenth centuries, the more it became apparent that the idea that laughter might derive from simple good-natured *joie de vivre* unalloyed with negative passions was losing out. For Rabelais, joy and laughter had been synonymous, and were a sure mark of French gaiety of spirit. This was no longer thought to be true. Many contributors to the debates went out of their way to refute any positive evaluation in this regard. This was the case, for example, with René Descartes. His *Des passions de l'âme* (1649) argued powerfully that the joyful component within the laugh was always mingled with hate. The English philosopher Thomas Hobbes, who had spent much of the 1630s in Paris, wrote in 1640 that all laughter was in essence rejoicing in the misfortunes of others. 'The passion of Laughter is nothyng but a suddaine Glory arising from the suddaine Conception of some Eminency in our selves by Comparison with the Infirmityes of others...' For Hobbes and his followers, all laughter was derision. Cureau de La Chambre was in general agreement: although it might seem that laughter would be associated with pleasure, he noted, in fact it was usually the expression of 'contempt and indignation'.

Scholastic debates on laughter in early modern France thus both endorsed and widened Castiglione's advocacy of modes of laughter which were restrained, controlled, stoical, decorous, seemly, graceful, health-conserving, and which, while demarcating the boundaries of gentility, had the social mission of castigating vice. Pulling in very much the same direction was Erasmus's pedagogical best-seller, *De civilitate morum puerilium* ('On the Civility of Childrens' Manners'). Published in Latin in 1530, this brief work went into huge numbers of editions and was translated into over a dozen languages. Its precepts penetrated, in diluted form, the *Bibliothèque bleue*, the cheap popular texts sold by pedlars all around the country. It was also a major source of the highly popular *Les Règles de la bienséance et de la civilité chrétienne* ('Rules of Decorum and Christian Civility' (1703)) by Jean-Baptiste de La Salle, founder of the Christian Brothers, one of France's main teaching orders.

Both Erasmus and de La Salle presented a neo-stoical programme of reform of conduct aimed at inculcating in children the precepts of 'civility'. The latter term was preferred to the 'courtesy' propounded by Castiglione and his epigones, but resembled it in all essentials. Like Castiglione, both authors drew on forebears from Antiquity. Laughter should be moderated and Rabelaisian extremes firmly resisted. 'The wise man', Erasmus argued, 'is hardly heard laughing at all.' He continued, 'Only fools laugh at everything that is said and done ... The burst of laughter, the immoderate laugh which shakes the whole body ... is indecorous at any age, especially in childhood.' And then again, he regarded as utterly unseemly

> opening the mouth horribly wide to laugh, creasing one's cheeks and showing all one's teeth. This is how dogs laugh ... [On the contrary], the face should express gaiety without any deformation or any sign of natural corruption.

De La Salle was equally categorical. Showing one's teeth in laughter was 'absolutely against decency, which commands that one should never see the teeth exposed'. Deploying the argument from design, he held that God would not have given humans lips if He had wanted the teeth to be on open display.

The stress on civility in these texts was echoed in probably the most influential of late seventeenth-century conduct books, Antoine Courtin's

Nouveau traité de la civilité qui se pratique en France parmi les honnestes gens ('New Treatise on Civility As It Is Practised in France Among the Persons of Quality' (1679)). The huge numbers of individuals aspiring to be 'persons of quality' ('*honnêtes gens*') who read this popular work learnt that all forms of mouth behaviour should be sophisticated, refined, and utterly unplebeian. One should smile both modestly and with one's mouth firmly shut. The new civility—or *honnêteté*—represented a rigid form of face control.

These precepts of civility had greater substance and social impact by the late seventeenth century because they were incorporated within a programme for the reformation of manners to which both Church and State subscribed. Courtin's text aimed to bring the notion of civility in line with the precepts of Christian charity, while his general rule for the conduct of an *honnête homme* was that 'he imitate a great Prince, all of whose actions are effectively rules of decorum'. The reformation was to be achieved by, among other things, the systematic policing of bodily orifices. The mouth was only one such orifice. Quite as much on the hit list as indecorous mouth abuse were all those orifice-related transgressive behaviours in which Rabelais had gloried. War was thus declared as much on uncontrolled sphincters as on uncontrolled mouths. Picking the nose, eye-rubbing and squinting, cleaning out the ears, scratching the arse, and, especially, unrestrained farting were taboo. There was to be no tooth-picking (especially with a fork after eating), no nail-biting or yawning in public, no aimless spitting, no sneezing without the aid of a handkerchief, no tongue-lolling or other facial grimaces. As regards laughter, the usual sort of prohibitions applied: one should not laugh loudly in bursts, nor rock helplessly in mirth, nor laugh in ways that were aimless and indiscriminating and that involved unseemly gestures.

In the wake of the Council of Trent, the Counter-Reformation Catholic Church proved keen to join the fight. A gloomy disapproval of humour in all its forms was of course a well-established theme within the Christian tradition, but during the Middle Ages it had often been tempered by a more tolerant, optimistic approach. Saint Thomas Aquinas, for example, had followed Aristotle in believing that laughter was a form of behaviour in which only humans engaged, and that it was thus permissible for a Christian to laugh, albeit only under strictly circumscribed spiritual conditions. Such an attitude emerged too in Erasmus's work—most notably in his *In Praise of Folly* (1511), where perceiving humour in the ways of the world was viewed as providing a pathway towards a new, more internalized piety. Yet as the sixteenth and seventeenth centuries wore on, these seemed to be voices crying in the wilderness. Laughter was subject to stern ecclesiastical review by a Church ever keener to tame—or even eradicate—the Rabelaisian culture of laughter condemned in contemporary books of manners. Just as discourses of civility sought to distance 'persons of quality' from the raucous plebs, so the post-Tridentine Church informed the faithful that all collective hedonistic and mirth-making activity was ungodly and spiritually abject. The carnivalesque in all its forms was now under attack: mardi gras cele-brations, charivaris, excessive and unseemly collective behaviour, wearing masks, festive cross-dressing, feasts of fools, burlesque processions, and so on. These practices were condemned: first, as popular and plebeian (though in truth in the past they had been a focus for all social groupings and classes); and, secondly, as politically dangerous vestiges of a pagan past. All Chris-tians, it seemed, and not only gentlemen, should have the manners of gentlemen.

Drawing on impeccable authorities stretching back to the early Church fathers, churchmen now endlessly preached that Jesus had never laughed in the Bible, only cried. 'To laugh and rejoice with the world is fitting only for a madman', had been Saint Jerome's—rather typical—view. 'Don't laugh', equally typically echoed Ignatius de Loyola, the founder of the Jesuits, the most important teaching order of the early modern period. There was really only one form of humour which the post-Tridentine Church unequivo-cally supported, and that was the sometimes dark, cruel, and unpleasantly *faux*-jocular argumentation aimed at ridiculing spiritual opponents. This drew intellectual justification from Aristotle's view that laughter was a way of reproving and countering vice. Disputatious preachers and polemi-cists gloried in fine-tuning every type of rhetorical technique so as to elicit from their audience contemptuous laughter at the expense of their spiritual opponents. Reformation and Counter-Reformation were full of joyless derision.

Abbé Jean-Baptiste Thiers's *Traité des jeux* ('Treatise on Pastimes'), published in 1686, was an extreme but not uncharacteristic late seven-teenth-century text in this regard. It was grounded in the belief that all human pastimes derived from the Fall. Original Sin dictated, it seemed, that the godly could laugh only with *gravitas* and decorum. They should avoid excessive mockery and affectation, grimaces and gesticulations, touchings and kissings, and only use decent and discreet terms in joking talk. Taboo subjects for humour were God, religion, the Church, the saints, religious relics, ceremonies, rituals, funerals, and sermons—plus anything relating to friends, those less fortunate than themselves, and the great and good. Sex and other forms of impurity were well beyond the pale. Discreet laughter was permitted, but preferably not on workdays, Sundays, holy days, and during Lent and Advent. Any sign of mirth within churches, in religious processions, or in cemeteries was sternly frowned upon. Laughing time and space was clearly at a miserabilist premium in the world according to the abbé Thiers.

With Thiers sketching out a mirth-free world, bishop Bossuet of Meaux joined the fray. Bossuet was the most eminent churchman of his day, Louis XIV's close confidant, and a key ideologist of Divine Right kingship. In his thunderously gloomy 1694 tract, *Maximes et réflexions sur la comédie* ('Maxims and Reflections on Theatre'), Bossuet flatly condemned just about any form of humorous recreation. Joking was, it seems, 'unworthy of the gravity of human manners', a view which he found triumphantly confirmed in scripture, in the Church fathers, in the customary teaching of the Church, and indeed in life itself. The point was all the more apposite for a king, especially one like Louis XIV who claimed to rule by Divine Right. If Jesus had never laughed, then how unseemly it would be for his chosen representative on earth, or others in his purview, so to do. 'A mocking discourse is intolerable in the king's mouth', Bossuet fulminated. And again: 'the goodness of the prince consists in repressing scandal-mongering and outrageous joking'.

Bossuet was picking up on an existing line of thought concerning the royal mouth that concurred with both religious sermonizing and Divine Right Realpolitik. Cardinal Richelieu, principal minister of Louis XIV's father, Louis XIII, had set the tone. For good government, Richelieu advocated the maxim, 'talk little and listen a lot'. 'Greatness in kings', he held, 'resides in nothing offensive coming out of their mouths.' Absolute monarchy thus promoted a political culture of closed mouths, in more ways than one. Louis XIV seems to have been temperamentally suited to (but had also been trained for) such an approach. Even when, as a lad, he had teeth, one court lady noted, the king had rarely smiled. He had loosened up in adolescence, it is true. 'In public, he is full of gravity', noted the papal ambassador at the French court, 'and very different from what he is in private.' He became an ardent pleasure-seeker for a while. He had serial mistresses; he danced and gambolled; and he laughed loud and long at Molière's plays. But as he aged, public and private behaviours tended to merge and his outlook became more austere again. Louis returned to the sombre moodiness of his early years, especially after the relocation of the royal court to Versailles in 1683. The curé of Versailles remarked how the king in the latter decades of his reign always had 'a serious appearance and look'.

Given this highly pessimistic and gloomy reading of human nature after the Fall, spontaneity and jest were in increasingly short supply at Louis XIV's court. The facial regime dictated in court protocol highlighted a grave, steady, and fixed look. The heavy, all-encompassing, and automaton-like rituals of Versailles ceremonial emphasized majesty, a kind of hyperbolic dignity attaching to the most minute of daily occurrences. Frivolity had no part to play in such an ambiance—as the fortunes of the post of court fool proved. Since the fourteenth century, kings of France had maintained a jester as an official, salaried post in the royal household. These were customarily allowed the liberty of holding up a moral mirror to the manners of the age, of reminding the monarch and his counsellors of their duties—and of making them laugh. In the past kings had allowed such figures free rein. Chicot, the fool of the great Henri IV at the turn of the seventeenth century, had familiarly addressed his ruler as 'mon petit couillon' ('my little bollock'), and had him in stitches. Louis XIV was having no such indignities. The institution of the court jester became obsolete. An absolute monarch did not want to be reminded of the folly of his ways or the vanity of his wishes. Laughter was not high up in his list of royal priorities. The monarch really did not want to rock with laughter any more.

'It's a strange business, making persons of quality laugh'; Molière's no doubt heartfelt comment in 1663 was even truer as the seventeenth century wore on, as the atmosphere at court became darker and more sombre. Part cause, part symptom of this was the king's relationship with Madame de Maintenon, his mistress from the mid 1670s and his morganatic bride from 1683. Madame de Maintenon (who incidentally was as toothless as her spouse) was sternly devout and shunned worldly pleasures, pushing Louis along the same route. Prudery took up position at the helm of state. New versions of Rabelais expurgated his text of the crudest sections, to the extent that his writings became utterly unfunny and indeed, it was said, incomprehensible to courtiers. Louis had once been a follower of the earthy comedies of the Comédiens-Italiens, but he stopped frequenting them in 1689 and closed the company down altogether in 1697 after an alleged affront to his wife. 'Old Wrinkly', as one outspoken courtier called her (at least behind her back), was soon 'pushing him to suppress theatre altogether', something that, in the event, he did not quite manage.

One way or another, then, the impassive, emotionless, unsmilingly immobile face evident in Rigaud's 1701 royal portrait—and, as we shall see in the next chapter, in court-endorsed portraiture—came very easily to Louis XIV. Spiritual solemnity and the traditions of courtly civility, combined with the ruler's own melancholy disposition, meant that he did not have to try very hard to fix on his visage that seemly and imperious *gravitas*. Even had he kept his teeth, in other words, the king would not have looked much different.

The power of royal example

Louis XIV's penchant for unsmiling facial impassivity impressed itself forcefully on the mores of his courtiers. According to the underpinning logic of court societies, expertly analysed by Norbert Elias, most courtiers sought to follow the example of their prince in everything he did. This could even take them into some rather masochistic territory. In 1686, the year after his dental saga, Louis had to be operated upon by Premier Surgeon Félix for an anal fistula, a procedure even more fraught with danger, indignity, and physical pain than his mouth operation the previous year, but which once again was crowned with success. According to court practitioner Pierre Dionis, the condition of having an anal fistula became straight away 'very fashionable'. Dionis cited around thirty cases of courtiers who approached him confidentially. Each of them 'had mild cases involving a weeping wound on the anus or even just haemorrhoids, [but they] did not hold back from presenting the surgeon with their behinds for him to make incisions'. Furthermore, Dionis recorded, openly puzzled and no doubt tongue-in-cheek, 'they appeared upset when I told them there was no need for it'.

If the courtiers at Versailles were not averse to sacrificing their behinds so as to stay fashionable and to mimic their master, they would certainly do as much with their face. Louis's impassive visage was the default position for any aspiring courtier. The impassive, tight-lipped face and the controlled smile within Louis-Quatorzian court culture had wider resonance too. It passed beyond the boundaries of the royal court and established itself in the capital. As La Bruyère noted, the city of Paris was 'the court's ape', and it took its cues from court fashion—and this was as true of smiles as of wigs and clothing.

This pattern of emulation played out in debates on the social reach and meanings of the model of courtesy sketched out by Castiglione and adapted in the royal court. 'The words courteous and courtesy are beginning to age and are no longer in good usage', noted Father Bouhours in 1675. 'Now we say civil and *honneste*, and civility and *honnesteté*.' Some writers still believed that it was only at court that one achieved the polishing of character necessary to make a gentleman. Significantly, Courtin had presented his highly popular work on civility as a surrogate for those who wanted to model their behaviour on their courtly betters 'but had neither the choice nor the means to come to the court in Paris so as to learn the rules of *honnêteté*'. The work also sought to provide a code of behaviour with which the socially aspirational might distinguish themselves from their inferiors. One of Courtin's allies was rather alarmed by the thought that the practices of civility might extend to common Parisian tradespeople on the Rue Saint-Denis and even to country-dwellers: such unseemly aping of one's betters was ridiculous. Yet this was a minority view. It came to be widely believed that the kinds of behaviour originally prescribed by Castiglione, Courtin, and their ilk for the denizens of royal courts could profitably be followed by most of the social elite. A 'person of quality', or '*honnête homme*', as the phrase went, might be a courtier but could equally be an individual who had acquired the precepts of gentility by other means— such as reading about it in the work of Castiglione or Courtin. The *honnête homme* was thus replacing the courtier. Indeed, the term courtesy was increasingly regarded as antiquated and anachronistic, as Bouhours noted. Rather than courtesy, one now practised civility (or *honnêteté*) as it was practised at the royal court.

The hegemony of court culture and the Church's ingrained pessimism about laughter *tout court* meant that it was difficult to avoid laughing at, rather than with, fellow humans. Just as the Church deployed humour as a weapon of contempt against enemies of the faith, so courtiers used it to mock their social, moral, or aesthetic inferiors. This kind of laughter was invariably forced, unspontaneous, reproving, and denigratory. Revelling in ridicule, it was often heartless and cruel to boot. The term used to capture the facial expression often associated with this kind of mockery was *le rire sardonique* (*risus sardonicus*, the sardonic laugh) which was said to owe its name to a poisonous plant on the island of Sardinia which caused the mouth to contract involuntarily into a bitterly smiling rictus before death set in. In public life, hostility towards smiling and laughing thus meant that the default position of either was unbenign at best, actively aggressive at worst.

When characters in late seventeenth-century plays, romances, and imaginative writings engaged in smiling, this was in very few cases viewed positively. Molière evokes 'a smile charged with sweetness' (1671), La Fontaine 'a sweet smile' (1685), Fénelon, in his influential *Télémaque* (1699), 'a smile full of grace and majesty'. These were surprisingly rare examples. Smiles were much more likely to be 'sardonic', or else 'disdainful', 'bitter', 'ambiguous', 'proud', 'knowing', and 'ironic'. In all such cases the smile denoted not human camaraderie or spontaneous gaiety of heart but rather social distance, usually on the vertical axis *de haut en bas* so familiar at the court. The open, laughing mouth was viewed as an infallible sign of poor breeding, plebeian status, emotional disorder, or worse.

Besides simple emulation, there were other reasons why the king's fixed expression became the moral and aesthetic ideal at court. It could, first, be recommended as a strategy of promotion and indeed of survival. Letting one's face betray one's emotions was a sure way of giving rivals an advantage in the quest for favours. Symptomatically, La Bruyère held that courtiers acted as if their faces were made of marble like the palace they frequented: both were hard and polished. 'A man who knows the court', he went on,

> is master of his gestures, his eyes and his face; he is deep and impenetrable; he pretends not to notice injuries done to him; he smiles to his enemies, controls his temper, disguises his passions, belies his heart, speaks and acts against his real feelings.

On the battleground of self-advancement and deceit, the smile was a controlled and chilly weapon.

This was all the more the case in that the custom of shaving the face had become almost universal among Louis XIV's courtiers. The full beard in the style of Henri IV at the turn of the seventeenth century had given way to the adornment of the moustache under cardinal ministers Richelieu and Mazarin—and indeed the young Louis XIV. But by the time of the court's move to Versailles, the wearing of the wig and the shaving of the face had become the norm for king and courtiers. The naked face offered no safe hiding-place for expression. The absence of beards made the revelation of feelings much more visible—and therefore more problematic for individuals who wanted to veil their feelings.

Facial impassivity was reinforced, secondly, by the standardized use at court of face-whitening creams. White skin was viewed as integral to established notions of beauty, distinction, and purity, and where the skin-colour failed to have the desired effect, *le fard*, as these face-paints were called, offered compensation. *Le fard* was usually accompanied by strategic-ally placed blobs of rouge on the cheeks and the occasional silk 'patch' or beauty-spot. The whiteness often covered the lips, as if to make one overlook the existence of the oral orifice (or, worse, what might lie within). By blurring physiognomic differentiation, this kind of cosmetic regime highlighted uniformity in appearances. One could not see an involuntary blush through *le fard*, and if one wore such face paint anything more than the slightest of smiles was best eschewed, since it risked cracking the mask (physically as well as metaphorically, in fact). In addition, the metallic base to face creams caused teeth to rot—as, incidentally, did mercury-based treatment for venereal diseases, which were certainly not unknown at court. This was yet another reason for keeping one's mouth shut.

A third reason for buttoning the lips was the physiognomic folklore that equated certain features of the mouth with character traits. Although as we shall see, the ancient tradition of physiognomy was losing credence by the late seventeenth century, it continued to be a consideration in such a competitive atmosphere as Versailles. Thus it was held that long teeth designated the glutton; sharp teeth, the lascivious; big and broad teeth, the vain; and a lolling tongue, the irredeemably stupid. In his popular 1699 text, *Réflexions sur le ridicule* ('Reflections on Ridicule'), Morvan de Bellegarde held that keeping one's own mouth shut was the most effective way of avoiding being found ridiculous, being attributed character features on the basis of physiognomical lore, or just being laughed at. This seemed the best advice going for courtiers. The philosopher aristocrat La Rochefoucauld was probably not untypical in estimating that he personally averaged about one laugh a year; and he thought that there was very little in life which was worth smiling about. The power games and jockeying for status that were staple features of court life left little room for humour to raise its head.

It is true that some at least within the court elite did begin to find this combination of progressively gloomy ceremonial hyper-seriousness and facial impassivity a little hard to swallow. By the last years of Louis's reign, such individuals, rejecting the glum unsmiling character of court life, took every excuse to slink off to indulge in the more worldly and agreeable pleasures to be found in Paris. From her residence in the Marais, the famous letter writer, Madame de Sévigné complained as early as 1676 that 'for some years, no one laughs any more'. But she did her best to compensate: her high-spirited laugh was famous for being audible a street away. Jovial smiles and laughter were already appearing to be more at home in Paris than Versailles.

Nevertheless, in spite of these few oases of mirth, wherever one looked in France in the final decades of the reign of Louis XIV, a mood prevailed which devalued smiling and laughing. In the Old Regime of Teeth, opening the mouth was a risky venture for sound biological reasons: loss of teeth, mouth disease, bad breath, and so on. Yet cultural constraints had come to provide further layers of aesthetic, behavioural, religious, cultural, and political reasons for remaining tight-lipped—as Rigaud's unsmilingly tight-lipped portrait of Louis XIV eloquently testifies. The laugh which hovered in the back of people's minds was still the nightmare laugh described by Laurent Joubert: low, plebeian, unseemly, excessive, passionate, out of control, dangerous to health. The aggressively sardonic laugh, or tight-lipped smile, prevalent in the facial regime of the royal court, was in some respects an effort to keep that nightmare image at bay and under control. These cultural factors, strongly present at the end of the seventeenth century, powerfully reinforced long-established biological problems with teeth. The open, friendly, and benign smile found few adherents in the last years of Louis XIV's reign.

2

The Smile of Sensibility

I n the first volume of Marcel Proust's *A la recherche du temps perdu* (1913), the central character Swann compares his memory of the sweetness of character and the bewitching beauty of his mistress to his recollection of 'the study sketches of Watteau, in which one sees innumerable smiles, here and there, all over and pointing in all directions' (Fig. 2.1). In making the comparison, Proust was evoking a new, less sombre and oppressive mood abroad in court culture after the death of Louis XIV in 1715 and during the period of the Regency in which Jean-Antoine Watteau flourished.

Fig. 2.1 Jean-Antoine Watteau, *Eight Studies of Women's Heads, and One Study of a Man's Head* (*c.*1716)

That mood at court was, however, to be as transient as the smile of Swann's mistress. The accession of Louis XV to full power in 1723 brought an end to the lightening of the emotional and ceremonial atmosphere at Versailles inaugurated in 1715. The facial regime of Louis XIV's court was reimposed, including as regards modes of royal and aristocratic self-presentation. Even so, the Regency mood had a more lasting legacy within the city of Paris than at Versailles. Indeed it contributed towards the emergence of a taste for sensibility among the urban elite which placed great store by emotional expression, and increasingly broke away from conventions of strict self-restraint that had held sway under Louis XIV. By the middle of the eighteenth century, a new facial regime was in gestation that made room for smiles.

Regency glimpses of the smile

In 1715, Paris was ready for change after Louis XIV's long reign and the aura of failure hanging over its last few years. There were surprisingly few Parisians who found much to regret in the passing of the old king. Louis 'the Great' was generally viewed as anything but. Admiration for the epic defeats he had inflicted on the rest of Europe in the early part of his reign had long since changed to dismay at his relentless war-mongering and the high taxes and social dislocation this had caused. Initially an emblem of European festive court culture, moreover, Versailles had become a morose, gloomy, unsmiling place under the joint stewardship of Louis and Madame de Maintenon. The times were right for change and high hopes now rested on the shoulders of the new king, Louis's great-grandson. Louis XV was still only six years old in 1715, and too young to reign. The Regency was entrusted to his great-uncle, Philippe, duc d'Orléans. At once the royal court left Versailles to install itself in Paris, and abandoned the stuffy ceremonial on which Louis XIV had insisted. Philippe of Orleans had always been Louis XIV's *bête noire,* and he had little respect for the old king's ways of doing things. With Louis barely cold in his tomb, the Regent unleashed a torrent of high living, relaxed morals, urbane sociability, political experimentation, intellectual openness, and a fundamental questioning of courtly values. Smiles, along with wit, humour, laughter, daring, imagination, and new thinking, seemed to be replacing po-faced solemnity and etiolated high seriousness. Suddenly monarchy was popular again, and the child-king Louis XV won the unalloyed affection of Parisians.

The sombre model of elite culture constructed by Louis XIV at Versailles seemed to be genuinely under threat from within the heart of the political system. Utopians and projectors of every stripe now flourished. The so-called 'System' of the Scottish financial wizard John Law introduced expansionist policies to boost the economy and expand France's colonies. The abbé de Saint-Pierre fizzed with schemes for representative government, world peace, and a new rational, phonetic language. The plays, polemics, and newspaper articles of Marivaux, who described his work as 'the production of a free spirit, who shuns nothing that amuses him along the way', evinced a humane, unstuffy tone which was the polar opposite of self-conscious courtly pomp. Even Marivaux's wit was eclipsed, moreover, by the early career of the brilliantly talented Voltaire, who seemed effortlessly to combine polemics with pamphleteering, the culture of the salon and the theatre with down-to-earth humour and satire. His young contemporary, Montesquieu, whose *Spirit of Laws* (1748) would make him the greatest political theorist of the century, was equally bold: his best-selling fantasy novel, the *Persian Letters* (1721), was a scarcely coded attack on Louis-Quatorzian absolutism, dressed up in the story of a visit to Paris by Persian ambassadors. Such a volume would have been unthinkable under Louis XIV's censorship rules—but in the Regency the press was freer than any other period until the French Revolution. Also on a light-hearted note, the convivial drinking society known as the Régiment de la Calotte, which was particularly strong among aristocratic army officers, assailed anyone in power with a scintilla of pomposity about them, irreverently holding them up to ridicule in pamphlets known as 'brevets'. In 1716, the Comédie-Italienne, consigned by Louis XIV and Madame de Maintenon to outer darkness in 1697, was allowed to re-form, putting a smile back on the face of Parisian theatre-lovers. There was a sense of connecting up with a lighter mood that had been repressed by Church and State in the late seventeenth century. 'After the mournful final years of Louis XIV', Voltaire was pleased to record, 'everything changed to gaiety and fun under the Regency.'

The writings of Anthony Ashley Cooper, Earl of Shaftesbury, seemed to offer a theoretical justification for this new mood of gaiety. Shaftesbury, who spent a good part of his life on the Continent, imagined society not as a collection of dark pessimists tainted by Original Sin, nor as a Hobbesian jungle of brutish self-interestedness, but rather as a space in which easy social interactions were like to produce individual gains and wider social benefits. Shaftesbury thought that the emotions had a positive value as long as they were handled in a spirit of politeness: humans were naturally prone to show sympathy for their fellow creatures, he held, and not contempt or hopeless disdain. Everyone, he held, 'possesses a moral sense that signals to us through sentiments like pity, love and generosity'. And everyone had something to gain from easy-going polite sociability: 'we polish one another and rub off our Corners and rough Side by a sort of *amicable Collision*'. The Regency was full of such 'amicable collisions'. Interestingly, Shaftesbury fine-tuned his theories by examining the individual's propensity for happiness. He made a specific contrast between what he called '*jocositas*' (joyfulness), which was characterized by the proud and aggressive taking of pleasure in the misfortunes of others, and '*hilaritas*' (mirthfulness, gaiety), which comprised amicable and happy feelings fuelled by the sight of the good and the beautiful. '*Hilaritas*' could have stood as the unwitting motto of the Regency, in contrast to the '*jocositas*' that had distinguished Louis XIV's Versailles.

Anything goes, was the dominant Regency mood; and Watteau sought to exemplify it. In 1717, he sent as his reception piece for the Academy of Painting a picture of a *fête galante*, the dreamily ethereal depiction of an entertainment particularly popular with the aristocracy that involved dressing up, party games, and a general letting-down of hair. Reception pieces for the Academy were supposed to be examples of history painting (the depiction of episodes in biblical and ancient history and myth), which was regarded as the most prestigious of all forms of painting. The Academy realized that Watteau's dreamy, bitter-sweet depiction of an aristocratic party scarcely counted as history painting—but admitted him anyway, thereby instituting the *fête galante* as a new artistic genre. The Regency seemed all about bending rules when they couldn't be broken.

In the event, however, the hedonistic, optimistic experimental Regency mood did not last. Orleans died in 1722, the precocious victim of louche living. Even before then, the writing was on the wall. John Law's famous 'System' exploded spectacularly in a massive financial crisis, bringing a hasty return to former ways of operating state finance. Watteau died tragically young. The abbé de Saint-Pierre became widely viewed as a lunatic. Marivaux went bankrupt (though he recovered). Scandal caused by Voltaire's irreverence led him to flee to England so as to avoid persecution. And sexual licence in the Regent's circle and among the high aristocracy triggered a mood of public outrage. The *fête galante* had transmuted into something altogether more unsavoury. Louis-Quatorzian values were consequently soon back in the saddle, not least thanks to the new king.

Any hopes that Louis XV, when he came of age, would abandon the stiff protocol and rigidity of manners which Louis XIV had implanted at court were sadly misplaced. The affection which Parisians initially showed for their young prince was almost totally unreciprocated. At the first opportunity—in 1723—he moved his court from Paris back to Versailles. The old ceremonial manuals that had been placed under wraps in 1715 were disinterred and applied intact. By 1726, the king was making it abundantly clear that as regards his style of rule he 'wished to follow the example of [his] great-grandfather in everything'. His perspective would remain substantially unchanged. Half a century later—he reigned until 1774—Louis confessed, 'I do not like undoing what my forefathers have done.' His core position was an unshrinking hostility to anything which detracted from the spirit of Louis XIV's Versailles. His great-grandfather's rules of court conduct had been creaking badly by 1715 but they were now reinforced, with rules of protocol made even more exacting. From 1759, court presentations were restricted to women with a noble genealogy predating 1400. The king broke the rule in the case of his own mistresses, notably Madame de Pompadour, the daughter of a maverick financier, and Madame du Barry, illegitimate offspring of a cook and a hairdresser. And he ruthlessly policed open criticisms of either, forcing even the jokey Régiment de la Calotte to disperse. Rules relating to aristocratic *entrées* at the various daily ceremonials of the king such as the *Lever* and the *Coucher* were tightened up too, as was the right to use the royal carriages when the king hunted. The court became stuffier and more elitist than it had been under Louis XIV.

Louis XV's coming of age in 1723 thus put paid to the adventurous and imaginative cultural mood of the Regency, and wiped the smile off the face of official culture, literally as well as figuratively. The reinstatement of Louis XIV's protocol involved the reaffirmation of the facial regime long current at Versailles, which La Bruyère had satirized in the 1680s. The face remained unchanging even as, over the course of the century, the growing empire of fashion and *la mode* produced a dazzling pageant of fine clothing. The prestige of snow-white skin persisted, and the pasty whiteness of *le fard* among female courtiers was unblemished (and was becoming widespread among male courtiers too). As in the past, court society looked askance at facial displays of emotion, and continued to value a fixed, neutral expression. In the hyper-competitive court world, expressing an emotion risked

giving oneself away, inviting ridicule or providing rivals with an advantage
and an intimation of one's own inferiority.

The prevalence of expressionlessness in public life affected the way that
courtiers chose to have themselves portrayed. The artist Jean-Marc Nattier
made his fortune from the late 1730s onwards producing a veritable assembly line of flattering portraits of members of the royal family and the court
(Fig. 2.2). Women subjects were dressed in mythological costumes with
their hair swept back from their faces which artfully featured lilywhite skin
set off with standard-issue blotches of court rouge. The women's delicately
poised and untroubled faces were either free from expression or else were
permitted the luxury of the mildest and most enigmatic of identikit-like,
tight-lipped smiles—smiles which, however, gave nothing away in terms of
feeling, and indeed which often looked snooty and superior. This air of
courtly exteriority was also revealingly celebrated in François Boucher's
notorious portrait of Madame de Pompadour applying make-up in the
ceremonial of the toilette. This daily ritual was a moment when Pompadour
received her clients and thereby celebrated her power and her influence
with the king. The official mistress's make-up brush coats powder over

Fig. 2.2 Jean-Marc Nattier, *Marie-Adelaide, daughter of Louis XV, as Flora* (1742)

Fig. 2.3 François Boucher, *Madame de Pompadour at Her Toilette* (1758)

a face-paint that seems to metamorphose into war-paint for the struggles of the Versailles jungle (Fig. 2.3).

This portrait style highlighted the role that the court still retained in all matters regarding artistic taste. The codes of facial expression that Nattier, Boucher, and their like displayed in their art-works revealed the continuing importance of Louis XIV's Premier Painter, Charles Le Brun. The latter had been a powerful contributor to the construction of the culture of Versailles, and took a large part of the credit for its decor. From even before the chateau's inception in 1683, down to his death in 1690, he designed and executed paintings, tapestries, and sculptures within it, influenced overall lay-out, and was himself responsible for numerous masterpieces. As Premier Painter, Le Brun also presided over the Academy of Painting and Sculpture, which had been founded in 1648. Reorganized by Louis XIV in 1665, the Academy sought to champion the conventions and norms of best artistic practice. In order to establish these, Le Brun engaged in theoretical work on the approved range of facial expressions within art practice. These were expounded in his *Conférence sur l'expression, générale et particulière* ('Lecture on Expression, General and Particular') which he delivered in 1668.

The *Conférence sur l'expression* is an important, hybrid work. First, it displayed a close awareness of the implicit conventions that had governed facial expression in Western painting back to Antiquity and also to theoretical works on the subject since the Renaissance by Alberti, Lomazzo, Leonardo da Vinci, and others. Secondly, it also evoked the cryptic codes of physiognomy, the ancient body of knowledge that claimed to locate in the human face an individual's underlying character. Developed in Antiquity, the subject had been taught in medieval universities, gained in intellectual urgency during the Renaissance, was found in manuscript and printed sources in just about every European language in the early modern period from Icelandic to Welsh, and was published in every imaginable print format from learned infolios through to cheap almanacs and broadsheets. Up to and during the Renaissance, physiognomy had been grounded in a cosmology expressing itself in correspondences between substances and qualities both within and between the supra- and sub-lunar worlds: there were thus supposed to be associations between facial features on one hand and on the other the qualities inherent in heavenly bodies within the cosmos. In certain hands, physiognomy transmuted into an arcane and mystical occult science. But it just as often boiled down to unfalsifiable claims that people with red hair had a fiery temper and that, as we have seen, those with long teeth were gluttons. The Scientific Revolution of the seventeenth century was blowing to pieces the cosmology on which physiognomy had been founded and making occult physiognomic lore seem out of date.

The third influence that Le Brun's *Conférence* registered was the cutting-edge physiology of René Descartes. Descartes's oft-cited motto, *cogito ergo sum* ('I think, therefore I am'), highlighted his championing of deductive reasoning. But he was also famous for his work on human passions, developed in his *Des passions de l'âme* ('On the Passions of the Soul' (1649)) and in his posthumously published *Traité sur l'homme* ('Treatise on Man', published in 1662 but written in the late 1630s). He argued that the human soul was positioned in the pineal gland, which was within the head, between the two lobes of the brain and behind the bridge of the nose. The gland was where thought was formed, and this influenced the flow of animal spirits to the brain, and then outwardly towards the facial muscles. Le Brun developed Descartes's analysis into a far-ranging system of expression.

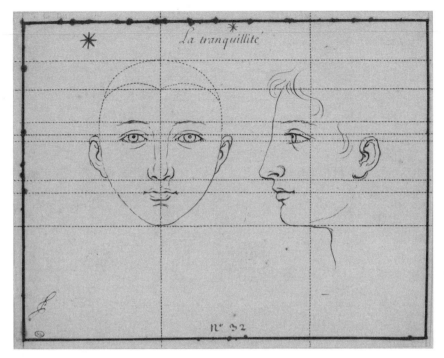

La tranquillité

Fig. 2.4 Charles Le Brun, *La Tranquillité*

When the face was perfectly at rest, the soul was calm and unmarked. Inner tranquillity registered as a degree zero of passionate disturbance (Fig. 2.4). Yet when the soul was agitated, Le Brun argued, this expressed itself on the face particularly around the eyebrows, the facial feature located closest to the pineal gland. The eyebrows were thus 'the motor of the face'. Le Brun went further than Descartes, in arguing that the more extreme a passion was the more contorted the muscles in the upper part of the face became—and the more the lower part of the face was also affected. In this light, incidentally, it is possible to regard Rigaud's 1701 portrait of Louis XIV (Fig. 1.1) discussed in the previous chapter, as conforming very closely to Lebrunian precepts: for whereas the king's mouth is dealt with in the insouciant manner we have evoked, his forehead shows not a wrinkle, thus highlighting the ruler's supposed tranquillity of soul.

Le Brun made his points graphically, by drawing a striking gallery of faces purporting to show the fine calibrations of emotional expression according to this Cartesian rationale. The purportedly scientific status of his work gained additional traction by linking to the established physiognomical

Fig. 2.5 Charles Le Brun, *Le Ravissement*

maxim which held that the upper part of the face, and especially the eyes, were more spiritual than the lower part of the face. His drawing of *Rapture*, for example, drew heavily on Raphael's *Galatea* (1512), reputed since the time of Vasari to represent ideal beauty, and frequently exemplified in the saintly figures of the Bolognese baroque artist, Guido Reni, and others (Fig. 2.5). Generally speaking, Le Brun regarded the mouth as more earthly and appetite-driven. In his gallery of the passions, it is opened slightly in the depiction of rapture, and also in wonder, esteem, horror, love, desire, sorrow, joy, and weeping. And it is wide open to denote terror, physical fear, despair, rage—and laughing. Revealingly, Le Brun's face denoting laughter ('*le rire*') has a malevolently sardonic air about it which links it with the contemptuous smile which was then, as we have seen, much in vogue in the courtly circles within which Le Brun moved (Figs. 2.6, 2.7). (It was the drawing of joy ('*la joie*') which came closest to Shaftesbury's '*hilaritas*'.)

Taken overall, the upshot of Le Brun's work was to endorse the convention that, in Western art, if one wanted to be portrayed pleasantly

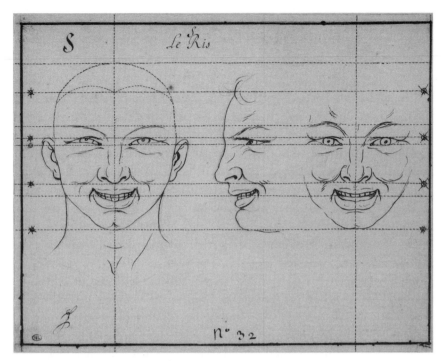

Fig. 2.6 Charles Le Brun, *Le Ris*

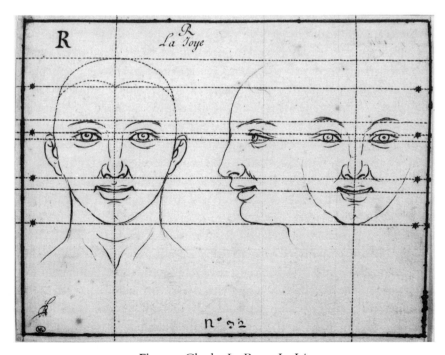

Fig. 2.7 Charles Le Brun, *La Joie*

smiling (as opposed to laughing), then it was best to smile like Leonardo da Vinci's *Mona Lisa*. Her smile—which, though admired was not in fact a great favourite in Enlightenment France—had been gracious, genteel, controlled, and mild. The same was true of Nattier's blue-blooded sitters. Had she, or they, opened their mouths to smile, they would have infringed implicit, rarely stated (but still closely observed) precepts about the representation of such a gesture. These precepts expressed in visual form the codes of civility and decorum formulated, as we have seen, by Castiglione, Erasmus, and their disciples from the Renaissance onwards.

The *Mona Lisa* was thus not alone in smiling, but she was also best minded to keep her mouth firmly shut. For individuals to have their mouths open in a painting in Western art, back to Antiquity, generally signified that, if they were not in the grip of extreme passion, as outlined by Charles Le Brun, then they were plebeian or insane. Ribera's painting of a Spanish peasant boy (1637) in the Louvre shows the lad opening his mouth to reveal dirty and deformed teeth—and he has a club foot to boot (Fig. 2.8). Individuals from the urban popular classes were also represented in this way. Their uncouth open mouths displaying teeth were featured when they were engaged in Rabelaisian high jinks. The teeth often resembled those of a human skull (and indeed, quantitatively speaking, the largest proportion of human teeth to be represented in Western art from the Middle Ages onwards are on death's heads). Although plebeian mouths were frequently used for comic effect, they could also imply threat or danger. The dark, forbidding facial orifices of beggars, gypsies, strolling players, and other social marginals portrayed by Caravaggio, Georges de la Tour, Velazquez, and others fitfully generate a sense of menace. Caravaggio's *I Cavadenti* (1608–9) shows sinister tooth-pullers hard at work among assorted low-life. The display of open mouths in George de la Tour's *Rixe de musiciens* ('Fight between travelling musicians' (1625–30)) is no more edifying (Fig. 2.9).

A further connotation of the open mouth in Western art is folly. Velasquez painted King Phillip IV's court jester Calabacillas comically and toothily smiling (1637–9) but it was broader than that (Fig. 2.10). Those in rational control of their feelings keep their mouths closed so as to evoke a *dignitas* and *gravitas* which is beyond the reach not only of the lower orders but also of those who have lost their reason, temporarily or permanently— or are simply, more comically, somewhat dim or mentally impaired. Merry or drunken figures fit within this rule. Seventeenth-century Dutch-genre painting by Jan Steen and Frans Hals, for example, portrayed endless

Fig. 2.8 Jusepe de Ribera, *Club-footed Boy* (1637)

cavaliers and their drinking companions laughing merrily (and open-
mouthedly) in their cups. Yet if one of them wanted to be memorialized
in a portrait, he left the tavern for the artist's studio. Then even a 'Laughing'
Cavalier (as instanced by Frans Hals) would keep his mouth firmly buttoned
as a sign of seemly *gravitas* and reason. Singers, often itinerant minstrels from
the lower orders in fact, were similarly shown with their mouths open in
song while their reason temporarily wobbled. Then again, depictions of
children gaily laughing and displaying open-mouthed smiles constituted

Fig. 2.9 Georges de La Tour, *Fight between Travelling Musicians* (1625–30)

Fig. 2.10 Diego Velázquez, *The Court Jester Don Juan de Calabazas* (1637–9)

Fig. 2.11 William Hogarth, *Shrimp Girl* (1740–5)

another type of painting which in fact endorsed rather than invalidated the general rule. William Hogarth's delightful *Shrimp Girl* (1740–5) was still a child yet to attain the age of reason. Maturity would soon enough make her and others like her button their lips (Fig. 2.11).

A particular tradition, to which we shall later return, is also worth noting in this respect, namely the custom of representing the Greek philosopher Democritus with his mouth fixed in a grin revealing his teeth. From the time of Seneca and Juvenal in the ancient world, Democritus was often, as by Rubens in 1603, paired with Heraclitus, the 'weeping philosopher', whose observation of worldly follies inspired tears of grief rather than peals of mocking laughter. Democritus was the exception who triumphantly proved the artistic rule about the open mouth. For he is, above all, the mad philosopher, who hides his deeper reason beneath the external appearances of folly. Precisely by acting the fool himself, Democritus laid claim to wisdom about the foolish ways of the world, by showing—as Montaigne noted in his *Essays*—that 'our condition is as ridiculous as capable of laughter' (and contempt, he might have added). One of Rembrandt's many self-portraits (1669) had shown him in this guise. Unsurprisingly, in view of his unstuffy and subversive attitude towards official culture, we also find Watteau adopting this pose (Fig. 2.12). His Democritan laugh mocked the closed, tight, prim, decorous mouth of courtly civility that the Regency seemed to be bidding to erase (but which Louis XV soon restored). As both

Fig. 2.12 Jean-Antoine Watteau, (attributed), *Self-portrait, Smiling*

Le Brun and Watteau would well know, plebeian manners, ungodly thoughts, sheer tomfoolery, and Democritan play-acting were all most unwelcome at Versailles.

The Regency had thus been something of a false dawn in official court culture. Louis XV reinstated Louis-Quatorzian templates of behaviour at Versailles. In terms of fine art, Le Brun's rule book for the representation of the passions continued to hold sway, its influence recordable in the palette of emotions displayed by successive generations of court painters. Its influence may also be judged by the fact that the images from the *Conférence* went into numerous editions. Significantly, the article on 'Passion' in Diderot's great *Encyclopédie*, the Bible of the Enlightenment, in 1765 drew heavily on Le Brun's categories. The images also provided the primers by which individuals of breeding learnt how to draw. And they were very heavily utilized by actors: actor manuals are full of Lebrunian grace notes. Despite the tantalizing glimpses under the Regency, therefore, the smile would have to make its own way in the world, Versailles seemingly having shut its doors to it.

Nevertheless, although this persistent Lebrunian influence testified to official culture's unequivocal return after 1723 to the facial regime of Louis XIV's court, there were still some signs that chinks were appearing in armour-plated expressionlessness. La Bruyère, the lucid analyst of court mores under Louis XIV, had noted how at court one needed to be a master of one's gestures, eyes, and face, and that 'one averts one's face to laugh and to cry in the presence of the Great'. He affected surprise 'that we should laugh so easily at the theatre and that we should be ashamed of crying'. It was precisely this latter relationship which changed in the early eighteenth century. People—even courtiers—learned to cry at the theatre. For some at least, tears spread contagiously into every aspect of their lives, ushering in a new world of emotionality, which, as time went on, would find time and space for a new kind of smile.

'Smiles on the mouth and tears in the eyes'

Writing in the 1770s, Denis Diderot highlighted a particular performance of a play at the Comedie-Française half a century earlier—in 1723 in fact, on the cusp of the transfer from Regency to Louis XV's personal reign—as heralding a new regime of theatrical emotionality. The play in question was

Antoine Houdart de La Motte's tragedy, *Ines de Castro*. At a moment in the play where the female protagonist is supposed to throw herself on the mercy of the king of Portugal, the leading actress, Madame Duclos, brought her own two children onto the stage (along with their nurse) to plead the case. Taken aback by the gesture, the audience shifted uneasily, and began to titter nervously. Turning squarely to face the audience, however, La Duclos proudly exclaimed, off-script, 'Laugh then, foolish stalls, at the most beautiful moment in the play.' At which moment she wept, her children wept, the nurse wept, the king of Portugal wept—and the entire audience found itself crying uncontrollably.

This startling *coup de théâtre* had a powerful impact. Voltaire claimed it marked 'the most affecting subject in all theatre'. Marmontel would write a moral tale upon it. Publicly pondering what it could possibly mean, Marivaux concluded that it showed the heart was superior to the head. The young Montesquieu noted how foolish the incident made the social convention appear whereby 'everything relating to natural feelings seems to be low and plebeian'. It implied, he thought, that a capacity to feel was a universal human attribute. The incident thus seemed to invoke a new, classless economy of feeling which reclaimed the experience of strong emotions from the lower orders and bade to transcend the kinds of stiff civility diffused throughout the royal court. Soon even state ministers, dukes, and imperious marshals of France would be found in Parisian theatres, away from Versailles, snivelling quietly into their handkerchiefs. They were not an exception: Parisians in general had discovered that they had tears—and were prepared to shed them now, even in public. The theatre thus kept alive the fizz of emotions that the Regency had all too briefly stimulated.

Grasping the shift in public taste, playwrights began to exploit the propensity for tears in a systematic way in a new genre of comedy known as *comédie larmoyante*—or 'tearful comedy'. However oxymoronic-sounding, the phrase referred to plays in which, as Voltaire put it, 'the same person within the space of fifteen minutes both laughs and cries at the same thing'. The most eloquent and successful proponent of this genre, picking up where de La Motte left off, was the prolific Pierre-Claude Nivelle de La Chaussée. While following the broad conventions of comedy, his plays placed non-heroic figures in plots and predicaments which often caused them suffering, and whose misfortunes touched the audience. Thereby—so the theory ran—they inspired audiences towards virtue. It was not that such plays had not existed in the past, even back to Antiquity. But they had never become a genre nor inspired theorization and the high degree of sentimentality as now they did. The astonishing success of the *comédie larmoyante* eclipsed both conventional comedy and tragedy in terms of public reception. The genre's success was such that even Voltaire, the great tragedian of the age as well as the author of numerous successful conventional comedies, tried his hand at the new style, notably with *L'Enfant prodigue* (1736) and *Nanine* (1749). Comedies in the repertoire grounded in humour suffered, with even the great Molière becoming unfashionable and performances of his works getting scarcer. 'The theatre is deserted, when [his] comedies are being performed', Voltaire noted in 1739. 'Hardly anyone goes to see *Tartuffe*, which used to attract the whole of Paris.' Molière seemed to be too unrefined and too unemotional for palates attuned to *comédie larmoyante*: 'scrupulous exactness as regards decency', noted another writer in 1764, 'does not permit us to laugh as people used to when Molière was alive'. Tragedy also went into steep decline under the assault of the *comédie larmoyante*. The great examples of the genre suffered the fate of Molière's comedies, being less and less popular.

In 1757, the *philosophe* Denis Diderot turned his hand to drama, seeking to improve upon and refine *comédie larmoyante*. His comedy, *Le Fils naturel* (1757), produced such a powerful impact that spectators wept far more copiously than for any tragedy. One critic was moved to write that 'three comedies like that will kill tragedy altogether'. Diderot's modification of the *comédie larmoyante* style developed into what became known as 'bourgeois drama'. This genre highlighted naturalism and the kinds of characters and circumstances of everyday life characteristic of Paris's largely bourgeois theatre audiences. Louis-Sébastien Mercier, whose own bourgeois dramas were pitched defiantly against any backsliding, claimed to be representing in them 'the picture of our mores, the interior of our homes, this interior which is to an empire what the entrails are to the human body'. Bourgeois drama invariably involved moral dilemmas and the shedding of copious tears.

Unsurprisingly, official court culture was neither shaken nor much stirred by these developments. Louis XV detested *comédies larmoyantes* and bourgeois dramas and always struck them off the Versailles play-lists. Though off-duty courtiers and state servants might crowd the lodges of the Parisian theatres, handkerchiefs to the ready, public taste was increasingly dictated by a far larger, mainly bourgeois theatre-going public, who cheerfully ignored the prompts from Versailles as regards what was and what was not worthy of attention. La Bruyère, analyst of Louis XIV's court, had noted contemptuously how Paris was nothing but 'the court's ape', instinctively mimicking its mores, values, and priorities. The *comédie larmoyante* suggested that this was changing very dramatically. Paris had developed tastes and values completely independent of courtly prescription.

In time, there would be some, even within the Parisian theatrical world, who came to deplore this soggy cascade of public tears. The actor Charles Collé blamed women, who always wanted 'a play which makes them snivel'. Voltaire, a sometime convert to the genre, subsequently said it made him weep that people were weeping at comedies, and he was upset that 'metaphysics and tears' had taken the place of real comedy. 'It would be a great impertinence today', another author ironized, 'to undertake to make the public laugh, when they claim that they only want comedies of tears.' Yet the cascade of tears did allow space for other expressions of emotion. Indeed, it was Voltaire himself, in the preface to his play, *L'Écossaise* (1760), who hit the pertinent note:

> As for the play's genre, it is the high comic mixed with the genre of simple comedy. The *honnête homme* smiles the smile of the soul, always superior to the laugh of the mouth. There are episodes sad enough to move to tears, but without however any of the characters seeking too zealously to be pathetic.

Through the tears, in other words, a smile was gently emerging. Voltaire's 'smile of the soul' was, as we shall see, the new smile of sensibility.

We can gain purchase on the slow but sure increase in the value attached to smiles by analysing the recurrence of the word, '*sourire*' in French literary works of the period. The occurrence of the term in the late seventeenth and eighteenth century was very low, as we have noted. Moreover, the adjectives or adverbs which most frequently contextualized these usages included such terms as 'forced', 'disdainful', 'bitter', 'mocking', 'proud', 'sardonic', and 'ironic'. There were exceptions of course, but in general terms, a smile most characteristically constituted a gesture made by individuals in a situation of superiority. Very often, this was social superiority in fact: those who smiled were often aristocrats and courtiers, condescending to and inwardly laughing at their inferiors. The smile thus generally fell within the classical theory of laughter, as discussed in the previous chapter. By smiling, as by laughing, one condescends, one shows contempt, and one is amused by the misfortunes of others. A gentleman's smile was a marker of social distinction.

But change was on the way. First, there was a dramatic step change in the frequency of the term 'sourire' in literary texts from the 1730s, and particularly in the 1740s, 1750s, and 1760s, marking a massive increase between the early decades of the century and the reign of Louis XVI. It was, in addition, a question of quality and context as well as quantity: from the 1740s and 1750s in particular there was a palpable shift in the way in which the meaning of the smile was understood. Smiles were now more likely to be 'enchanting', 'sweet', 'good', 'agreeable', 'friendly', and 'virtuous'. It was not that the old, ironic, disdainful smile had totally disappeared. It was too rooted in the facial regime of the social and courtly elite to vanish overnight, and it continued to play a role, but often now as a counterpoint to a more pure and authentic smile that was increasingly on view.

The works which more than any others produced the breakthrough in usage in French literary culture were the great novels of the English author Samuel Richardson, namely *Pamela* (1740), *Clarissa* (1748), and *The History of Sir Charles Grandison* (1753), which were translated into French in 1742, 1751, and 1755 respectively. The latter two volumes, entitled in French *Lettres anglaises* and *Nouvelles lettres anglaises*, were translated by the abbé Prévost, already famous as the author of the powerful moral drama, *Manon Lescaut* (1731). These English novels of sensibility found no difficulty in acclimatizing themselves in France. The taste for Richardson in France was overwhelming. 'You cannot go into a house without finding a *Pamela*', noted one French observer. Along with *Clarissa*, it would be the most-found English novel in the libraries of French families down to the end of the century. In the translations of Richardson's novels, usage of '*sourire*' far outdistanced anything found in previous works.

Diderot, the zealous apostle of bourgeois drama, eulogized Richardson in the most lavish terms, placing him in his personal pantheon alongside Moses, Homer, Sophocles, and Euripides. Although the length and moral scrupulousness of the Englishman's novels are emphatically not to our modern tastes, Diderot's eulogy is striking testimony to the extraordinary effect they had in Enlightenment France. Diderot loved them for similar reasons that he loved the idea of bourgeois drama (and that he also, as we shall see, warmed to the sentimental moralizing of Greuze's painting): their sublime domestic ordinariness, and, consequently, their humane relevance. In a novel by Richardson, the backdrop is the world in which we live; the plot is true; the individuals in it are completely real; its characters are drawn from the middle rungs of society; its actions are based on the customs of all nations; the passions that it paints are just like those I myself feel; they are moved by the same things that move me . . . it shows me the general course of things that surround me . . .

The naturalistic sense of the real that Richardson's novels radiated was heightened by their epistolary format. This was also true of Jean-Jacques Rousseau's *Julie, ou la Nouvelle Héloise* (1761). Manifestly written under Richardson's influence, *La Nouvelle Héloise* became one of the best-selling novels of the eighteenth century, and it too offered a striking revalorization of the smile. Both Richardson and Rousseau eschewed an authorial voice, and allowed the plot to unfold through the simple device of the exchange of letters. Both authors played their readers along with the notion that the novels were merely 'found correspondences' and were in fact authentic scenes from the everyday life of real individuals. The subtitle of *La Nouvelle Héloise* was *Lettres de deux amans habitants au pied des Alpes* ('Letters of Two Lovers, Living at the Foot of the Alps'). Letter-writing was one of the obsessions of the age, and the truth-to-life effects that Richardson and Rousseau achieved made the impact of their work on Anglo-French audiences all the more powerful.

The English divine William Warburton claimed that both the French and the English had been prepared for the impact of Richardson and Rousseau by the French writer Marivaux, in his post-Regency days. His plays and then his post-Regency novels—notably the *Vie de Marianne* (1735–41) and *Le Paysan parvenu* (1735)—had replaced the medieval tradition of 'barbarous romances' with studies of imagined lives and manners from a familiar and recognizable modern world in a way that was 'entertaining to an improved mind, or useful to promote that improvement'. Their mixture of psychological acuity and moral investigation chimed with the authors of *Clarissa* and *Julie*. Each of the latter novels constituted a moral lesson grounded in the misfortunes of virtue—a virtue that was objectified in the character of a beautiful young woman, a fact which seemed to promote both identification and protectiveness. Reader response to their plots was highly charged and nakedly emotional. 'Come, fellow men and learn [from Richardson]', Diderot exclaimed, 'how to reconcile yourselves with the evils of this life. Come and we will weep together over the unfortunate characters in his fictions and we shall say, "If fate strikes us down, at least honest folk will also weep for us."'

As Diderot would freely have admitted, he was speaking the language of sensibility. The term 'sensibility' was becoming one of the most redolent buzzwords of eighteenth-century French literary and visual culture. It owed some of its prestige and cultural reach to the assumption that it purported to be describing scientific fact. In the late seventeenth century, the English philosopher John Locke had argued that human identity and individual consciousness were derived from the material impact of the environment on the raw matter of the human body. Whereas Descartes—with his '*cogito, ergo sum*'—had stressed the cognitive role of the human reason in this process, Locke and his French followers, such as Étienne Bonnot de Condillac, in his *Traité des sensations* ('Treatise on Sensation' (1754)), placed much greater emphasis on the role of the senses. This 'sensationalist' philosophy powerfully subverted Descartes's physiology, with its emphasis on the material presence of the soul in the pineal gland. The soul was now increasingly viewed as dematerialized, and freed from the humoral system that characterized the Galenic system of medical thought.

Following the work of the physicians Thomas Willis, Hermann Boerhaave, and especially Albrecht von Haller, the human body was coming to be viewed less as a kind of clumsy container in which humoral fluids sloshed around, than as an assemblage of raw matter composed of fibres, which showed greater or lesser sensitivity to external stimuli. Under stimulation, fibre was characterized by 'irritability', while the nerves had 'sensibility'—a word and an idea that was concurrently making its way in the world of the novel.

Fibre was, for Haller and the physicians, simply a material property of matter, but over the course of the century the term sensibility increasingly came to be used in an active and moral as well as a passive and material sense. 'What is sensibility?', Diderot rhetorically demanded, only to answer: 'the vivid effect on our soul of an infinity of delicate observations'. An essential quality of humanity was consequently the ability to be, and to feel, moved—morally, spiritually, emotionally. Diderot claimed that Richardson's novels had the ability to 'lift up the spirit, touch the soul, and radiate everywhere the love of good'. This moral hypersensitivity expressed through the language of sensibility converged with notions of sympathy as a quintessential human trait being developed by Scottish philosophers such as Francis Hutcheson and Adam Smith. The human imagination was hardwired to feel sympathy and pity for the problems of others. The inner man or woman present in every human being had a capacity to be emotionally

moved by the spectacle of human suffering, through imaginative identification with another's ills. Sensibility was thus not just an automatic reaction;
it was a positive and formative moral response to external stimuli which
fully engaged the mind.

This view of sensibility as a kind of opening oneself up to vivid impressions was, needless to say, at the antipodes of the classical theory of laughter,
with its insistent contempt for the misfortunes of others. Sensibility fostered
not an air of superiority but a sense of humane equality and fellow-feeling.
One person's misfortune was now another's opportunity for remedial
action. One was sympathetic when confronted with the spectacle of
human suffering, and the tears that one shed underlined the intrinsic
goodness of wider humanity. The cult of sensibility thus came to nurture
the notion of philanthropy and *bienfaisance* ('benificence') a term that was
brought into the language in 1725 by the Regency-period veteran, the abbé
de Saint-Pierre. Unlike traditional Christian charity which, it was now said,
was grounded in donors' selfish concern with the fate of their souls,
bienfaisance was a secular virtue with its roots in the human condition. It
held out the prospect of a better and more humane society, and better
human beings.

Tears, the most obvious expression of an individual of true sensibility in
the novels of Richardson and Rousseau, thus had an almost sacramental
quality in regard to human nature and identity. They were an outward and
visible sign of an inner and invisible grace, the grace of humanity. They also
highlighted the strategic importance of the smile. This was evident in the
comparative frequency with which the term '*sourire*' appeared in the novels,
and also in the egregiously tearful contexts in which smiles often appeared,
the significance attaching to them, and the meanings they expressed.
Thus the plot of *Clarissa* at times reads like a contest of smiles. On the
one hand, there is the traditional mocking smile which plays around the lips
of arch-seducer Lovelace, one of the eighteenth-century's most memorable
(and attractive) villains, and his partners in the hunt for female favours.
Lovelace is notable for 'the misleading sweetness that he has in his smile, in
his language and his whole countenance'—misleading, of course, since it is a
weapon in his arsenal of seduction. His smile is as artificial as the gestures of
his rival for Clarissa's hand, the repulsive Solmes, whose smile we are told 'is
so unnatural when set against his facial features that one might take it for the
grimace of a madman or a lunatic'. For Lovelace, the smile is a smile of
betrayal in another way too: 'I have managed to lay siege to more than one

[young woman] through an immoral book, or by a risqué quotation, or by an indecent painting, especially if I see them ogle and smile. Then we have always, Old Satan and I, marked them down as ours.' For better or worse—in this case, for worse—the smile has become the facial gesture that offered a transparent window into an individual's innermost being.

In powerful contrast, the target of Lovelace's wiles has a smile which does not mask a lustful interior but instead transparently transmits a sublimely virtuous character. If Clarissa occasionally smiles with disdain, it is only at Lovelace's gamey obscenities. Otherwise hers is a hauntingly lovely smile, 'a smile mixing tenderness and concern', full of charm, beauty, and fellow-feeling. Clarissa's long, drawn-out death scene, lasting many pages of the novel, sees her surrounded by her friends and servants, all in a tableau of lachrymose unison. Yet at the very end, we are told, as she states her hope in the afterlife, 'a sweet smile beamed joy over her countenance'. Despite her apparent death which triggers 'a violent burst of grief' from the assembled, she revives weakly to die pronouncing the words 'blessed Lord—Jesus'. 'And with these words', we are told, she 'expired: such a smile, such a charming serenity overspreading her sweet face at the instant seemed to manifest her eternal happiness already begun'.

The transcendent death-bed smile of Clarissa Harlowe haunted French imaginations much as it already had the British. It certainly seems to have stayed in the mind of Jean-Jacques Rousseau. The plot line of his *La Nouvelle Héloise* similarly showcased feminine virtue under trial and ultimately resplen-dently triumphant—and made of his Julie one of the great virtuous heroines of eighteenth-century literature. As in *Clarissa*, the novel's heroine dies serenely after a marathon death-bed scene (Fig. 2.13). As with Richardson's heroine, the tear-soaked environment of the egregious Julie's death-bed is pierced by a smile. The last day of Julie's life, we are told, was spent with her facing her end not simply with Clarissa-like serenity, but also with a word of consolation for all around her who are lost in grief and sobbing. Despite her suffering, an observer notes, Julie's 'gaiety was not constrained, even her mirth was touching. There were smiles on the mouth and tears in the eyes.'

It was precisely this smiling through the tears—'smiles on the mouth and tears in the eyes', in Rousseau's words—that made the novel so seductive. The cocktail of strong emotions, pioneered in *comédies larmoyantes* and in translations of Richardson, here reached its climax in terms of audience response. The mixture of emotions within *La Nouvelle Héloise* was thun-derously echoed in a wave of voluptuous grief which seized those who consumed its contents. Readers vied with each other in their expressions of delicate sensibility. Julie's creator received a deluge of fan mail, detailing the 'tears', 'sighs', 'torments', and 'ecstasy' which had accompanied individual reading of the novel. The weeping was contagious: people reread key passages to trigger more 'delicious outpourings of the heart'; they read it to their friends so that weeping could be general and unconstrained; they read it behind closed doors so that the servants could not hear them sobbing (or worse, join in); they read it in small portions so as to make the pain bearable; they postponed reading it so that their health could stand the force of the unleashed emotions. 'One must die of pleasure after reading this book', one reviewer of the book opined, '... or rather one must live in order to read it again and again'. Julie's final act seemed to constitute a life-and-death issue almost as much for *Julie*'s readers as for Julie herself. One noble-woman broke down completely at the death-bed scene: 'I was past weeping. A sharp pain convulsed me. My heart was crushed'. Another

Fig. 2.13 Jean-Jacques Rousseau, *Death-bed Scene* from *La Nouvelle Héloise* (1761)

reader had to spend a week in bed after exposing herself to the fateful chapter. 'Never', a retired army officer proudly puffed, 'have I wept such delicious tears . . . I would gladly have died during that supreme moment.'

Rousseau's fan mail is a tear-saturated monument to the way in which the cult of sensibility stimulated new forms of behaviour and fashioned new forms of subjectivity. The author Louis-Sébastien Mercier, in his role as theatre critic, turned the Cartesian *cogito* on its head: recording his experience in a theatre he noted, 'I cry and then, voluptuously, I know that I am a man.' Yet historians and literary critics have perhaps been so overwhelmed with this declaration of '*Fleo, ergo sum*' ('I cry, therefore I am') and with the torrents of unleashed tears in the cult of sensibility that they have lost from sight the smile which—as the two critical death-bed scenes in the most sensationally best-selling novels of the century attest—played a critical role in the culture of sensibility.

Tears and smiles were to have been all the more powerful, moreover, because of their apparently contagious quality. This contagion could take place in theatres—from *Ines de Castro* onwards. We can also be pretty sure that it happened in real life situations too. Twenty-first century psychologists note that the smile does have a contagious quality in interpersonal relations in our own day, in that the gesture tends to be responded to by a smile from the smiled-at, which then confirms the positive feelings of the original smiler. It is thus plausible to imagine these processes of 'emotional contagion' occurring in the eighteenth century in the context of this movement of sensibility, for tears and smiles combined. Furthermore, the Rousseau correspondence also shows how these strong emotions could be passed on from the pages of a book. Smiling and weeping contagions could, it seemed, leap from the page into the heart and onto the face of the reader.

The smile of sensibility in question in all of this was Voltaire's 'smile of the soul'. It mingled elemental passions—pain and pleasure, enjoyment and grief—in a dramatic, infectious mix. This kind of smile revealed the true and beautiful character of the virtuous heroine. It was at the opposing pole from the smile of contempt and disdain which had traditionally dominated literary, philosophical, and aesthetic discussion. In the new world of heightened sensibility, the smile was becoming a kind of crystallized encapsulation of identity. It revealed what was truest and most authentic about one's inner being and sense of identity.

This new kind of perception is also evident in the famous letter in *La Nouvelle Héloïse* in which Julie's lover, Saint-Preux, chastises her for having her portrait painted. In his eyes, though graceful, beautiful, and lifelike, the portrait was simply not her. The painter had failed to put liveliness into the eyes, and had got the hairline and cheek-colour wrong, giving her an artificial air. Worse, however, was to come: he had wrecked her mouth, by seeking to idealize her appearance and by failing to depict a distinctive facial blemish: 'Ye Gods! Was this man made of bronze? . . . He has forgotten the little scar that remains under your lip.' Above all, however, he had failed to convey her smile:

> But tell me, what has he done with these little cupids' nests hiding at the corners of your mouth . . . ? He has not given them their full graciousness, he has not given your mouth the ability, both agreeable and serious, suddenly to change at your slightest smile and penetrate the heart with some unknown enchantment, some sudden inexpressible ravishment. It is true that your portrait cannot pass from seriousness to a smile. But that is precisely my complaint: to display all your charms, you would need to be painted in all the moments of your life.

In the literature of sensibility, the smile had become the badge of human identity, the fleeting but almost unrepresentable sign of self.

Visualizing the smile of sensibility

Inscribed within the discourses around the smile of sensibility a new and optimistic account of human nature had emerged. Voltaire's phrase for the new smile of sensibility, 'the smile of the soul', was to ricochet around the discussions of the new smile in the following decades. Writing in 1773, for example, Louis-Sébastien Mercier would define 'the smile of the soul' as a 'refined, delicate and peaceful smile as far distant from tumultuous joy as pleasure is from debauch'. Unlike what he called 'the machinal [or instrumental] smile' which did not speak to the soul, the smile of the soul 'sweetly applauds what is respectable, noble and touching'.

Rousseau had highlighted the resistance of the loved one's smile to representation, its simple ineffability. But his contemporaries were less withholding in imagining what this 'smile of the soul', the sublime smile of sensibility, actually looked like. Voltaire was categorical: 'a beautiful individual will lack grace on their face, if in smiling their mouth is closed and without a smile'. The white-tooth smile was on the horizon.

Richardson also provided clues as to the visualization of the smile, notably in his *Sir Charles Grandison*. As in *Clarissa*, there are smiles in abundance in the novel. These were sometimes 'forced', 'mocking', 'flattering', 'puerile', and 'ironic' smiles—for every drama must have its villains. (And in the 1780s, Laclos was to provide an even wider and more sinister array of perfidious smiling in his *Les Liaisons dangereuses*.) But of more dramatic effect in Richardson were 'charming' and 'tender' smiles and smiles 'without affectation' associated with the novel's female protagonist. She smiles with a fearless, revealing transparency: 'her first smile will show you her heart painted on her face'. 'Each look of complaisance, each smile that I saw shining on this loveable face', one of the characters notes, 'I attributed to her natural goodness, to her frankness, to the gratitude of a generous heart.' This is a smile which accommodates more extreme emotion and rises above it: 'the charming girl! She managed to smile through her tears [revealing her] innocent sensibility.' The author continues:

> This form of open, smiling, virtuous beauty may take the form, of this kind of grace that the French call physiognomy and that we might call expression . . . Her cheeks? I have never seen such beautifully-formed cheeks. The mildest smile creates two charming dimples in them . . . Her mouth . . . there has never been a mouth so divine. And why be surprised? Vermillion lips and teeth both even and white would give beauty to any other mouth.

A beautiful mouth, white teeth, and a charming smile seem to be coming into a new conjunction. The heroine Miss Grandison is thus described:

> her colouring is not of striking whiteness, but she has a delicate and clear skin. Her features are generally regular . . . her teeth extremely white and very even. I have never seen anything so loveable as her mouth. An air of reserve and modesty inspires both respect and love and is accompanied by the most charming smile.

This marks a significant moment in the emergence of the smile of sensibility. The smile now shone out from *comédie larmoyante* and bourgeois drama, and, with the sentimental fiction of Richardson and Rousseau, it bade to become a primary marker of identity. The new smile had overturned the hierarchy of facial expression established by Charles Le Brun on the basis of his observations on Western art. Whereas it was formerly the eyes that had emblematized spirituality and the higher emotions, it was the mouth—traditionally the site of appetite and fleshly passion—that now did so. Similarly, whiteness of skin, previously the very cynosure of purity and beauty, shrank in significance in comparison with whiteness of teeth. Significantly, the great natural historian Buffon, in his celebrated *Histoire naturelle*, highlighted the mouth as the most mobile and therefore the most expressive of the organs in giving a sense of character.

These clues in literary and scientific works as to the morphology of the new smile of sensibility were endorsed in the world of painting, most notably in the *oeuvre* of Jean-Baptiste Greuze, who began to achieve fame from the late 1750s, just as the breakthrough of the smile of sensibility was occurring. Greuze specialized in genre painting, notably the depiction of scenes from everyday domestic life, even though he retained the loftiness of vision evident in history painting. He animated and gave narrative drive to his scenes in ways which recalled contemporary drama or fiction. Diderot, principal theorist and practitioner of bourgeois drama, saluted him as the first painter 'to link together events in ways that would enable the writing of a novel'. One can indeed imagine the dramatization and moralization of virtues in, for example, Greuze's *L'Accordée de village* ('The Village Bride' (1761)) or *La Piété filiale* ('Filial Piety' (1763) or *La Mère bien-aimée* ('The Well-Loved Mother' (1769)) which could have passed muster as plausible scenes from the novels of sensibility, or from Diderot's plays in fact. This emerged particularly in Greuze's very close attention to the facial and gestural expression of the characters. In this, he was reflecting a more general concern with French painters' ability to depict the emotions more naturalistically than Charles Le Brun's famous drawings. In a way, this echoed the Zeitgeist sensibility. 'I want a soul that speaks to my soul', the philosopher Condillac had opined when discussing the place of the expression of feelings in painting. Greuze sought to supply just this.

Greuze's virtuosity in expressing a wide range of 'soulful' facial expressions is evident in the dignified painting, *Epiphany* (the *Gateau des Rois* (1774)), a moment in which the simple joys and pains of a large peasant family play off against the stoic dignity of the paterfamilias (Fig. 4.3). The latter, interestingly, has his mouth shut, but all the other dramatis personae are shown in a state of excitement and expectancy with simple, sincere, and naturalistic expressions which feature open mouths and, indeed, white teeth. The innocent virtues of peasant life are thus rendered through the white-tooth smile emergent in the literature of sensibility. Similar naturally expressive smiles of sensibility are on view in *La Mère bien-aimée* (1765) (Fig. 2.14). The serene face of the exhausted mother surrounded by adoring but demanding children in this painting was widely recognized as an

Fig. 2.14 Jean-Baptiste Greuze, *The Well-loved Mother* (1769)

adaptation of Rubens's depiction of Marie de Medici in *The Queen in Childbirth* (1621–3). Yet where Rubens's happy but exhausted Marie was tight-lipped, Greuze's mother characteristically opens her mouth to reveal her teeth in a wan yet transcendent smile. Diderot thought Greuze had surpassed Rubens in this image.

The smile really had changed. And this new smile of sensibility had teeth. From the middle decades of the century, the cult of sensibility evident in fiction, drama, and painting had revalorized the smile as a marker of inner and outward beauty and as an emblem of identity. It seemed an implicit reproach to the glum facial fixity associated with Bourbon court culture. There was a kind of missionary zeal about the cult of sensibility that Louis-Sébastien Mercier, whose *fleo, ergo sum* bade to replace Descartes's *cogito ergo sum* as a motto for human existence. The smile associated with those tears now showed teeth. Furthermore, those teeth could be better cared for than ever before. Dentistry was coming into focus.

3

Cometh the Dentist

Every day, from some time in the 1710s until his death in 1757, Jean
Thomas stood on the Pont-Neuf, alongside the *cheval de bronze*, the
famous equestrian statue of Henri IV at the bridge's centre, and offered to

GRAND THOMAS avec son panache,
Est la Perle des Charlatans :
Il vous guérit le mal de dents,
Quand il vous les arrache.

Fig. 3.1 *Le Grand Thomas*

pull out the teeth of all and sundry. *Le Grand Thomas*, as he was familiarly known (or, in homage to his extraordinary girth, *le Gros Thomas*, 'Fat Thomas') was a colourful and striking offshoot of what we have called the Old Regime of Teeth (Fig. 3.1). It would be untrue to say that he was the last of his kind, for similar figures would be found touring European countrysides through to the early twentieth century, and indeed they may still be found today in the marketplaces of cities in the developing world. But it is true to say that by the time of Jean Thomas's death in 1757, an alternative form of practitioner had emerged within Paris. This figure not only differentiated himself from the tooth-puller of old but was also recognizably similar to the modern dentist. Indeed, the term 'dentist' ('*dentiste*') was invented specifically to describe him. This institutional and professional development would have a major influence on the history of the smile. In conjunction with the blossoming of the smile of sensibility within the cultural ferment of Enlightenment Paris, it would produce the city's Smile Revolution.

The Pont-Neuf tooth-pulling carnival

The latest link in the chain of tooth-puller showmen who had colonized the bridge since its earliest days, *le Grand Thomas* was a worthy heir of Pont-Neuf practitioners such as Ferranti, Tabarin, Contugi, Carmelina, and Barry. Like them, he spawned a literary industry. This celebrated the mythical status in Parisian popular culture of a man who had fashioned himself in the heroic mode. His portrait proudly proclaimed:

> Our *Grand Thomas*, beplumed in glory,
> The Pearl of Charlatans (or so's the story).
> Your Tooth aches? You need never doubt
> *Le Grand Thomas* will yank it out.

Epithets rained hard around the head of this 'Pearl of Charlatans'. The 'Honour of the Universe', 'Massive Aesculapius', 'Terror of the Human Jaw', 'Sans-Pareil', always dressed in an outsize scarlet coat, trimmed with gold, with a solar medallion jangling on his chest. The imposing wig that he wore over his swarthy face was half-hidden by a colossal tricorn hat bedecked with peacock feathers and a colourful cockade, while at his side was a huge military sabre, its handle a decorative eagle. The stage of 'the Illustrious Thomas' was a colourful mobile cart, with a roof to keep the

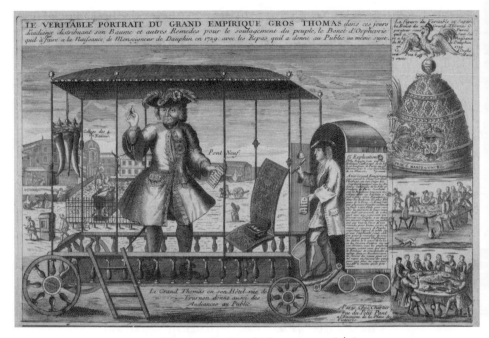

Fig. 3.2 *Le Grand Thomas en son hôtel*

elements at bay (Fig. 3.2). An enormous tooth, dubbed 'Gargantua's awe-some molar', hung on one corner, surmounted with a coronet, and on another there was a bell to summon custom. His usual troupe comprised two Savoyards who performed with trumpet and violin. There was a small enclosed place on the stage which may have acted as his consultation chamber, as well as serving as changing room for his troupe. Like any good charlatan, Thomas combined tooth-pulling prowess with a reputation as a salesman of orviétan and other sure-fire remedies that claimed to ensure the health and embellishment of the mouth, and also to clear up what his handbills called 'secret' (i.e. venereal) illnesses.

The demeanour of *le Grand Thomas* was such that it seemed that he could terrify peccant teeth into submission. Everything about him exuded mythic power. The medicines he prescribed were made up in doses suitable as much for a horse as a man. He himself weighed the same as three men, and ate and drank for four. His barking voice could be heard across the city. If a client's tooth resisted his assaults he would, it was said, make the individual kneel down in front of him and then, with the strength of a bull, lift him three times into the air with the hand still clenched on the recalcitrant tooth. His flag bore the device *Dentem sinon maxillam* ('the tooth, and if not, the jaw'), evoking his claim that he could pull out a jaw faster than his fellow practitioners could manage a tooth. One mock-heroic piece of doggerel celebrated the epic, daily struggle which Thomas waged against the forces of darkness from his redoubt on the Pont-Neuf:

> Once it was, on shore of Seine,
> Dwelt sombre Death, a cruel sovereign . . .
> But *Grand Thomas,* appearing on this strand,
> By his divine secrets stemmed Death's cruel hand . . .
> Endless efforts, in vain its might,
> Proud Death's sent crashing into endless night.
> Then Thomas, triumphant, full of glory,
> Allows us taste of his great victory . . .
> Fever before him trembles and slips out;
> Away too, vanquished, hobbles Gout.
> All ills are banished by his salutary art.
> He restores our pleasures, gives us all good heart,
> As the Universe blesses him in full admiration
> So stops my singing muse and all this peroration.

This mythical figure prided himself on relieving suffering in a way few physicians could manage. In a play, *Le Vaudeville*, produced at the Opéra-Comique in 1743, he appears in the guise of 'The Operator' and comments approvingly on his tooth-pulling fingers which 'have effected more cures than all the Faculty'. When upbraided for lack of respect to his superiors, he replies:

> Beware the lure of windy exaggeration
> Which doctors use – for our assassination.
> Tho' I, Thomas, am tongue-tied in truth
> At least I can help with the ache of a tooth.
> I pull it right from the root.
> Crack! Right from the root.

Thomas engaged in exploits worthy of attention by the literary muse. The birth in 1729 of a Dauphin, Louis XV's first son and heir, had been the occasion for outpourings of Parisian joy. On 9 September, Paris's Opéra-Comique company gave free performances of a playlet entitled *L'Impromptu du Pont-Neuf* ('The Pont-Neuf Impromptu'), which purported to show all the stock characters of the Parisian landscape, including, of course, *le Grand Thomas*, giving thanks in their own distinctive ways. Two days previously in fact, the living legend had erupted into action. When Louis XV passed the Pont-Neuf on his way to Notre-Dame cathedral in order to give thanks for the birth of his son, Thomas was ready and waiting for him. He was dressed, accounts revealed, 'like a second Phaeton on his chariot', 'more like [the God] Silenus than the men of our own age', 'in the manner of the elephants of Darius, his head bowed down under a hat-brim more suitable for stuffing a mattress than for acting as headgear'. A fanfare of trumpets greeted the passage of the ruler, and Thomas beat a drum, 'crying out "Long Live the King!", in a voice so loud that he made himself heard above everyone else'.

Thomas sought to prolong the royal festivities. In a handbill which he circulated round the city, the *Avis salutaire au public* ('Salutary Advice to the Public'), he portrayed himself speaking from his 'chariot' on the Pont-Neuf 'like an Emperor on his throne', and he urged the public to take 'rejoicing pills watered down in a pint or two of bacchic celebrations'. He went on to announce that 'in celebration of the happy birth of Monseigneur the Dauphin', he, Thomas, would be pulling teeth gratis for a fortnight, besides 'washing them, cleaning them and rendering them as white as milk'. (Interestingly, even traditional tooth-pullers, it seems, had begun to recognize a growing demand for white teeth.) He would also distribute his medicines free. In addition, on Monday 19 September, he planned to hold open table on the Pont-Neuf from morning to night, to be followed by a firework display. He prepared by marking out an enclosed area round the Henry IV statue and laying on provisions of wine, sausage, and much besides. The excitement was such that individuals with windows overlooking the bridge hired them out for the forthcoming spectacle.

Wretchedly, the open-handed beneficence of our Pearl of Charlatans blew up in his face. The Paris Lieutenant de Police banned the feast the afternoon before the great day, and confiscated all the refreshments. In the morning, however, the invited guests turned up in huge numbers, filling the bridge and the surrounding quais. When they realized that their fun had been thwarted, they took matters into their own hands. One report stated:

> They marched to Thomas's home on the Quai Conti where he was skulking under virtual police arrest. There they hit out insolently, saying that the public was sacred and that they would not be lightly mocked. *Le Grand Thomas* appeared at his window as at a tribune, thinking to pacify the hungry by the sight of his august face and that public eloquence of which he has long had

the knack. But starving stomach has no ears. The guests mutinied, forcing Thomas to bring out to them the only plate of food that the police had left him ... The host spent the day seeing his windows being broken ...

Nor were Thomas's humiliations at an end. For at around the same time he was subject to an impressive practical joke by medical students the narration of which reached Germany. A report in Berlin's *Vossische Zeitung* recorded how

> several students played a humorous practical joke on the familiar tooth-breaker named 'Great Thomas' who has his shop standing on wheels on the Pont-Neuf. They bound four large rockets to the underside of his little house and ignited these at exactly the time that he was in the middle of extracting a tooth from a patient. Whereupon the latter fell to the ground and the Great Thomas fell on top of him, which caused a great deal of laughter from the crowd of people gathered round him.

Much fun was clearly to be had in making fun of a figure of fun, in carnivalizing the carnivalesque. The incidents highlighted the continuing Rabelaisian humour that was still associated with the tooth-pulling arts. Now couched in the fashionable language of the mock-heroic genre, the recounting of such an episode probably added to rather than detracted from the charisma of *le Grand Thomas*. The latter certainly kept his sacred place on the Pont-Neuf, and his tooth-pulling exploits continued in style, for the author and dramatist Louis-Sébastien Mercier, who was born in Paris in 1740, fondly remembered having seen him at work in his regular spot during his own childhood. This 'Corypheus among Operators', as Mercier called him,

> was recognizable from afar by his gigantic shape and the size of his clothing. His head held high and coiffed with striking plumes, his virile voice made itself heard on both sides of the river Seine. Surrounded by a trusting public, toothache seemed to approach, only to expire at his feet.

In 1757, the living legend died. An anonymous obituary poem for Thomas envisaged him down in Hell—for he had proved too fat to ascend the ladder into Heaven—keeping his hand in by sharpening the teeth of Cerberus at the gates of Hades. The success of his former business was more than evident in the inventory of his possessions drawn up in March 1757 after his death. The notary solemnly recorded a medallion with a sun motif, the decorated hat, the scarlet coat with gold trimmings, plus in the stable 'a dismantled cart which served the deceased when he placed himself on the Pont-Neuf to pull out teeth and to sell his merchandise'—plus sacks of gold coin worth a princely 54,000 livres. There was a fortune to be made from looking after the teeth of Parisians, it would seem. Indeed, such was the growth of demand for white teeth, there were any number of fortunes to be made.

A tale of two dentists

Thomas had lived and prospered, keeping the flame of the charlatanesque tooth-puller-cum-showman tradition alive and well at the heart of Paris far into the eighteenth century. Yet by this time, a divergent tradition of mouth care had also begun to establish itself in the city—one which, as we shall see, was altogether more accommodating to the act of smiling than the gung-ho extractionism of Thomas and his ilk. It differentiated itself sharply from the *Grand Thomas* style. Rather than revel in plebeian acclaim, it foregrounded scientific credentials, preventive care, and functional efficiency. It was first and best embodied in the person of Pierre Fauchard. In Fauchard's life and work we begin to glimpse for the first time in European history the world of modern scientific dentistry—and the decline of the Old Regime of Teeth.

There was nothing that we know about Pierre Fauchard's early life that would have marked him out as different from the colourful world of theatrical tooth-pulling of a *Grand Thomas*. Born in 1678, possibly in Vannes, Fauchard practised from the late 1690s mainly in the west of France around Angers, seemingly on a semi-itinerant basis, like a traditional *arracheur de dents*. For some time, he recounted, he also worked under a naval surgeon, Alexandre Poteleret. Dental care was a particular issue in the navy because of the impact of scurvy on the teeth, and Poteleret had made mouth care a particular interest. Fauchard started his practice in Paris in 1719 at which moment *le Grand Thomas* was already installed on the Pont-Neuf. Fauchard probably had no more and no less formal surgical qualification than his tooth-pulling nemesis.

Pierre Fauchard lived and worked on the Left Bank, in the Rue des Fossés Saint-Germain (now Rue de l'Ancienne-Comédie in the Sixth Arrondissement). Although this was physically only a couple of hundred metres distant from the Pont-Neuf on which *le Grand Thomas* and his ilk practised their craft, it was light-years away in terms of what the two men came to offer. The publications of *le Grand Thomas* had combined dog Latin and literary *jeux d'esprit* with crude advertising handbills. Fauchard, in contrast, could boast a weighty, two-volumed work, *Le Chirurgien-dentiste, ou Traité des dents* ('The Dental Surgeon, or, Treatise on Teeth'). 'The fruit of assiduous research and thirty years of experience', the magnum opus was published in 1728—at around the same time, in fact, that Thomas was having his troubles with banned feasts, exploding fireworks, spoil-sport policemen, a mutinous public, and all the rest. It is probably the most influential book in the early history of dentistry in any language. It also coined the term *dentiste* that has remained within the language (passing into English in the 1750s, for example). It is on this work that rests Fauchard's claim to be the first modern dentist. It was a response to the emerging demand for the white-tooth smile of sensibility that was just beginning to take shape in the post-Louis-Quatorzian period. In a way too, Fauchard made it happen.

In the introduction to *Le Chirurgien-dentiste*, Fauchard highlighted the academic neglect which the study of dentistry had suffered in the past. There was no continuous or even substantial body of work from Antiquity on which to draw, and the Moderns had been almost as silent on the topic as the Ancients had been. He could cite only two post-Renaissance works focused on the teeth that were worth their salt, even if both were manifestly uncomprehensive in Fauchard's view. These were Urbain Hémard's *De la vraye anathomie des dents* (1582) and Bernardin Martin's *Dissertation sur les dents* (1679). Despite their pioneering status, neither of these works could pass muster as works of erudition in eighteenth-century terms. Martin in particular amassed his own untrained surgical observations alongside passages lifted wholesale from surgical texts and also traditional remedies (cat droppings for teeth cleansing, for example).

At the time that Fauchard wrote, it was still the case, he noted, that there existed in print 'no public course, nor specific surgical course in which the illnesses associated with the teeth [were] amply covered'. Even when surgeons dealt with the matter, as in the case of generally well-regarded manuals of the period—such as René-Jacques Croissant de Garangeot's *Traité des opérations de chirurgie* (1720) or Guillaume Mauquest de La Motte's *Traité complet de chirurgie* (1722)—they were invariably reticent on the score. Fauchard was especially critical of Garangeot. Furthermore, although the *Cours d'opérations chirurgicales* of the eminent practitioner Pierre Dionis (1708) had devoted a whole section to a rather thoughtful account of the teeth and their illnesses, it still only occupied less than thirty pages out of a two-volume work of over 600 pages in total. Moreover, as we have seen,

Dionis effectively warned off aspirant surgeons from getting too involved with such a plebeian occupation as pulling teeth which 'smack[ed] of the charlatan and the mountebank'. This advice was symptomatic of a more general wish among many socially and scientifically ambitious surgeons to distance themselves from the kinds of routine body maintenance (bleedings, purges, shaving, hair-dressing and -cutting, tooth-pulling, etc.) that had traditionally been the province of surgery, or at least barber-surgery.

Dionis's depreciatory comments on tooth-pulling need to be set in the context of institutional squabbles taking place within the world of surgery and medicine from the late seventeenth century down to the French Revolution of 1789. Surgeons sought, with growing success, to extend the range and prestige of their practice, and to achieve freedom from the traditional controls that physicians customarily exerted over them. A key factor giving surgeons greater institutional clout was the centralization of surgery across the land: from 1668 all surgical communities passed under the jurisdictional authority of the king's Premier Surgeon. By early in the following century, Dionis was hailing Parisian surgery as already the best in the world, arguing that its quality was expressed in a fundamental commitment to fusing theory and practice in the interests of more efficacious techniques, and an institutional framework that allowed frequent experimentation. Paris surgeons were probably more tightly organized and better led than any comparable professional corporate grouping in France. From the 1720s, marshalled by successive Premier Surgeons (and also by the astute Montpellier-trained court practitioner, François de La Peyronie), they increasingly took the battle to the physicians, as represented by the somewhat hidebound Paris Medical Faculty. In 1695, a new surgical amphitheatre had been opened in Paris in which the surgical community was permitted to offer public courses in the theory and practice of their discipline, thus complementing the popular courses which Dionis had started in 1673 at the Jardin du Roi, the royal botanical gardens. Louis XV had a personal liking for surgery and operations, and he subsequently established professorial chairs attached to the amphitheatre, and then in 1731 created an Academy of Surgery (there was not to be a full Academy of Medicine until the nineteenth century). Increasingly, the Paris Medical Faculty was obliged to slacken its grip over surgery, and by mid century the surgeons, thanks to royal support, were effectively autonomous.

The ascent of Parisian surgery was also predicated on a greater hierarchy within the body of Paris surgeons itself. Over the course of the sixteenth and seventeenth centuries, long, drawn-out and venomous struggles had taken place within their ranks. These pitted 'long-robed' academic surgeons, who had ambitions to emulate physicians, against the 'short-robed' barber-surgeons who were closer to small tradesmen, who could boast very little in the way of academic learning and who made their living by offering routine body maintenance. Dionis, for example, contrasted the ideal of what he called 'a good anatomical surgeon', open to theoretical knowledge about the body, but also well versed in practical knowledge, with, on the other hand, the often barely literate and semi-trained surgical empiric working according to trad- itional routines. This latter group included the kinds of crude and charlatan- esque 'operators for the teeth' that gave surgery a bad name.

Towards the end of the seventeenth century, however, matters came to some sort of resolution. A realignment of guilds throughout France led to barber-wigmakers drifting off into an independent corporative framework separate and distinct from surgical communities. Parisian master wigmakers surfed the wave of the extraordinary vogue for wigs, and their number rose from 200 in 1673 to over 700 in 1731, by which time they were completely independent of surgery. Their corporation drew in many barber-surgeons, simplifying the institutional map. Then, in 1699, Paris surgeons organized a new hierarchy within their own ranks, similarly aimed at differentiating scientifically oriented and socially ascendant elite surgeons from their profes- sional inferiors. The 1699 regulations introduced the title of 'expert' into a number of defined subaltern surgical fields. These comprised care of the teeth and the eyes and operations to remove gallstones, kidney stones, and bladder stones (the future specialisms, in fact, of dentist, oculist, and lithotomist). Similar arrangements were also made for the makers of herniary trusses. The new 'experts' were not required to have the full extent of surgical training which would qualify them to become surgical masters and to practise all established surgical techniques. They were to be ancillary members of the Paris College, and were also placed under the jurisdiction of the king's Premier Surgeon. Aspirants to the 'expertise' had to undergo a two-day examination, conducted by members of the Paris surgeons' guild, in the theory and practice of their craft. By these arrangements, the surgeons effect- ively distanced themselves from subfields within the discipline, allowing them to maintain their lofty condescendence towards mouth care, for example. But they retained and consolidated control over these disparate inferior groupings.

The 1699 institutional framework, slightly amended in 1768, would remain in place until the end of the Ancien Régime. The title *'expert pour les dents*' was a definite social promotion and scientific validation for those individuals who had formerly styled themselves 'operators for the teeth' (*opérateurs pour les dents*) or, even more prosaically, 'tooth-pullers' (*arracheurs des dents*). If *le Grand Thomas* could almost certainly be counted among the Parisian 'experts', so too, as we have suggested, could Pierre Fauchard.

Yet if indeed both *le Grand Thomas* and Pierre Fauchard were licensed to practice under the 1699 regulations as experts for the teeth, the two men made strange bedfellows. Fauchard's reponse to the difference between them was to erect a theoretical distinction—as Dionis had done with surgeons—between good and bad. On one hand he acknowledged the excellence which a number of prior operators had displayed 'in a part of surgery which is certainly not contemptible in itself', and which could well be adjudged the equal of 'other parts of surgery no more useful or important for the conservation of Man'. He cited in this respect the former Pont-Neuf denizen Carmelina. Even if a surgeon had much more general knowledge, a specialist in mouth care could be preferable within the bounds of his specialism.

At the other extreme, however, Fauchard expressed nothing but contempt for bad operators, whose conduct led the public to disdain all practitioners of the tooth-pulling arts as ignorant, deceitful, and lacking in knowledge or skill. Such individuals were wont, he noted, to dupe the public using a variety of impostures:

> Some say that they cure toothache by particular essences; others by plasters; others by prayers and the sign of the cross, promising to perform miracles; others have specifics to kill the worms that they imagine are gnawing the tooth and causing pain.

Fauchard was particularly scathing towards the unscrupulous tooth-pulling fairground-style practitioners who practised on the Pont-Neuf. Although he did not mention *le Grand Thomas* by name, it is crystal clear that it was he whom Fauchard had in his sights when he went on to attack 'the alleged skill' of such figures which consisted merely in

> winning over some poor wretches who mix in with the crowd listening to the string of promises the impostor is making. The paid fakes come forward and the would-be operator, who holds in his hand a tooth already enveloped in a very fine membrane containing the blood of a chicken or some other animal, puts his hand in the mouth of the fake sufferer and hides the tooth in the mouth; after which he has only to touch the tooth with a powder or straw, or

with the point of a sword or to ring a bell into the ear of the alleged patient for him to break open what has been placed in his mouth; and one sees him then spitting up blood and a bloodied tooth which is, however, merely the tooth that the impostor had placed there.

Fauchard's way of distinguishing between the immoral and unscrupulous operator for the teeth—a.k.a. *le Grand Thomas*—and the good, experienced one (such as himself) also had a linguistic dimension: he invented a new word. Bad operators were simply 'charlatans'; good ones were henceforth 'dental surgeons' (*chirurgiens-dentistes*) or 'dentists' (*dentistes*).

What was at issue was social class as well as linguistic distinctiveness and professional competence. While *le Grand Thomas* exuded a popular fairground aura, a proper dental surgeon like Fauchard rubbed shoulders with ultra-respectable figures within the core of the surgical and medical communities. In the preliminary pages at the front of *Le Chirurgien-dentiste*, eminent physicians and surgeons queued up to pay homage to the dedication of Fauchard and the public utility served by his publication. Case studies which he narrated, moreover, showed him being respectfully consulted by surgical luminaries including La Peyronie, by Parisian faculty members and even by the king's Premier Physician, Dodart, to whom the work was dedicated.

Fauchard professed to learn from his surgical betters as regards the professional image he sought to project. The engraved portrait which he included in the *Chirurgien-dentiste* (Fig. 3.3) presented an image of gentlemanly science which can fruitfully be contrasted with the image of *le Grand Thomas* as 'the Pearl of Charlatans' (Fig. 3.1). The eye-popping finery of the charlatan in his outdoors, Pont-Neuf setting contrasts powerfully with the academic robes, sumptuous domestic environment and Louis-Quatorzian wig of the scholar. Thomas holds aloft a tooth extracted from the hapless jaw of the apprentice sitting at his feet. Fauchard, in contrast, is shown with his supple hand resting on two volumes which we can assume are his own creation, and he points vaguely but significantly towards a library of bound texts. All previous book-learning on his subject, we are being encouraged to think, is crystallized in Fauchard's two-volume work—and in his eloquently poised hand. Finally, the 'Pearl of Charlatans' street-doggerel motto in the Thomas engraving strikes a contrastive note compared with the sententious Latin inscription beneath the image of Fauchard, which may be (freely) translated as:

> O Fauchard! who through hand and pen
> Calms the sufferings of our teeth,
> Guards their health, keeps their charms;

Hold envy's bleeding fangs in scorn
Which on your virtues break.

As we shall see in the next chapter, practising privately (not on the public thoroughfare), foregrounding tooth conservation (not extraction), and establishing practice on sound anatomical and surgical principles (rather than on 'secret' lore), dentists gained new consideration not only for health but also for the welfare, appearance, and the sensibility of their clients, and for the wider social utility they served.

Fig. 3.3 Pierre Fauchard, from his *Le Chirurgien-dentiste* (1728)

Like *le Grand Thomas*, the new dentist could live and prosper through his art. After the publication of *Le Chirurgien-dentiste* in 1728, Fauchard's practice boomed. The work went into further French editions in 1746 and 1786, and was translated into German. Fauchard knew about reaching his client base, and as his engraved portrait suggests, was not so wrapped up in his science as to neglect self-promotion. At the end of the second edition of his *Le Chirurgien-dentiste* in 1746, for example, he included a full-scale puff for his own services:

> The author also keeps fine sponges, specially prepared roots, opiates, powders, waters and liquids suitable for the conservation of teeth and gums. He executes all dental pieces, artificial palates and mechanisms described in this book. [He and his pupil would be happy to supply] all the aid of counsel and hand necessary to embellish the teeth and to remedy the diseases of the mouth.

A good marriage to the daughter of a famous actor from the Comédie-Française allowed Fauchard in 1734 to purchase the manor-house of Grand Mesnil near Orsay to the south of Paris. Once the love-nest of King Francis I and his mistress, the duchesse d'Étampes, the property, which came complete with lucrative seigneurial rights, cost the dentist-of-the-manor nearly 100,000 livres. By 1740, the chronicler of Parisian life, Edmond Barbier, was remarking that Fauchard was 'the first man in all of Paris for the teeth', and that he had 'many friends among persons of rank'. He built up an extensive practice, though his personal happiness took some knocks: the death of his wife in 1746 led to a new marriage which, however, went sour, with the couple separating in 1760. Yet the business prospered. His first wife's brother, Laurent Tugdual Duchemin, was trained in anatomy and joined the family firm in the 1730s, and Fauchard had a number of other pupils. He was also wealthy enough to have his son train for the law and achieve a decent office as royal counsel in the Admiralty courts. In 1763, six years after the death of his legendary rival, *le Grand Thomas*, Fauchard passed away aged eighty-three. He too died a rich man.

Enlightened Parisian teeth

The impact that Fauchard's work was to have in terms of the emergent discipline of dentistry and the developing professional group of dentists owed much to the changing intellectual and cultural climate of Paris in the middle decades of the eighteenth century when he was making his breakthrough. By that time, the city of Paris had become one of the principal hubs of the pan-European Enlightenment. Contemporaries had a strong sense that they were living through an 'age of lights'—*un siècle des Lumières*. Those points of light were natural philosophers, or *philosophes*, who used the yardstick of human reason to advance knowledge, and to subject existing institutions and values to rational scrutiny. The *philosophes* comprised a European movement with a Parisian base. The most venerable among them were figures like Voltaire and Montesquieu who, as we have seen, had emerged into Parisian public and intellectual life in the sunny interval of the Regency. Such figures led a sceptical assault on established practices and values across most areas of eighteenth-century life. They did so with a smile on their faces, that they hoped would be contagious among their countrymen and women.

The *philosophes* offered an optimistic general account of human progress. They rejected the old theology-based scholastic science which the universities, under the aegis of the Church, had proffered since the Middle Ages. Instead, they revered the great figures of the Scientific Revolution of the seventeenth century who had highlighted the human capacity to understand the world without recourse to explanations derived from scriptural revelation or from the dogmatic assertions of the science of Antiquity. Galileo's writings on astronomy, William Harvey's on the circulation of the blood, and, most famously of all, Isaac Newton's theory of gravity were viewed as brilliant triumphs of human reason which owed nothing to accepted dogma or to scriptural injunction (and which indeed ran counter to the traditional teachings of the Church). Furthermore, if scientific method based on empirical observation was proving to be a means of unlocking the secrets of the universe, it also promised to be, for the *philosophes*, a way of changing the world for the better. The *philosophes* railed against sterile, unproductive forms of knowledge. Their aim was to use knowledge to improve society materially and morally and to make men and women happier, in this world rather than the next. Social utility was the golden thread running through all bodies of enlightened knowledge.

In the optimistic, progressive account of the history of humanity that the *philosophes* collectively formulated, the torch of human reason was held to be growing ever brighter, producing happier individuals and a more humane society with more socially rational values. Human perfectibility seemed a real possibility which, if distant, was still taken seriously. Optimism in the future, based on trust in human ingenuity and goodwill, should replace the gloomy pessimism about human nature derived from the doctrine of the Fall. The movement went on to mock the dark gloom of traditional court and ecclesiastical culture in France. It condemned the Dark Age of Miserabilism upheld in the past by absolutist divine right monarchy and an intolerant Catholic Church. The *philosophes* nurtured a gaiety of spirit that drew on the free-wheeling mood of the Regency period but also connected up with the vestiges of a 'Merry France' evident in Rabelaisian literature and rumbustious folkloric survivals.

Smiling and laughing were highly prized in the Enlightenment as a badge of collective gaiety. 'One must laugh at everything', was the advice for living that master-*philosophe* and Regency veteran Voltaire gave. 'That is the only way to be.' And then again, 'I take the liberty of poking fun at everything, and laughing at everything. Such a regimen is very good for one's health and I am hoping it will cure me.' Voltaire's use of laughter as a weapon sometimes recalls the *de haut en bas* reactions of the ambitious, self-protective courtier (that at one stage of his life he actually was), and his sardonic astringency could turn bitter: 'The world is a war, and he who laughs at the expense of others is victor.' But such tendencies were balanced by a sense that the laughter that he proposed ran counter to the '*perfidium ridens* which took joy in the humiliation of others'. Voltaire viewed the laugh as an ultra-rational gesture, a collective burst of good humour by reasonable men in the face of the follies of the age. There was both safety and laughter in numbers. He and his fellow *philosophes* saw themselves as conducting a cheerful campaign of human betterment against the dark forces of superstition, intolerance, and ignorance. If there was a smile on their faces, it was the smile of reason.

In retrospect, the *philosophes* of Voltaire's generation were sometimes accounted dry rationalists resistant to feeling. This was far from true. Although they lacked the extra frisson of sensibility that Rousseau would impart to the movement, their critique of existing institutions and values chimed harmoniously with the account of human nature and the re-evaluation of the passions deriving from the scientific and imaginative literature of sensibility that we discussed in the last chapter. Significantly in this respect, the *philosophes* also drew heavily on Shaftesbury's theories of morality and politeness which had started to become popular under the Regency. For Shaftesbury, individuals were naturally sociable: what he called 'herding'—individuals getting together in groups for their collective safety and pleasure—was every bit a natural

appetite as eating and drinking. Humans had a natural propensity to sympa-
thize with others, and through free-and-easy sociability human freedom and
individual happiness might be achieved. Shaftesbury's 'amicable collisions' of
face-to-face interaction produced socially harmonious behaviour, a greater
sense of respect for others, and what by mid-century was coming to be called
'civilization'.

'Gaiety, activity, politeness and sociability', the radical *philosophe* baron
d'Holbach maintained, formed the true character of Frenchmen. He spoke
for the movement as a whole, with the added caveat that the truest of
Frenchmen were to be found in Paris, which in cultural terms constituted
the quintessence of the nation. 'Good philosophy', the Italian writer Louis-
Antoine Caraccioli stated, 'consists in being gay.' And nowhere else in all
the world but Paris was such gaiety to be found. Paris was 'the model for
foreign nations', and 'the home of laughter'. The city buzzed with 'a
moderated gaiety which consists not of great bursts of laughter but of a
cheerful [*riant*] countenance'. Such was Parisian gaiety that even beggars
smiled as they politely requested alms. The Jesuit writer Joseph Cérutti,
who was said to have 'the smiliest and most imaginative language', agreed
with his compatriot Caraccioli about the 'cheerful countenances' to be seen
around the city, and claimed that laughter was 'the distinguishing characteristic' of the French. The German philosopher, Immanuel Kant, in 1764
noted how though the taste of Italians ran to 'thoughtful beauty', the French
always prized most highly 'smiling beauty'. The celebrated theorist of
physiognomy, Johann-Caspar Lavater, was in general agreement. The
French were always smiling: 'I know [the French] chiefly by their teeth
and their way of laughing.' Voltaire compared his compatriots to cham-
pagne: brilliant, bubbly, producing laughter. Paris had all of that.

In Paris the smile was hailed as a symbol of national character that
confirmed the narrative of human progress and happiness at the heart of
the Enlightenment. According to Louis-Sébastien Mercier, writing in the
1780s, a 'revolution in people's ideas' had taken place in the French capital:
'the Parisian was very different before the reign of Louis XIV from what he
is today'. The change had been particularly acute since around 1750. Since
then his native city had become 'a delicious location for anyone out to enjoy
themselves', a place which 'had more public amusements than any other in
all the world', and which above all was 'a superb and cheerful city where
one lives as one likes'.

English tourists largely bought into the myth. William, Viscount Pulteney who visited the city in 1749 thought it 'the centre of all gaiety and pleasure'. Visitors could, however, sometimes be irritated by the exhausting social smiling that went on in public places. The choleric Scottish physician and novelist Tobias Smollett, who visited the city in the early 1760s, for example, growled ferociously about the fawning smile endlessly playing around the lips of his hosts. Many English men and women regarded smiling in any form as a symptom not of sincerity and transparency, however, but of hypocrisy, untrustworthiness, and artificiality. (The French in contrast found the English morose and melancholic, splenetic and unsmiling: there was evidently a law of gravity in England, noted one French commentator, which closed down the possibilities of English gaiety on the French model; the English placed parapets on their bridges to prevent citizens hurling themselves suicidally into the water.) Furthermore, hardened British Francophobes claimed resentfully that the typically French smile had started to make progress on English lips. A Swiss visitor to England in the late seventeenth century had considered one of English women's main deficiencies that of 'not taking care of their teeth', but the historical writer John Andrews a century later gallantly noted that 'of late years... the English women are become more careful of their teeth then they were used to be'. They had seemed to have acquired the taste from the French, for Andrews noted on his visit to Paris in 1783 that 'there are two objects of which the French ladies are peculiarly solicitous to make a display, their eyes and their teeth; in the brilliancy of the first and the whiteness of the latter they think no woman can surpass or equal them'. The Parisian smile seemed to be ready to conduct a war of conquest across the Channel.

This triumphant smile was still less in evidence in Versailles, however, than in Paris. Face-to-face interactions in public were of course a staple at the royal court. But sociability in Versailles was a chilly thing that still paid homage to strict, Louis-Quatorzian codes of conduct that were ploddingly respectful of social hierarchy (rigorous body control, emotional impassivity, facial immobility). The Versailles norm was, moreover, emulated within all the official organs of the Bourbon state. One did not speak out of turn, if at all; and turn was governed by precedence and rank. Meetings and greetings at the royal court were still performed at a seemly distance and with a self-defending formality, whereas in the Parisian public sphere kissing and handshaking were breaking down social distance, and unaffected smiles were establishing the basis of open conversation and encounter between like-minded souls.

Paris was thus the capital of Enlightenment not merely because the most eminent *philosophes* lived and published there, but also because its polite sociability was optimally geared towards the production of collective happiness. This was apparent in the emergence in the city of new fora of interaction which intensified Shaftesbury-esque, enlightened 'herding' and 'amicable collisions'. A public sphere had emerged of voluntaristic, informal groupings. This new kind of civil society prided itself on resisting the dead hand of courtly mores. There were salons, in which upper-class women provided a forum for the mingling of social elites with the artists, musicians, and writers of the Enlightenment. There were coffee-houses, where debate was free, open, excitable, and both stimulating and (thanks to caffeine) stimulated. There were masonic lodges where highfalutin mystical ceremonial overlay more mundane, collective, leisured indulgence. And then there were a congeries of bars, arcades, public parks and promenades, theatres, vauxhall gardens, ice-cream parlours, and the like where the pleasures deriving from relaxed and informal sociability held sway. These venues stimulated the circulation of sensibility that allowed the contagious character of smiling and good humour to thrive in an ambiance of politeness.

The profusion in Paris of these innovative forms of public sociability was closely linked to the growing commercialization of Parisian society in this period, which also helped to weaken traditional social hierarchy. French peasants went hungry when harvests were bad, and a needy under-class evolved in many of the larger cities. Yet overall the economy was booming, and urban elites (*a fortiori* Parisian urban elites) had money to spend and were increasingly willing to flaunt it. Indeed, Paris experienced a veritable consumer boom over the century, the city becoming a sparkling shop-window for urban consumption. More and more Parisian homes came to contain fashionable furnishings, possessions, and bric-à-brac. Food consumption became more mixed and variegated, with once-exotic and expensive colonial commodities such as coffee, sugar, chocolate, tea, and tobacco entering even the popular diet. The new substances linked to the emerging forms of sociability that we have described: coffee- and tea-drinking, drinking fine wines, consumption of confectionery, and the smoking of tobacco were as much collective as personal or domestic practices, which followed the dictates of fashionable politeness. (They also, incidentally, had the additional consequence, of damaging the teeth in ways that required medical attention—a point not lost on the city's dentists, as we shall see.)

Within this consumerist milieu, personal appearance was a particular area of delectation. Fashion reached well down the social scale, and the wardrobes of individuals from even quite lowly backgrounds diversified and were increasingly responsive to changing tastes. With so many desirable commodities becoming affordable, moralists worried insistently that the availability of cheap imitations had made it more difficult than in the past to discern social status. On the streets of Paris, it could be difficult sometimes from manifest appearances alone to tell a duchess from a dairymaid. In this world of fashion and display out in the Parisian public sphere, where facial as well as vestimentary appearances were taken increasingly seriously, 'the theatre is no longer in the theatre', Mercier opined; 'it is in the world in general'. And in that *theatrum mundi*, smiles and healthy white teeth were recognized as being at a premium. In terms of just general polite sociability, stated an English commentator, well-attuned to Parisian mores, the utmost care was needed over teeth (as well as hands and fingernails) in order 'not to offend peoples' eye and nose'. No wonder good teeth were the envy of all, added the dentist Beaupréau in 1764: 'the whiteness of the teeth is their main attraction, since they make the main charm of a beautiful mouth'.

Historian of the emotions, William Reddy has suggested that it is useful to think of the myriad venues of Parisian sociability in this period as 'zones of emotional refuge', where individuals did not fear to lower their guard and to engage on terms of equality and emotional openness with their fellow citizens. The description seems apt, but the word 'refuge' is really too passive a term, for in many ways these were expansive arenas where what had formerly been private forms of behaviour saw the light of day in public. The open, transparent smile of sensibility had hitherto tended to be confined within domestic settings. Now through these venues of polite sociability it penetrated the public sphere.

Furthermore, the Parisian public sphere accepted much greater social mixing than the official institutions of the monarchy. Women, for example, were more widely present in the institutions of the public sphere than anywhere else in Europe. The salons were invariably headed by a *salonnière* lady of the house. Voltaire adjudged that the unrivalled levels of politeness evident in the city derived from the cultural presence of such women, and indeed staked the progress of civilization on such female engagement. Socially too, there was evidence of fusion. At one end of the spectrum, it

was held, dukes and peers left their coronets at the door as they entered a
salon, so to speak, and could find themselves out-argued or even silenced by
their social inferiors in a coffee-house. At the other extreme, the leisure
venues reached well down the spectrum of urban society into and beyond
the ranks of the middling classes.

As we have seen, interchange within this increasingly commercialized
and dynamic public sphere was lubricated by a reworked system of politeness which set its face against the practices to be found at Versailles.
Emergent codes of *politesse* worked to modify and transcend the notion of
the *honnête homme* that had developed at the seventeenth-century royal
court. In point of fact, the vast bulk of behavioural conventions implicit
in the new *politesse*—policing of the bodily orifices, containment of bodily
fluids, a seemingly relaxed but in fact quite controlled disciplining of
gesture—derived from the same classical and Renaissance sources which
had inspired the template of the *honnête home*. The Enlightenment's con-
duct-books—notably the still-popular Antoine Courtin's *Nouveau traité de la
civilité* (1671) and Jean-Baptiste de La Salle's neo-Erasmian *Les Règles de la
bienséance et de la civilité chrétienne* (1703)—had been written well in advance
of the movement. Nonetheless, a more informal version of these prescrip-
tive texts emerged, bespeaking a quiet determination to adapt manners in
line with changing Paris-based modes of sociability and sensibility—and
away from Versailles-based codes that were now judged stuffy and formal-
istic, insincere and out of touch, nasty and brutish.

Versailles-style *honnêteté* was discredited and *dépassé*. It divided people and
highlighted difference; Enlightenment *politesse* brought them together and
stressed commonalities of interest. In the preface to his best-selling and
controversial *Les Moeurs* (1748), the writer François-Vincent Toussaint
urged: 'let us leave the condition of *honnête homme* to anyone who wants
to use it . . . The hallmarks of the *honnête homme* are arrogance, wealth, and
applauded vices. Virtue has nothing to do with it.' The *Encyclopédie* similarly
bewailed 'the abuse of an idea which expresses such a respectable notion
[and yet which] proves the progress of corruption'. In practice, 'gentleness
of character, humanity, openness without crudeness, accommodation without flattery, and above all a heart tending to beneficence' were beyond the
reach of those steeped in courtly civility.

True, sincere *politesse* was now viewed as being rooted in natural sensibility and authentic social virtues. For many commentators, the values of
the courtly *honnête homme* had dialectically transformed into their opposite.

The efforts of the nobility to ingratiate themselves within the new, urban spirit of *politesse* seemed unconvincing and artificial, especially as they were often held to be expressed in a rather excessive manner. This was caricatured in theatre, in visual representations, and in social commentaries in the guise of the *petit-maître*, whose smirking, wheedling condescension was not much of an improvement on the impassive white mask that had distinguished the courtier at Versailles. In this model of fashionable insincerity, 'the heart was in the manners, while vice was in the heart', as future revolutionary Bertrand Barère put it. The smile of the *petit-maître* was viewed at best as an unseemly hypocritical grimace.

At court and among the nobility, Louis-Sébastien Mercier maintained, 'the smile of malignity' still reigned in an emulative arena where 'laughs are never true and caresses countefeit'. 'If we want to spread generalized corruption', Mercier added, sarcastically, in his *Du théâtre* (1773), then 'we will need marquises, counts, and little dukes, with their silly language and their disdainful smiles'. In her pedagogic novel, *Adèle et Théodore* (1782), Madame de Genlis was even more acerbic. While lavishing praise on her heroine—'her glance, her smile, everything about her is open, natural and without artifice'—she poured contempt on one of her aristocratic characters:

> Monseigneur imagines that as soon as he smiles everyone must be enchanted with him. But this affected smile, which is just a grimace and a habit will become agreeable and obliging only when Monseigneur really wants to be liked. Otherwise this forced expression will always appear stupid and ridiculous.

The former *honnête homme* had thus transmuted into the *petit-maître*, a preening courtly fop, whose efforts to fit in were transparently insincere and who was quite as hypocritical as he was fawningly excessive in his civility.

The adoption of the code of politeness by the nobility thus left much of Paris unimpressed. Long before the Bastille had fallen, the cultural hegemony of the Bourbon court was being steadily sapped by the vaunted values of a smilingly polite and natural virtue. Desirable and desired smiles were now not courtly smirks, but 'smiles of beauty', 'smiles of happiness' between individuals on a basis of moral equality. And those smiles increasingly sported white teeth. Overwhelmingly 'virtuous', 'sweet', 'tranquil', 'tender', 'loveable', 'gracious', 'angelic', 'enchanting', 'charming', 'serene', they were

obliged, however, to make their way in the world in the context of contemptuous grimaces presenting as tight-lipped smiles—cold, haughty, ironic,
sardonic, constrained, wicked, treacherous, insulting, and disdainful, or else
wheedlingly hypocritical.

The smile of sensibility shaped up as a political missile targeted at the facial
regime still dominant at the royal court. 'The smile of the people', stated the
dramatist Marmontel, 'is worth more than the favour of the king'. The
presence of the 'people' (who had a solidly bourgeois core) legitimated the
view that the new public sphere somehow collectively transcended individual differences, social rank, and gender and represented the views of the
mass of the population. 'Public opinion' was in gestation. Formerly a dirty
word, it was now considered a useful term for denoting the overall intellectual mood of the manifold organs of Enlightenment sociability.

Yet it must be noted that the Parisian public sphere was less inclusive and
certainly less popular than the benign universalism of its own rhetoric
implied. In spite of the suspicion of nobles muscling in on their sociability,
a sizeable fraction of the high nobility still maintained a good deal of social
and cultural heft within the Parisian public sphere. On the other hand, the
latter was more grudging in its acceptance of women and the lower orders
than pronouncements implied. Women were more passive players in the
Enlightenment than civilizing discourses suggested: the *salonnière* Madame
Necker likened her facilitation of Enlightenment conversational exchanges
to 'taking up the shuttlecock when it falls from the racquet', hardly a
powerful role. There was also a concern to defend the public sphere against
contamination from below, from the popular classes. In line with Shaftesbury's philosophy of sympathy and the affective prompts of sensibility,
politeness resonated with the spirit of beneficence—and also condemned
vulgarity and plebeian conduct. Mercier might vaunt Paris as the home of
'true politeness', but he condemned the popular classes of the city who 'only
speak of ordure and who coin thousands of louche crudities which make
them roar with laughter'. (Significantly, he blamed the nobility for setting a
bad example.)

Enlightenment politeness assailed the old Rabelaisian, side-splitting
laughter quite as fiercely as Louis-Quatorzian *honnêteté* had done. Open-
throated (*à gorge déployée*) laughter had become outdated and uncivilized,
Mercier held: moderation and restraint were required. The art critic
Claude-Henri Watelet expatiated on the virtues of this *via media*:

What characterizes a civilized nation, is the useful restraint that men place on most sudden and unconsidered expressions of soul and body. Free and natural movements would trouble society and bring reproach. People are careful to moderate them.

And, following much the same reasoning, Lord Chesterfield put his finger on it in his famous letters to his son. 'Having mentioned laughing', he noted, in words that echoed back to Antiquity,

> I must particularly warn you against it; and I could heartily wish that you may often be seen to smile but never heard to laugh while you live. Frequent and loud laughter is the characteristic of folly and ill manners...

Such views recalled Mercier's advocacy of 'the smile of the soul', which cut itself off from 'tumultuous joy' of any description. And they highlighted Caraccioli's characterization of the city of Paris, cited earlier, as the 'home of laughter', which eschewed 'great bursts of laughter', that is, the plebeian belly-laugh. The city now buzzed with 'a moderated gaiety' where 'a cheerful countenance' was the rule. The true social virtues were thus to be found somewhere along a bourgeois *via media* situated between the aristocratic snigger and the plebeian belly-laugh, which Chesterfield disparaged as 'the mirth of the mob'. Paris was an arena for emotional contagion, where a smile seemed, much to the displeasure of grumpy English tourists, on everyone's lips. That polite, restrained Parisian smile was viewed as a sign of national character that confirmed the narrative of human progress and happiness at the heart of the Enlightenment.

4

The Making of a Revolution

The Abbé Galiani, the 'laughing philosopher', as English historian Edward Gibbon called him, was widely reputed to be one of the wittiest and most brilliant conversationalists of salon society in Paris, where he served as Neapolitan ambassador from 1759 to 1770. His laughter and his conversation were temporarily staunched, however, by his exile from Paris after a diplomatic misdemeanour—and by the progressive loss of his teeth. In his gossipy correspondence with *salonnière* Madame d'Épinay back in Paris, he regretted both his exile from the home of sparkling sociability and his disappearing teeth. In a gloomy count-down, he recorded that he still had fourteen remaining in June 1770, but only eight in August 1771. By then, any untoward movement of his tongue while he was talking led to his teeth springing out of his mouth. His conversation, he complained, had become a mixture of unintelligible mumbling and inadvertent whistling which baffled his friends. He began to have dreams in which his teeth grew back. Chance would be a fine thing. By mid 1772 all his teeth were gone; he was in his early forties. The nascent tragedy had a happy ending, however, and his dreams (sort of) came true; at Madame d'Épinay's prompting, he imported a set of false teeth from a Parisian dentist, which allowed him to rediscover his habitual articulacy. He re-entered the Enlightenment of free-flowing, engaging conversation.

This story was far from exceptional. Late eighteenth-century Paris witnessed a golden age of dentistry that impacted on the quality of people's lives. From roughly mid century, the skills of Parisian dentists working in the wake of Pierre Fauchard became internationally renowned, and were appreciated not only in Paris but all over Europe and across the globe. Before she sent her daughter, Marie-Antoinette, to France in 1770 to marry the Dauphin (the future Louis XVI), the Austrian Empress Maria Theresa thought it wise to summon to Vienna the very best that Europe could provide to reposition some of the princess's teeth so that they would look 'very beautiful and well arranged'. Her choice fell on Parisian dentist Jean-Baptiste Laverand. On the other side of the Atlantic, when the future first President of the United States, George Washington was having toothache troubles in the early 1780s, he too availed himself of the expertise of a French expatriate dentist, one Jean Le Mayeur. Then again, his charms failing and his teeth falling out, the Italian *roué* Casanova himself turned in desperation to Parisian dentures on the eve of the Revolution.

By the same token, Grand Tourists now made their stay-over in Paris the opportunity for a dental check-up. The ardent Francophile, the Earl of Chesterfield, who had spent lengthy sojourns in the French capital in his youth, recommended the dentist Claude Mouton to his son, for example. The English diarist Anna Francesca Cradock recounted a passing visit in 1786 to the famous Parisian practitioner, Étienne Bourdet:

> and we waited for more than half an hour before he deigned to appear, his valet having come to advise us that his master never entered the operating room before he had had his morning coffee. The moment arrived, [and] ... this grand person (but excellent dentist) [attended to me].

The dentist had arrived. 'This grand person' even had valets. In no other city in the world was the dentist such an established feature of the urban landscape. Nowhere else could such a figure boast a more willing, devoted, and well-heeled clientele. Furthermore, as we have seen, Paris's intellectual and social ferment was inspiring new forms of sociability which provided a theatre for the smile to flaunt itself. In the public sphere emergent over the middle decades of the century, better-off Parisians were increasingly regarding good teeth and a capacity to smile Voltaire's 'smile of the soul' as more intellectually, morally, socially, and even politically desirable than ever before.

A Smile Revolution was in the making, then, and the pickings for those who wished to forge a career in smiles were consequently rich. The smile constituted a physical gesture that was the focus of a new facial technology grounded in forging individual identities and seeming to offer a bright new way out of human misfortune. Inspired by the smile of sensibility that they found in the popular novels of the period, Parisian dentists working in the wake of Pierre Fauchard opened up a career path which aimed to make that smile available to ever larger numbers of people. Paris became the home of what was in effect a proto-industry of smiles that catered for a burgeoning demand for more beautiful and healthy teeth and mouths, and deployed considerable entrepreneurial skill to boost that demand. As we shall see, that smile played out essentially in the public sphere that had developed in Paris over the course of the century. Significantly, the royal court, which had set the template for bodily comportment under Louis XIV, was largely bypassed. Versailles was still in thrall to the Old Regime of Teeth, even as Enlightenment Paris was beginning to experience a Smile Revolution. Indeed to some, the Parisian Smile Revolution aimed to eradicate the courtly facial regime altogether.

Fauchard's heirs

The golden age of Parisian smiles nurtured, and was nurtured by, the rise of dentistry as a vocation. The capital's sociability of politeness created a new demand for a smiling mouth with benefit of dentistry. This expressed itself in the emergence of a cadre of dental specialists who collectively developed a new vocation self-consciously contrasting with the tooth-pullers and operators of yore. The group had been set a dazzling example by Pierre Fauchard, and they followed enthusiastically in the footsteps of that new model dentist. By mid century, 'dentists' in Paris numbered around thirty individuals and they hovered between thirty and forty down to the Revolution. Some of these men had taken full training as a surgeon, and were entitled to call themselves 'dental surgeons' (*chirurgiens dentistes*), while most others continued to practise under the auspices of the 1699 Paris regulations (updated in 1768) that had created the status of '*experts pour les dents*'. By mid century, however, it was no longer done to trade under the status of '*expert pour les dents*'. Rather such men gloried in the new identity of *dentiste*.

Among those who styled themselves *dentiste* were individuals who maintained or might have the luck to fall back on the mores of the old tooth-pullers. It was still possible to secure from the Crown a licence to sell the alleged wonder-drug orviétan, for example, and to do some old-style tooth-pulling on the side. A quarter of individuals authorized to sell orviétan in the middle decades of the eighteenth century called themselves dentists (deploying much poetic licence as they did so). Surprisingly Étienne Bourdet—one of the most proficient of dental surgeons of the new model and, from 1760, *dentiste du roi*—had gone down this route, only handing over his orviétan-selling business to his brother Bernard in 1764. Louis

Lécluze, a distinguished dental practitioner who published well-regarded works, in 1757 secured the position of 'inspector of operators', which gave him rights of control over all the orviétan-sellers in the kingdom. The world of old-style razzmatazz tooth-pulling thus lived on in Paris, at least vestigially. In addition, Jean-Baptiste Ricci combined private dental practice with public tooth-pulling at the annual Saint-Germain fair, where he also exhibited exotic animals. In 1751, he commissioned a sea-captain to bring back from Africa for him lions, tigers, leopards, camels, and ostriches. In 1762, he was exhibiting a five-footed, two-tailed calf at the Saint-Germain fair. Yet such cases were increasingly the exceptions. Overall, Parisian *dentistes* exuded seriousness, stability, and respectability. They could pride themselves on the fact that no other city in Europe boasted more than a handful of such dental specialists (and indeed, most Europeans still depended on the tender mercies of tooth-pulling operators and worse).

Following the vocational template established by Fauchard, the new community highlighted strong scientific credentials. There were two dimensions to this. On the one hand, despite the back-sliding of certain of their number, they denounced the misdeeds of tooth-pulling charlatans of every stripe for their ignorance, venality, and disastrous technical deficiencies. On the other, they stressed the closeness of their relationship to Parisian surgeons, whose star, as we have seen, was in the ascendant. Dentist Robert Bunon, for example, contrasted the 'frivolous operator' with the 'applied dentist who practices with honour a significant part of the estimable art of surgery'. The surgeons still examined and certified dental 'experts' under the 1699 and 1768 regulations. If Parisian dentistry could claim to be the best in the world, this was partly at least because Parisian surgery was even more markedly world-class. The operative success of the surgeons in many areas of practice, including childbirth, smallpox inoculations, treatment for venereal disease, and lithotomy, was widely trumpeted. This, their exceptional anatomical knowledge, and their gift for scientific instrumentation had given them a pan-European reputation. The old menial, enema syringe-wielding Molièresque figure of fun was being consigned to the scrapheap. As the century advanced, surgeons seemed even to be overhauling physicians in public esteem and scientific credentials. Dentists were thus well-advised to hang on to the coat-tails of their surgeon betters, and to claim that surgeons' practical and theoretical excellence had rubbed off on them.

The mimetic posture that Parisian dentists took up in regard to their surgeon superiors was evident in their keenness to publish. Like Fauchard, they followed the lead of Paris surgeons in highlighting scientific transparency as the gauge of their disinterestedness and their commitment to public utility. Even operators in the past who had been talented dentists *avant la lettre* had left nothing of their learning in print. Indeed most operators regarded manual tricks and drug-recipes as trade secrets (when they were not pieces of arrant deceit), which either died with them or else were passed on to heirs. In contrast, by publishing openly, Fauchard and his ilk placed the professional capital which such knowledge comprised solidly within the public domain. Fauchard pointedly noted that 'I am giving the most exact descriptions possible, even though this is to the prejudice of my own interests.' Altruistic commitment to scientific transparency overrode personal self-enrichment. It was a sentiment that dentist Robert Bunon echoed: 'I am betraying without scruples', he confessed, 'the most important secrets of the Art.' These protocols of professional science had become routine as regards academic surgery for more than a generation, and they now extended to dentistry.

A new body of dental-surgical writing emerged at an accelerating rate over the course of the century. Already by mid century, works included Claude Géraudly's *L'Art de conserver les dents* (1737), the *Essai sur les maladies des dents* by Robert Bunon (1746), and the *Essai d'odontotechnie* by Chesterfield's consultant, Claude Mouton (1746). Later classic works in the same erudite tradition included Étienne Bourdet's *Recherches et observations sur toutes les parties de l'art du dentiste* (1757), Louis Lécluze's *Nouveaux éléments d'odontologie* (1754) and Anselme Jourdain's *Traité des maladies et des opérations réellement chirurgicales de la bouche* (1778). All highlighted, and most paid direct tribute to, Fauchard's learning and his lead position within the new field of dental surgery. Within a few years, Bourdet noted how people were saying that there was 'a larger number of writers [on dentistry in France] than there is any other branch of physic'—an exaggeration, but a telling one. The point would be echoed in the early nineteenth century, when the surgical author, Jacques-René Duval, noted how 'the French seem to have paid more particular attention to the dentists' art than perhaps any nation, if we may judge from the scientific books which have been written upon the subject'. The Spanish, Italians, Dutch, and Germans managed a number of serviceable works in the course of the Enlightenment, the best of which were influenced by Fauchard. The English were particularly backward. Though

John Hunter's *Natural History of the Human Teeth* (1771) was the most impressive study of dental anatomy in the European Enlightenment, it was manifestly not a work related to dental practice. No other nation could hold a candle to the French, or rather, the Parisians, when it came to understanding and practising the proper care of teeth and mouths.

Fauchard's writings sought to demonstrate how a thorough grounding in anatomy allowed an expansion of the range of activities in which a dentist could engage. At the turn of the eighteenth century, surgeon Dionis had identified seven activities in the work of the 'operator': operations required to prise open the mouth (particularly in cases of lockjaw and hysterical reactions), cleaning dirty teeth, preventing them going bad, filling cavities, filing uneven teeth, extracting bad teeth, and supplying artificial teeth. Fauchard doubled this number, adding to Dionis's list the separation and reduction of teeth; cauterizing, straightening, and positioning; 'firming'; 'trepanning' (drilling to release infected matter); and transplantation. Dentists also whitened as well as cleaning teeth, knew how to care for the gums and the soft parts of the mouth, and might specialize too in the creation of dental pieces and dentures. As Fauchard and his heirs were aware, these were also operations which had the additional effect of maintaining and enhancing the beauty of the mouth.

Where Dionis had talked unspecifically about illnesses afflicting the teeth, moreover, Fauchard added an impressive precision: he claimed to have encountered no fewer than 103 different illnesses. Forty-five of these sprang from external causes, he calculated, seventeen from 'secret' causes—that is, from causes which were not visible to the eye and which had to be isolated deductively (such as toothache caused by abcesses in the gums), while forty-one were 'symptomatic'—that is, they formed part of a larger pattern of somatic illness. Dentist authors often presented evidence through case studies (another format popular with current surgeon authors): Fauchard provided seventy of them, Courtois supplied thirty-three, Jourdain hundreds. And then authors would foreground their own experience: Géraudly claimed forty years of it and Courtois thirty. Lecluze could boast a mere twenty—but he could throw in five military campaigns in Flanders and access thereby to over 80,000 military mouths.

Parisian dentist authors followed the example of Fauchard, who had studiedly cultivated the rhetorical style of natural science deployed by surgeons and physicians. At their most convincing, dental texts spoke in impersonal, value-neutral French. There were anatomical engravings aplenty,

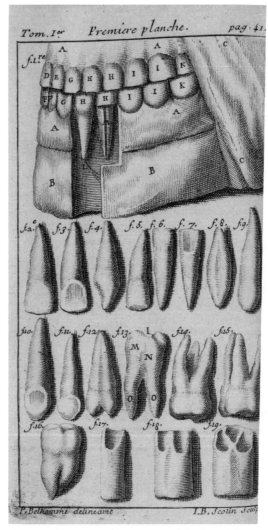

Fig. 4.1 Anatomical engraving (1), from Pierre
Fauchard, *Le Chirurgien-dentiste* (1728)

plus footnotes or else appropriate referencing of sources (Figs. 4.1, 4.2).
Acknowledgement was duly given where due, both to the previous literature
and to research assistance. The emphasis was on how far dentists had transcended purely manual (as opposed to cognitive) skills. Claude Mouton
contrived to make the dentist's art seem like a form of advanced civil engin-
eering: 'The head must act alongside the hand, so to speak, and the architect of

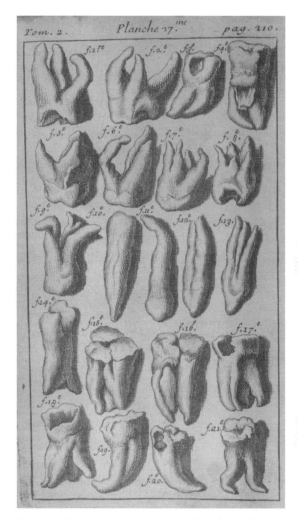

Fig. 4.2 Anatomical engraving (2), from Pierre
Fauchard, *Le Chirurgien-dentiste* (1728)

a mouth must always measure, combine, reason, foresee and keep in mind
these three objectives, namely, decorativeness, convenience and time.'

By dint of such training and experience acquired from their surgeon
teachers, Parisian dentists prided themselves on the dexterity and skill they
had, and the wide range of technical operations which they could consequently perform. Proven ability to extract teeth was not even half of it. The
new dentistry was all about conservation, a notion that fitted in with a
wider emphasis in Enlightenment medical science of avoiding illness

through improved hygiene. Traditional tooth-pullers had existed for emergencies. Although they might sell pills and potions on the side, their core business was extracting bad teeth to minimize pain. In contrast to this, 'conservation instead of destruction' (as Bunon put it) was the dentist's watchword. For his part, Fauchard made it a point of professional honour *not* to pull out teeth. He poked fun at individuals who were 'so impatient [about pain] that at the slightest twinge they have their teeth out'. Toothache sometimes could pass. Like Dionis before him, he knew there were times when teeth had to go—when they were shaky and infirm, where they were rotting towards invisibility, where there was tooth overcrowding, and so on. Yet his overall stance was resolutely and passionately anti-extractionist. The Marshal de Saxe, perhaps the greatest military theorist of the day, once maintained that the sign of truly great generalship was to go through one's entire career without engaging in a single battle. Fighting, even winning battles, caused such irreparable loss of human life that they had to be avoided at all cost. In much the same way, the sign of the dentist for Fauchard was that he preserved, rather than wastefully discarded, teeth. Extracting teeth might vanquish pain, but at a considerable cost in terms of an individual's comfort, appearance, and identity.

Conservation was also the lodestar in regard to general regimen. Fauchard and his followers held that there were particular forms of behaviour which could be especially damaging to health. These included consuming rich and spicy foods and more exotic commodities such as those 'seductive poisons', sugar and tobacco. Though Fauchard's instructions on care of teeth was generally pretty straightforward—keep them clean, notably by a daily regime of rinsing (one's own urine was a good mouthwash, he held), combined with a modicum of rubbing and some deft tooth-picking—he was more direct in regard to treatments which he regarded as harmful. Abuse of metal toothpicks, cleaning with the new-fangled tooth-brushes (which he deplored), and use of rather dangerous tooth-whitening substances were firmly disapproved. So, of course, were rampant tooth-pulling and bad dentistry.

Even though they had abandoned the tooth-puller's attachment to the street, dentists prided themselves on their accessibility. In the 1780s, Mercier could still remember with some nostalgia *le Grand Thomas* touting his wares on the Pont-Neuf. But he warmed even more to the convenience of new dental practices, which almost resembled a shopping experience:

If your tooth starts to plague you in the course of a stroll in the streets, look up; almost certainly you will see somewhere near at hand a dentist's sign. One enormous molar, the size of a bushel measure, with a hand pointing and the words, 'First Floor'. The dentist offers you a chair, throws back the lace at his wrist grips, adroitly tweaks out the offender, and offers you a decoction to gargle. After which you pay and continue your stroll in comfort. What could be more convenient?

This was science placed as a marketable commodity at the disposal of society. It dovetailed neatly with the wider Enlightenment aim of bettering the lot of the individual within the modern, commercialized city.

In keeping with the times as well as the place and also bearing in mind their known aspirations to be considered as gentlemen scientists, Parisian dentists professed a polite science that was stronger on politeness than on science. (In fact, despite the rhetorical gloss and the sweeping claims evident in dental publications, the careful reader can detect in them a notable degree of plagiarism and some tell-tale slips of vocabulary. Dentists' vaunted scientific status was often merely a veneer.) They sought social validation through acting sympathetically in regard to the needs of elite urban consumers. As Mercier's example suggests, convenience now came politely wrapped. Dentists offered their services in the homes of their clients, usually in the morning, and received in their own homes in the afternoons. Fauchard had set the bar characteristically high in this respect. In 1746 he moved his practice to the Rue des Cordeliers (present-day Rue de l'École de Médecine VIe.) in a residence with a *porte-cochère*—a nice touch of gentility for an *arriviste* practitioner whose clients could thus attend their appointments by carriage. This was a far cry from the public tooth-extractions of the Pont-Neuf pranksters.

Dentists strove to produce the kind of social setting in which their largely bourgeois clients could feel at home. Thus, as we have seen, Mrs Cradock could wait in peace and comfort for Monsieur Bourdet to finish his morning *café au lait*. Post-mortem inventories of the homes and possessions of prominent dentists reveal a material culture of distinct, even lush comfort among practitioners. On his death in 1751, Claude Géraudly had a residence on the Rue des Deux-Écus to the north of the Louvre replete with expensive paintings, including portraits of his patron, the duc d'Orléans. In the same year, Claude Mouton's dwelling on the Rue de Richelieu (where his neighbours included the Président d'Aligre from the Paris Parlement and the archbishop of Paris) could boast stables with eight horses and three carriages. François Le Roy de La Faudignière's estate in 1786 was even more commanding: it included over 300 paintings highlighting the Dutch school and French masters such as Oudry and La Tour, numerous drawings and engravings, plus a well-stocked library. Étienne Bourdet's possessions at his death in 1789 were if anything even more impressive: a wine-cellar laden with choice burgundies and clarets, a stable with a cabriolet and five horses, a rich artistic inheritance, a dazzling array of mirrors of every description, an orangerie with eighteen orange trees, a brass-fitted bathroom, a billiards room, a cabinet with stuffed birds (plus a living grey parrot), and so on. Revealingly, when the veteran Parisian dentist Jules Ricci died in 1819, his extensive possessions included engravings of Greuze's classic reproductions of the eighteenth-century art of sensibility such as *The Village Bride* and *Epiphany* (Fig. 4.3). In the case of

Fig. 4.3 Jean-Baptiste Greuze, *Epiphany* (1774)

the latter, this visual array of white teeth on display on the walls of the dental antechamber must have acted encouragingly on the morale of nervous clients in attendance, and made them feel at home.

Scientific Parisian dentistry proved to be commercially savvy and socially successful by being attuned to the cult of sensibility and the codes of politeness current in the public sphere. Driven by a concern for the sensitivities and lifestyles of clients, it also showed awareness of practitioners' changing views on health. Although most of the scientific writings of dentists still paid homage to a humoral view of mouth disease which was becoming increasingly obsolete among physicians, as the century wore on more dentist authors manifested an openness to emergent nerve theory. Following those who wrote in the wake of von Haller, practitioners showed themselves aware that the nerves of certain types of body (women, children, the highly strung, academics, . . .) were more sensitive than others—and that overstimulation could trigger pathological convulsions. It was thus medically essential, socially desirable, and commercially unthinkable not to overtax the nervous state of clients, but to present a friendly and soothing demeanour.

Since the days of Ferranti in the early seventeenth century, public tooth-pullers had showcased their physical strength by using only thumb and forefinger to pull out recalcitrant teeth. The forte of tooth-pullers in the *Grand Thomas* tradition was the overpowering force of their interventions. Such men used an ambiance of power and terror to command recalcitrant teeth to leave the mouths of their clients. Feats of raw strength had no place, in contrast, in the new dentist's armamentarium. The mark of the dentist was, through immersion in anatomical theory, a hand that was, as Fauchard put it, 'light, steady and skilful'. Fauchard preferred to use instruments to do the work of extraction in ergonomically less taxing ways which carried fewer risks of ancillary damage (such as, for example, the accidental removal of much of the hapless Louis XIV's jaw). Indeed, he redesigned many classic dental implements and invented others to achieve optimum effect (Fig. 4.4). In addition, dentists chose to trade in reassurance, not fear. 'I say to the sick', noted the dentist Louis Laforgue, 'that I will have to deprive you of this tooth, or extract it, or take it out. This seems gentler to the individual who has to have the operation.' 'Tooth-pulling' was evidently a word that was banned as too frightening in this sensitive world (and indeed, the French '*arracher*' does sound rather scary).

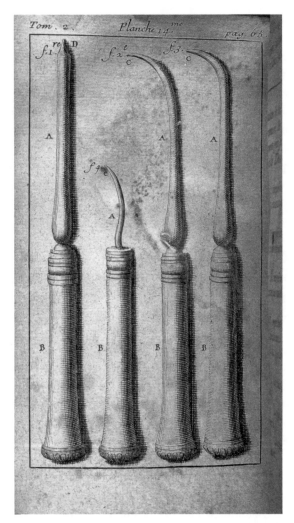

Fig. 4.4 Dental instruments, from Pierre Fauchard,
Le Chirurgien-dentiste (1728)

By deferring extraction to the moment when absolutely everything else had failed, Fauchard elevated tooth loss almost to the level of human tragedy:

> I only decide to extract teeth with great regret, not at all because of the violence of the operation (which is never great) nor because of the pain that this causes nor because of any side effects. If I hesitate, defer, and evade tooth-extraction this is because I set such great store by teeth in terms of their utility and importance.

The dentist's sensibility now vibrated sympathetically with the fragile body and mouth of his patients. Highlighting the dental mantra of conservation, Anselme Jourdain—probably, in fact, the most scientifically adept practitioner of the century after Fauchard—noted how 'the smallest destruction done pointlessly ought to be a reproach to the sensibility of a worthy soul'. It was as if a lost tooth might be a cause for weeping hot tears (for both dentist and patient), uttering words of genteel consolation, with much soothing of the furrowed brow. The mark of the new dentist was the avoidance of the ostentatious use of destructive violence and in addition the efficient deployment of skill, intelligence, and scientific insight in order to conserve teeth.

This generation of '*dentistes sensibles*' offered, in the words of one of them, 'an intuitive sense of delicacy, tact, great skill and a real sensibility'. The new, studied scrupulousness as regards the feelings of the patient emerged in other forms of dental behaviour too. On Fauchard's recommendation, dental implements had to be kept well out of the sight of clients so as to avoid triggering patient terror. Dentists were to be ultra-careful too about letting cold metal obtrude too brutally on vulnerable open mouths—in certain cases, implements should be draped in cloth which made contact with vulnerable soft tissue less frightening. If there was a choice, one started work on the more robust lower jaw. Also significant in this respect was the decision to shift the site of the dental encounter off the public highway, as Mercier's example showed. The operator's preference for publicly displayed tooth-pulling was now a thing of the past: patients could snivel and sob in private, feeling that their dignity was still being respected. Practitioners were also advised to situate their consulting room on an upper floor, so that the screams of patients could not be heard from the street.

Dionis (no less) had obliged dental patients to sit on the floor at his feet, to allow him to grasp their head between his knees (*le Grand Thomas*, it must be noted, had at least provided a low stool) (Fig. 3.1). Fauchard had harsh words ('indecent', 'dirty') for this generalized practice among operators. By the same token, Lécluze maintained that the custom of gripping clients round the neck with their head under the armpit was more than a trifle shocking, especially for the ladies. The stiff, powerful rigidity of the tooth-puller's posture contrasted with the suppleness of the dentist's, as the latter moved lightly and unobtrusively around the body of the patient discreetly establishing the best and least troublesome angle of approach— 'the least awkward for the patient and the most effective for the operator', that is. A padded armchair was now *de rigueur*, and even, for working on back teeth, a reclining sofa. Soft furnishings were the order of the day for the dental encounter.

The entrepreneurialism of the '*dentiste sensible*'

Parisian dentists thus built up trust among their client base not only by stressing their scientific status within the world of medicine but also by adapting themselves in ways that responded to and indeed became part of the mood of polite sensibility evident in the Parisian bourgeois public sphere. They honed their gentlemanly science around sensitive mouths, bodies, and minds. Of these, there was no shortage in Parisian polite society.

Dentists sought to build up their client base among the groupings of the city that had most money to spend. Around half of the *dentistes* practising in the city in the last decades of the *Ancien Régime* were located on or close to the Rue Saint-Honoré, just to the north of the Louvre palace. The area was not only the elite shopping zone of the city and the centre of the fashion trades, it was also quite the swankiest part of town, where were to be found the luxurious residences of the high financial sector of the national economy (Farmers General and the like), mixed in with a sprinkling of the old aristocracy. Around a quarter of Parisian dentists resided in the Marais to the east of the city, which was home to much of the legal elite of the city, notably many members of the Paris Parlement. And a further quarter of dental practitioners were located on the Left Bank behind the Pont-Neuf, in or close to the elite Faubourg Saint-Germain. To the west of the area, that neighbourhood was dominated by the old aristocracy, but to the east it abutted the Rue Saint-Jacques, where Parisian publishing houses clustered: self-promotion through print was, as we shall see, a particular consideration.

Despite the homing instinct that dentists showed towards the neighbourhoods of the Parisian elites, those neighbourhoods were still more mixed in the eighteenth century than later became the case. The poorer classes still tended to dwell at street level or in the garrets of the wealthiest houses. Such groups were consequently not outside the remit of the new dental practitioners. For example, as a boy, very much from a plebeian background, Jacques-Louis Ménétra, future glassmaker and future revolutionary *sans-culotte*, was taken by his mother to see the dentist Jean-Baptiste Ricci when he had a tooth problem. By the same token, individuals from the lower orders were among the case studies of many dental authors, suggesting they enjoyed a broad client base. Dentists also publicized *pro bono* work on behalf of the poor in their books, pamphlets, and advertisements. They emphatically did not turn their backs on those lower down the social scale who were anxious to emulate their betters in the Parisian human comedy.

The emphasis within Parisian culture on the importance of fashionable appearances on the social stage helped to ensure a strong demand for the services and commodities of dentists. This was boosted by the fact that many of the substances ingested in the homes of Parisians and in their sites of public sociability were toxic to teeth. Although most dentists did not necessarily account it a problem, it does seem that the advent of sugar (by way of coffee, tea, ice-cream, soft drinks, and sweetmeats of every description) into the diet of not just the elite but the broad run of urban consumers wreaked havoc on teeth. Tobacco also had a deleterious impact. Archaeological evidence from eighteenth-century cemeteries suggests that teeth had never been as bad in the whole history of humanity. Toothache could claim to be the *mal du siècle*, the great illness of the age. Its effects were all the more devastating for threatening the white-tooth smiles that seemed to be becoming the passport of enlightened sociability. Stricken by toothache, the Swiss-Dutch writer, 25-year-old Isabelle de Charrière confided in self-referential, hysterical despair to a friend about her own plight:

> What can one say of a person who has suffered so much with heroic courage . . . the most horrible pains in the mouth, in the neck and on the brain; and who after nearly fifteen months spent peacefully without any suffering now despairs that her teeth, which look beautiful are not good at all; and who at every moment thinks she will lose them; who dreams of this at night; who looks at them a hundred times a day; who imagines one is good for nothing when one does not have perfect teeth; and who is amazed at the thought of finding friends, lovers, a husband . . .

A strong admirer of Rousseau, de Charrière was evidently worried that she could not live up to the sweet smiles of Julie, the 'nouvelle Heloise'. The literature and iconography of sensibility had set the bar high for personal appearance in matters of the teeth, breeding an anxiety that predisposed individuals to heed dental advice. Being forced out of the smiling circuit of enlightened sociability seemed a threat to one's very being.

Where Rousseau's *La Nouvelle Héloise* did not instigate smile anxieties in young women, dentists did their best to do so. Writing in 1780, dentist Jules Ricci graphically highlighted the future for those who lost their teeth:

> The most beautiful mouth is no sooner deprived of teeth than it loses its charms; the cheeks that these little bones supported cave in; the chin gets longer and becomes pointed; pronunciation, formerly sweet and sonorous, becomes laborious; the air producing the voice is no longer modified as hitherto, so that the voice's sound gets sharp, false, disagreeable; and finally, saliva, which is always ready to escape the mouth while talking, dribbles out of the mouth as if one were old.

The spectre of the horrors of the toothless mouth was here being painted in a deliberately lurid and ghastly manner. Preying quite openly and calculatedly on the anxieties of clients was a key part of the sales pitch of the Enlightenment dentist.

There certainly was a strong demand for dental services. But as the Ricci example shows, dentists further boosted their indispensability by stimulating and expanding social demand by artful entrepreneurship. Tooth-pullers hawking their services on the markets and crossroads of the city had been their own advertisement. Even with a signboard on a street, the closeting away of the actual dental encounter posed a potential problem of promotion within the public sphere. That problem was largely solved through the medium of print. Print allowed dentists to grow their client base and to diffuse information about their services immeasurably more efficiently than if they had depended on mere word of mouth. The bourgeois public sphere was full of avid readers and browsing consumers who could flick from, say, an account of Clarissa's white-tooth smile to an advertisement for dentifrice.

Print acted to bring together suppliers and clients eager to possess fashionable commodities in every sector of the economy. Publicity thus offered a route to potential commercial success for dentists. As the century wore on, it became apparent that their publications tended to be less scientific than commercial in their aura, and were targeted less at surgical and scientific peers than at the domestic world of polite consumption. The highly scientific Étienne Bourdet, for example, produced a pocketbook, *Soins faciles pour la propreté de la bouche* (1752), aimed to promote his services and to blow the trumpet for the science of dentistry. (He would follow this up, in 1786, with a work, unusually enough, on care of the feet. Doubtless many a smiling pedestrian had both books.) Other examples of the populist genre with an overt consumerist bent included Claude-Guillaume Beaupréau's *Dissertation sur la propreté et la conservation des dents* (1764), Le Roy de La Faudignière's *La Manière de préserver et de guérir les maladies des gencives et des dents* (1766; new edition 1772) and Jean Hébert's *Le Citoyen Dentiste* (1778).

At an even more basic level, Jean-François Botot's *Observations sur la suppuration des gencives* (1770), Pierre Auzebi's *Traité d'odontalgie* (1771), and Jean Hébert's *Réfutation d'un nouveau traité d'odontalgie* (1773) were simply advertisements for their proprietary mouthwashes. Though dressed up in scientific language, these texts were not far removed from the handbills of a *Grand Thomas*.

It is somewhat artificial to seek to divide dental publications into 'scientific' and 'commercial', for the overlap was extensive. Even the great Fauchard, patron saint of dental science, had not been immune from the itch of publicity, as we have seen. The entrepreneurial note was particularly evident in fact in newspaper advertisements. These formed a key element in a kind of 'Great Chain of Buying' linking producers and consumers, especially from around 1750, when the Paris-based advertisers, the *Affiches de Paris* and the *Affiches de province*, were established. Their influence was amplified by the fact that provincial news sheets often lifted copy from them wholesale, allowing the formation of print-driven national markets in a wide range of commodities.

Publicity allowed information to flow through to the public and also permitted the expression of a range of arguments designed to pique public interest. Health, especially in conjunction with beauty, was one of the most buoyant sectors within this virtual marketplace. Dental services and commodities formed a considerable element within this sector. Publicity stressed that good teeth were the *sine qua non* of good looks. The often explicit claim in medical advertisement was that the beautiful, white-toothed smile—as registered in the classic best-selling texts of the literature of sensibility—could be more than a novelist's fantasy: it could become a quotidian reality and a radiant badge of individual identity within the Parisian world of polite sociability. The 'Great Chain of Buying' spawned a 'Great Chain of Smiling'.

This was particularly true of women. Good teeth were one of women's facial armaments, as a Genevan dentist put it in 1790, that 'gives grace to their smile'. Yet beautification of the mouth applied to men as well as women in the Parisian public sphere. For Étienne Bourdet 'the beauty of teeth is not a point of coquetry', but applied emphatically to both sexes. 'If women lose much of their beauty through losing their teeth', concurred Jourdain, 'men are no happier'. The teeth were more prominent, moreover, in faces that were shorn of beards, in a style which in this respect still mimicked Versailles.

The Parisian world of sensibility encompassed both men and women, not least because good healthy white teeth were about more than good looks. They also facilitated convenience, comfort, and good health. Claude Géraudly itemized the multiple ways in which tooth care allowed an individual to fit into public-sphere sociability:

> Not only do [teeth] contribute to the constitution of good health, they also offer a cheerful physiognomy, an agreeable tone of voice, an easy and distinct articulation, sweet breath and a graceful air which makes them highly suited to the civil commerce of urban life.

In regard to children's teeth, dentists portrayed themselves as fighting an uphill but patriotic struggle for the hearts and minds of ignorant and benighted parents. It was not only the ignorant poor but many middle-class families as well, Bunon held, who neglected their children's teeth, for example, and even held that tartar strengthened (rather than weakened and diseased) the teeth. Those dentally off-message also pointed out that the children with the best teeth were grubby little Savoyard street-urchins, who would not recognize a dentist if they saw one. Adults could scoff at warnings about sweeteners: the duc de Beaufort had allegedly lived to the age of seventy with all his teeth intact yet had consumed an average of 4 kilos of sugar a day. Dental authors urged schools to resist such counter-propaganda against proper mouth care. Lécluze thought that schoolmasters should take their pupils to see a dentist twice a year. Others thought this rhythm far too relaxed, and that a once-monthly regime should prevail.

Dental writings emphasizing the social utility, both individual and collective, of teeth often referred to the issue of speech and enunciation. As Diderot's *Encyclopédie* noted, 'the loss of teeth disfigures the mouth and harms... pronunciation'. One needed teeth to be able to pronounce many words, comprehensibly at least. How, for example, could an *habitué* of the salons or the coffee-houses really function if they had no or few teeth—a question which, as we have seen, haunted the abbé Galiani? Nor was it only the aged who were affected by such matters of oral hygiene. Bad teeth meant bad breath. Furthermore, Étienne Bourdet also noted how 'both sexes, being continually inclined to laugh or talk, cannot pronounce certain words without saliva accompanying them, and without offering a most disagreeable spectacle'. Tooth absence led to saliva spilling from the corner of the mouth and other unseemly gestures that acted as a turn-off in polite conversation.

The preservation of the teeth allowed the face to retain its habitual order and regularity—without teeth, the lips, cheeks, and chin all caved in inauspiciously, as Ricci had noted. Loss of teeth was a step on the road to disenfranchisement from society and worse. The loss of teeth, Lécluze pointed out, 'causes deformities which leave the mouth in a disagreeable state, sight of which seems to proclaim the imminent destruction of the individual'. Toothlessness seemed to entail a loss of social identity in the Parisian public sphere. The pleasant mouth—the mouth that could smile the new smile—was inextricably tied up with individual subjectivity. 'Do we not often see', rhetorically enquired dentist Honoré Courtois, 'individuals . . . of the fair sex who cannot proffer the least remark, nor give the slightest smile, without allowing all to see the lack of care that they have taken of their teeth.' The recognizability and attractiveness of the face thus required the presence of the teeth, even if the mouth remained closed and if what remained of the teeth was invisible (a point that would not have been lost on Louis XIV's portrait-painter, Hyacinthe Rigaud). The dentist offered a reassuring sense of self in the the face-to-face encounters of the age of Enlightenment.

Dental authors dressed up their services in a patriotic and beneficent rallying narrative of social improvement in an enlightening society. The editorial rhetoric of the *Affiches* invariably highlighted, for example, how the advertiser conjoined the agreeable (*l'agréable*) with the useful (*l'utile*), and this was precisely how dentists presented their own services and commodities. In this they took their cue from other artisans of the body at this time: wig-makers in particular were prominent in stressing how their wares supplied good looks, comfort, convenience, and good health. So equipping individuals with the kind of teeth, mouth, and smile which allowed them to fit comfortably within the world of Parisian sociability was also an asset for the wider society. It also laid the groundwork for a functioning public sphere in which progress and societal felicity were to be found.

Dentists were thus willing and eager artisans in the construction of a body more attuned to the requirements of modern living. The working assumption was that healthy white teeth were a valuable asset for all adults. An ability to flash a dazzling smile was only one of a range of social advantages that one gained in having good (and preferably white) teeth. On the level of social utility as well as individual health and well-being, dental publicity represented poor teeth as both symptom and cause of sundry maladies. Dentists stressed the need for teeth to be conserved so that they could aid mastication and digestion. The old suffered chronic indigestion through lack of teeth which worsened their overall health. At the other end of the spectrum, children's teeth were a focus of particular concern in this dental literature, from the most scientific to the most popularizing examples. Good dentistry could prevent the perennial massacre of the innocents caused by fluxions and dehydration during teething. This fitted in with the populationist concerns of government over the period.

Readers of the burgeoning wave of dental publicity available in Paris from mid century onwards would thus gain the distinct impression that the dentist had only to wave his magic wand to achieve a host of mini-miracles. Where once there had been ugliness, there should be grace and good looks; where the pains of indigestion, comfort; where incomprehensibility, perfect elocution; where showers of spit, an agreeable and unembarrassing dryness; where wince-worthy and sphinctre-tightening halitosis, suavity of breath. This dreamy vision was held aloft as a goal that was realizable for every assiduous denizen of the Parisian public sphere. For the vision of good teeth and an agreeable smile was now no chimera; it was within the grasp of all.

Tooth conservation and beautification were held to start at home, and dental publicity supplied self-help advice on how, and how frequently, and in what conditions, to clean teeth. Most dentists favoured the use of a warm sponge plus a non-metallic toothpick and (if possible) a tongue-scraper (the latter was an invention of Lécluze). However, also emerging at this time and in this place was a new self-help technology destined for a long and glorious future in Western civilization: the humble tooth-brush. Constructed in much the same way as the tooth-brushes of our own day, these spared tooth enamel while penetrating into gaps in the teeth in an efficient and non-harmful way that soon made them an essential part of everyday toilette. Their daintiness and portability were particular assets. As the dentist Hébert noted, these basic technologies and practices allowed individuals to become 'physicians of the self' in all that related to enlightened mouth care.

For dentists to advocate self-help among their clients might seem like professional suicide. In fact, it took little Machiavellian cunning to realize that enhanced public interest in tooth conservation served rather than subverted the interests of the dentist. For a great many conditions of oral hygiene required more specialist care than the uninitiated could manage. The commercial logic in their position was that self-help could only achieve so much, and that once the idea of tooth-conservation had taken root with clients, the latter would always be back for more dental treatment. In theory, it might appear that if one acquired the habits of teeth cleanliness at an early age, one would have good teeth for life, so that future generations might come to a situation where dentists were a thing of the past. Dentists thought this was unlikely to be the case. Good dental habits were still only slowly making their way in the world. Moreover, diseases of the mouth might be reduced in impact but they were unlikely to disappear. Even those most committed to the Enlightenment notion of human perfectibility found it difficult to imagine that tooth problems would ever not be around.

Furthermore, although dentists did not make a song and a dance about it, many of the commodities that individuals required for looking after their own teeth were in fact supplied by dentists. The latter not only provided service; they also sold the wherewithal of personal mouth care. Self-help required the products that dentists marketed. Géraudly, for example, offered an *opiat* 'to clean and whiten' the teeth; an *elixir* which could be gargled and which 'conserves the cleanliness of the teeth, prevents pain and dissipates the bad odour of the mouth'; and an *essence* 'for calming and curing tooth-ache'. All came in handy three-livre pots. Géraudly claimed somewhat disingenuously that he had only been pushed in this commercial direction by his assistant Mademoiselle Calais (who, for reasons unknown, was in fact the only female dentist authorized to practise in the city in the course of the century). But in fact such sheepish modesty was unconvincing. The news-papers of the day abounded in advertisements for beauty products (many of which were aimed at men as well as women). We find shoals of publicity for tooth-powders and tooth-whiteners (as well as for lipsticks to set off tooth whiteness), mouthwashes, breath-sweeteners, toothpicks, tongue-scrapers, as well as the new-fangled tooth-brushes. Moreover, where at court *le fard* still spread a ghastly white over the face down to and including the lips, on the market now were rouges not just for highlighting cheeks but also for serving as lipsticks. Ruby red lips set off and showcased lovely white teeth. Two million pots of rouge were sold throughout France in 1781 alone— and the focus was now as much on lips as on cheeks.

However scientific dental publications might aspire to be, commercial concerns were thus never far away. It seems likely that many dentists derived a more substantial part of their income from such sources than from classic dental work on the mouths of clients. (The same had probably been true of some *arracheurs de dents*.) Le Roy de La Faudignière was an inveterate advertiser for his potions both in Paris and the provinces; he certainly plugged his wares in the *Affiches* in Bordeaux, Grenoble, Metz,

Picardy, and Normandy. When he died in 1786, his post-mortem inventory revealed, beneath the stairs, a laboratory containing no less than 5,500 little bottles (as well as a large bottle full of soap essence, twenty-one other bottles of thick glass, and forty-four pewter pots for his opiate). Similarly, the most valuable part of the moveable estate of dentist Pierre Billard, who died in 1751 was 57 lb of hippopotamus tooth, for cutting into (human) false teeth. As such examples suggested, dentists were still more salesmen than scientists. If there were careers in smiles to be made in Enlightenment Paris, this owed more to the dynamism of the market and the quality of dental entrepreneurship than to the institutional structures of science.

Meanwhile, in Versailles . . .

Where, one may wonder, was the royal court in these significant evolutions taking place in Paris around the mouth? After all, as we have noted, Louis XIV's Versailles had formerly set a cultural template for France's social elites. The fact was, however, that this was less and less the case. Versailles now followed the pace rather than set the tempo of the crazes for novelty and innovation evident in the French capital. Whereas the town had famously followed every court fad and fashion, now the flow was reversed: new ideas and forms of behaviour trickled up from the city to the court, from the marketplace to the palace, from bourgeoisie to aristocracy. As Mercier put it, the court had become 'a satellite revolving round a whirlwind'. The whirlwind was, of course, Paris.

The fashionable dentistry created in the enlightened public sphere over the century was far less in evidence at the court than in the city. Pre-existing codes of bodily and facial comportment at the court remained doggedly in place at Versailles, as if the critique of courtly manners just made the king dig his heels in. Louis XIV's successors showed hyper-fidelity towards the conventions of protocol established by 'Louis the Great' for almost every facet of court life. Louis XVI, after 1775, would be visibly embarrassed by some of the archaic-seeming rituals he put his courtiers through. But he did them all the same. A kind of mental paralysis in the face of change was in play. This was evident in state portraits, which were often deliberately modelled on Rigaud's swagger portrait of Louis XIV and still showed off a fine leg (but, interestingly, never implied an ageing or toothless mouth, as Rigaud had done so powerfully). The taste for fashion engendered in the

Parisian public sphere may have been penetrating court conventions, and it was certainly the case, as we have seen, that many court nobles sought to insinuate themselves within the Parisian public sphere. But these developments did not overthrow existing modes of behaviour at court. Wigs changed their forms and styles—but stayed on the head. The empire of *le fard* continued its reign on courtly faces—indeed its use may even have been growing among men. At court, rouge stayed on cheeks and if there was change in the use of beauty spots and patches, it only related to their exact location on the face.

This facial regime contrasted increasingly powerfully with a move away from the facial regime of rouge and *le fard* in Parisian circles. Here, the emphasis was on a more natural look that was assumed to signify virtue. The idea of truth-to-natural goodness had a Rousseau-esque tinge to it that gave the notion wide appeal. Whereas *le fard* had always offered to provide white skin for those who lacked it, vendors of cosmetics now offered products that would achieve a natural rather than a preternaturally bleached look. The creator of one *crème de beauté* stressed as its main selling point 'that it is actually impossible to notice that the beauty it gives comes from art'. Cheeks should have a natural colour, far from the eery brightness of traditional rouge, even if 'natural' transparency sometimes required a helping hand. In any case, the emphasis on whiteness of skin as symbol of natural virtue in courtly circles was being challenged in the Parisian public sphere by whiteness of teeth.

In private and informal settings, it is true, there was some movement away from Louis-Quatorzian models. Louis XV himself found his own court ceremonial irritatingly constricting, and reduced the number of days he passed at Versailles, preferring to spend more time in minor palaces around the Ile-de-France (Fontainebleau, Choisy, La Muette, Trianon, etc.) where he was accompanied by his mistress, Madame de Pompadour (later, Madame du Barry), and some trusted cronies. Even at Versailles on the numerous days he went hunting he eschewed state banqueting for light suppers, card games, and amateur theatricals with his circle of intimates. In such circumstances, the king could be less morose and even could look and feel relaxed—'though always with a grandeur that he did not choose to discard', as a courtier noted.

In these circumstances, many aristocrats now preferred to slip away from the patchy monotony of court rituals to immerse themselves in the giddy new world of Parisian indulgence and showiness, even if that meant, as we have seen, refashioning themselves as members of a public sphere that was bourgeois rather than aristocratic. Refugees from Versailles took to the conventions of politeness developed in the Parisian public sphere, partly in imitation and but partly too in opposition to notions of courtly civility and *honnêteté*. This allowed them to move in the circles of enlightened sociability that had developed in Paris—and indeed in some cases to dominate them. But as we have seen, their social inferiors found it difficult to trust them completely as equal citizens of the world. The overly effusive civility of nobles was invariably taken as proof of their insincerity and artificiality. Indeed, given the increasing fashionability for male courtiers to adopt the face-paint conventions of court, effeminacy was an additional charge. Jacques-Antoine Dulaure, a rare Enlightenment enthusiast for the beard, thought that the fad of *petits-maîtres* for being clean-shaven posed a threat to morality and indeed was a stimulus to homosexuality: 'the resemblances of the sexes seems to incline men towards those shameful debaucheries which polluted the glory of Greece and Rome'.

The putative effeminacy of courtiers and *petits-maîtres* was targeted for attack from other, less wacky perspectives too. Rousseau's strongly gendered writings criticized men for allowing women to be involved outside the realm of domesticity which was their favoured Rousseauean habitat: the charge was directed at royal mistresses like Madame de Pompadour, but significantly, *salonnières* in the public sphere as well. While men should dominate the public sphere, women should content themselves with the pleasures of domesticity—a vision that in fact ran athwart patterns of Enlightenment sociability. Rousseau's gendered writings were also an implicit critique of current standards of manliness, which had allowed women too much of a say in public life. Furthermore, medical men grounded in nerve theory increasingly endorsed the idea that women were unfit for any such responsibilities. In the middle decades of the century, sensibility had been a gender-free notion: men were as prone to the overt expression of the feelings as women. By the last years of the Ancien Régime, however, there was a tendency to see the nervous systems of women and children as overly sensitive (even hysterical) in contrast to a more even manly emotional keel.

This perspective found strong support from other quarters, for new idealized forms of virility were also entering public debate as regards artistic taste. From the 1760s, the writings of the German art theorist Winckelmann rehabilitated the calm, expressionless beauty of ancient Greek statues as a bodily ideal. The faces of the statues were virtually expressionless, while the beauty lay in their idealized bodies and graceful poses. A little later, and partly influenced by this, the history paintings of the highly popular Jacques-Louis David also pulled in the same direction. The inspiration again was Antiquity, but David's vision was more focused on Rome, where he had spent time as a pupil at the French Academy's École. David's early paintings had registered the continuing influence of Charles Le Brun's gallery of expressive faces, but in his mature historical paintings from the 1770s onwards the face is more restrained and rarely the centre of attention. The spotlight now falls not on the (rather doggedly set) faces but instead on the powerful gestures of muscular, sculpted bodies which betray the influence of Roman and Greek antecedents. Moreover, David sought to make of his paintings a form of public art with broader pedagogic and moralizing impact.

It was not inconceivable that his neo-classical idiom could have been picked up and adopted by the French monarchy as a propaganda tool: the demeanour of David's heroes was not so very far removed from Louis XIV's official portraiture. David received extensive royal patronage in fact, and was favoured by many in the court elite. But in the event, he prized the virtues that he associated with Roman republicanism over the values of the French monarchy. After 1789 he placed his talents at the disposal of French republicanism—with damaging effect, as we shall, see, on the popularity of the smile.

The relative fixity of royal protocol and the frivolity of court manners thus made the aristocratic body an easy target. The value of the dentist's services in facilitating a charming, polite, and sociable smile was far less appreciated at Versailles than in the public sphere in the French capital. The royal court lagged behind, and only slowly became aware of the improved technical expertise offered by Parisian dentists. Over the course of the eighteenth century, as we have seen, Louis XV gave considerable support to institutional reorganization of medicine in ways that favoured high-quality surgical practice. Yet the monarchy was far less accommodating with support for dentists.

An early sign of an only very hesitant responsiveness to changing manners was the gradual replacement of the old tooth-pulling operators by the new-style dentists in the court medical entourage. On 18 November 1719, Jean-François Caperon (or Capperon) had purchased for some 30,000 livres a *brevet d'assurance* which made him *opérateur pour les dents du roi*, following in the footsteps of Charles Dubois (Louis XIV's famous jaw-breaker). He held the position until his death in 1760, but long before that date the 'operator for the teeth' had come to prefer to style himself *chirurgien-dentiste*. It is not clear exactly when this happened. But in 1747, the duc de Luynes, assiduous chronicler of Louis XV's court, noted that a place had become vacant in the medical retinue of the king's daughters. It was, he bluffly remarked, 'what they call a dental surgeon, or, to use a more common term, tooth-puller. It is Capron [*sic*] who has for a long time occupied this office in the service of the king.' The disdainful annotation by the duke highlighted the progress of Fauchard's new nomenclature even in court circles.

In 1742 it was recorded that Caperon had broken two of the king's teeth during some repositioning of the teeth (this 'not being the first time that people have complained about him in such circumstances'). Yet this did not stop his steady rise—three years later the king ennobled him. He was also awarded sought-after lodging in the Louvre and property in the town of Versailles where he built a mansion. Succeeding him in post was Mrs Cradock's Étienne Bourdet, a published author with strong scientific credentials as we have seen. He too would prosper and end up being ennobled for his services. In 1783, he signed a contract with the Parisian dentist Vincent Dubois Foucou, whereby the latter became his *survivancier* as *dentiste du roi*. (On Bourdet's death in 1789, Foucou did indeed become Louis XVI's personal dentist.) The value of the *brevet d'assurance* which Dubois-Foucou paid for the post of *dentiste du roi* in 1783 was, at 120,000 livres, four times what Caperon had paid as an equivalent in 1719. This suggested a considerable (if, in relation to Paris, tardy) rise in demand for dental services at court.

Royal support for Parisian dentists was also evident in the increase in the number of posts for such individuals in the royal household, and in the service entourage of members of the royal family and the high aristocracy. According to the duc de Luynes, it was the king's practice to choose a different dentist from his own for other members of his family 'so as to stimulate emulation by multiplying the number of posts'. Following a mimetic courtly logic we have already observed in reference to everything from top to (literally) tail, the royal example was soon picked up by other aristocrats, who added a surgeon-dentist to their own medical retinues. The post of *chirurgien-dentiste de mesdames les filles du roi*, for example, in 1747 went to the Parisian dentist and author, Robert Bunon. Bunon died almost straight away and the post passed to Lord Chesterfield's Claude Mouton. Géraudly was appointed dentist to the duc d'Orléans, seemingly in the 1740s too. He was succeeded by royal dentist Bourdet, who was also in the service of the comte de Provence, Louis XVI's brother (the future Louis XVIII).

Yet how fast mores were changing in regard to teeth among the denizens of Versailles is very moot. The chronicler, the marquis d'Argenson, recounted a story about the duc d'Aiguillon, scion of one of France's most lustrous ducal families, whose mistress was the princesse de Conti, the widow of the prince de Conti (who as a Prince of the Blood had been only a few places removed from the throne). D'Argenson noted how the duke, growing weary of his mistress, and she of him,

> made her take another lover. He himself withdrew to his estates in Véretz in the Touraine, and called in a tooth-drawer. Shutting himself in with him, he proposed that the fellow should take out all his teeth, which were very fine. The tooth-puller refused, but the duke threatened to run him through with his sword, and on these grounds the tooth-puller operated. Monsieur d'Aiguillon made a packet of the teeth and sent them to Madame the princesse. He said that it was all so as to avoid the fluxions which were inconveniencing him. He now looks horrible, hardly talks and smiles not at all.

D'Argenson, who was a noble and had served as royal minister, was also a stern critic of court politics, and he was evidently almost as shocked as the tooth-puller at d'Aiguillon's conduct. But that was precisely the point. Courtly, aristocratic insouciance was still expressed within an unsmiling fatalism which (despite the sado-masochistic element in this tale) was solidly encrusted within the Old Regime of Teeth. Where Paris was finding fatalism about tooth loss shocking, Versailles shrugged and accepted.

Louis XV seemed supremely unconcerned about the state of his mouth (another example of his fidelity to the manners of Louis XIV). In 1742, he had a tooth extracted which was causing him some trouble. This tooth loss, the marquis d'Argenson noted, 'is going to disfigure his face when he talks and when he laughs'. Yet what irritated the monarch about the whole affair was that it forced him to stay at home and miss hunting for two whole days. The king's insouciance extended even to his lovers: one of his mistresses in the 1740s, the duchesse de Vintimille, had a strong reputation at court for stinking like a goat. The story differed little with Louis XV's successor. According to one of Louis XVI's pages, the new king had 'a very strong and fine leg' (a Louis-Quatorzian leg, no less) and 'his face was agreeable'. In contrast, 'his teeth were badly aligned and this made his laugh very graceless'. As for the comte d'Artois, the future Charles X, 'he continually had his mouth open, which made his physiognomy look less than intellectual'.

Some change was, however, detectable. The royal family started to avail themselves of the services of their dentists particularly for their children.

Highlighting how serious a threat to health teething problems in small children could still be, in 1748, the little Marie Thérèse, daughter of the duc d'Orléans, died at Versailles during weaning, after much suffering caused by a fluxion in the cheek. The autopsy report stated unequivocally that 'teeth were the sole cause of death'. Luynes reported a related, if less deadly, incident in the same year. It followed the decision of Claude Mouton, dentist to Mesdames (the king's daughters) to extract one of the teeth of the fifteen-year-old Madame Victoire. The young princess tried everything to postpone the operation, and managed to defer it a day at least. However, Luynes recounted,

> Finally the king determined to go and see her after vespers and remained with her for two hours and a half. M. the Dauphin kneeled down in front of Madame Victoire and to all the exhortations that religion and friendship inspired him he added some touching reflections about the goodness of the king, who could have ordered her to be seized and the tooth extracted by force and who however wished rather to accommodate her weakness and silliness; but that all the same she should not abuse the royal goodness. Indeed, the king could not resolve to give the order to have the tooth pulled out. He kept putting it off and Madame Victoire was endlessly thankful. She proposed to the king that he pull it out himself. One could say that it was a kind of tragi-comic scene. The queen . . . seeing that the king could not resolve to assume a tone of authority, represented to him the indispensable necessity of doing so. And Madame Victoire, finally seeing that she only had a quarter of an hour left to make her mind up, allowed the tooth to be extracted, but she wanted the king to hold her on one side, with the queen the other and with (her sister) Madame Adelaide holding her legs . . . When the operation was over, Madame Victoire said, 'The king is very good, for I feel that if I had a daughter as silly as I, I would not have suffered it with such patience . . .'

This tooth-pulling conflict set an absolute monarch against the temper tantrums of an adolescent daughter, who was either caught up in a phobic reaction or else merely being flighty and obstinate. The absolute monarch eventually (but seemingly only just) won the day. Despite his reputation for liking nothing better than talking about 'burials, deaths and surgical operations', the lugubrious Louis XV was indeed rather squeamish at the sight of blood. On another occasion, when the young Dauphin was having one of his milk teeth pulled out, Luynes told of how one of the consultant physicians 'seeing the king go pale, gave him a flask of *eau de Luce* (an antispasmodic) that he had in his pocket'.

Another symptom of change came in 1770 over princesse Joséphine de Savoie, who had recently married the comte de Provence. The ambassador of the king of Savoy at the French court reported to his master, criticizing the princess's toilette. His criticism focused on the upkeep of her hair and her teeth. 'Such things that are regarded elsewhere as mere minutiae, are essential business in *ce pays-ci*' (that is to say, at the court of Versailles).

Louis XIV would have turned in his grave to think women's oral hygiene had become 'essential business' at the royal court. Yet it showed that attitudinal change was in the air, even if it was still very tentative. The case of Queen Marie-Antoinette confirmed this. She had had prenuptial dental work done on her teeth, as we have seen, so as to enhance the appearance of her mouth. She too, like her sister-in-law, refused to take French court etiquette too seriously, a fact which triggered a dangerous wave of courtly hostility towards her. Yet though she rather gloried in being an exception to the rules, she did not overdo this propensity. This rebel against Louis-Quatorzian rituals might have smiled a lot for portraits. But she quite explicitly did not show her teeth.

As a young man, the great Romantic writer and subsequently Restoration diplomat, Chateaubriand, had been present at the royal court at Versailles in the middle of July 1789, as the revolutionary climacteric approached. Queen Marie-Antoinette, he later recalled cast 'a smiling glance in my direction'. He continued:

> Marie-Antoinette, when she smiled, shaped her lips so clearly that, horrible to relate, the recollection of that smile enabled me to recognize the jawbone of the daughter of kings when the head of the unfortunate woman was discovered in the excavations of 1815.

It was the distinctive Habsburg jaw, which we see in striking profile in a drawing of her severed head, attributed to David, and sketched minutes after her execution in October 1793. The queen's smile was defined by her jaw-line, and not her teeth which, we can safely conclude, she kept strictly within firmly buttoned lips. The Smile Revolution being fashioned within the Parisian public sphere had not yet cracked the codes of conventionality of the facial regime still enforced at the royal court.

5

The Transient Smile Revolution

Had Helen of Troy lost a front tooth, Louis-Sébastien Mercier noted in his *Tableau de Paris* in 1781, the Trojan War might never have taken place. This philosophical quip about the role of accidents in history has the additional merit of highlighting how much of human beauty and individual identity in late eighteenth-century France was thought to be invested in the smile, particularly the open-mouth, white-tooth smile of sensibility. The citation thus testifies to the progress that the gesture had made in Parisian society, powered by emergent dentistry on one hand and the re-evaluation of feeling on the other. Paris seemed to be on the cusp of achieving a Smile Revolution, and ending the chilly facial regime of the royal court, just at the moment when the great political and social revolution of 1789 loomed onto the horizon.

The years 1787 and 1788 witnessed the so-called 'Pre-Revolution' in French political life. In it, France's social elite blocked efforts by royal ministers to find a solution to the state's impending bankruptcy, and forced an unwilling Louis XVI to call the Estates General of 1789, heralding the outbreak of the Revolution proper in the summer of that year. The minds of Parisians were rarely, however, 100 per cent engaged in political affairs even in such tumultuous times. From the late 1770s to 1785, 'mesmerism', the odd and (it was claimed) sexually devastating health therapy of Mesmer, had created a stir. In 1783–4, everyone was obsessed by the fad for manned ballooning. And in 1787 and 1788, as if further to underline the moral of Mercier's casual remark, the talk of the town appeared to be the smile—and in particular the white-tooth smile. The two individuals who set the town talking were an unlikely couple: a painter, Élisabeth-Louise Vigée Le Brun, and a Parisian surgeon, Nicholas Dubois de Chémant, who manufactured dentures. In their very different ways, the two of them seemed harbingers of

the French Smile Revolution as it moved forward in step with the impending political transformation. In the event as we shall see, despite their best
efforts, the smile lost its position as a cultural icon just as the moment of its
apparent triumph. The Smile Revolution would prove to be an ethereal and
evanescent bubble waiting to burst.

The lady artist and the denture-maker

In the Academy of Painting in the early 1780s, the playwright and critic
Jean-François de La Harpe had praised Madame Vigée Le Brun for having
'the smile of Venus'. It was thus not the nature of her smile but its
representation on canvas that was an issue. In an incident that we discussed
earlier, her self-portrait displayed at the Paris Salon in 1787—and in which
her Venus smile conspicuously featured white teeth—provoked outrage in
artistic circles at such an unseemly innovation (Fig. 0.1).

There were two aspects to the shock this image had evoked. First, it was
out of step with emergent neo-classical aesthetics and notions of public art
that had developed since the 1760s, which favoured gravity, reserve, and
emotional containedness in facial expression. In the 1770s and 1780s, this
approach was particularly associated with the history paintings of Jacques-
Louis David who, as we have seen, had highlighted theatrical bodily gesture
and downplayed the expression of emotion through the face. A wave of
scepticism about the naturalism of facial expression in painting had indeed
been emerging: *Encyclopédiste* Denis Diderot attacked the 'simpering' of
portrait subjects, for example, and the artist Carmontelle criticized 'senti-
mentalist' (*sentimentaires*) female subjects who affected a 'passing sensibility'.

The opponents of affected posing which had distorted the original purity
of the notion of sensibility would have their day later in the Revolution.
At this stage these were outnumbered by traditionalists for whom the Vigée
Le Brun portrait seemed to transgress the age-old convention that the
display of teeth in a painting was indecorous and revealed the subject to
be plebeian, insane (or at any rate not fully in rational control), or else in the
grip of some particularly powerful passion.

The old conventions about the depiction of the smiling mouth were
already and increasingly under pressure by the 1780s. The white-tooth smile,
the smile of sensibility, had already been making its way in French culture for
half a century, as we have seen, and in some ways art connoisseurs and

portraitists were merely late-comers to the burgeoning Enlightenment smile-fest that we have described in the previous chapters. Stimulated by the taste for the expression of sensibility, and inspired by the 'smile of the soul' to be found in best-selling novels such as Richardson's *Clarissa* and Rousseau's *Julie, ou la Nouvelle Héloise*, many within the Parisian elite had adopted that smile and brought it into their lives. Testimony to the impact of the phenomenon within the wider cultural life was the emergence of the new vocation of Parisian dentist, the technologist of the Smile Revolution, who catered specifically for an open, transparent, healthy, and beautiful smile that showcased white, well-cared-for teeth. To modern eyes, Madame Vigée Le Brun might almost be taken to be an advertisement for Parisian dentistry. She had certainly embraced not only the smile but also the whole cult of sensibility with gusto. Her memoirs highlight the profundity of her emotion caused by reading Richardson's *Clarissa* just after her marriage, while the naming of her daughter Julie (shown in the 1787 painting) was a nice compliment to Rousseau's *La Nouvelle Héloise*. Later in her life she would undertake literary pilgrimages to the sites around Lake Geneva in which that novel had been set.

Furthermore the new smile had already started to infiltrate even artistic production. But it had tended to do so discreetly and without confronting the formal conventions attached to the most prestigious artistic genres. The sea-change, adumbrated during the Regency by the drowsily smiling figures of Jean-Antoine Watteau, was taken further by the quirky society portraitist Quentin de La Tour (Fig. 5.1). Besides his numerous subtly animated portraits, in which teeth floated tantalizingly in and out of focus, La Tour followed Watteau in depicting himself in the guise of Democritus, the wise fool who mocks the follies of the world by laughing at them—and laughing at them with teeth on full display. The radical materialist philosopher Julien Offray de La Mettrie had had himself quite deliberately portrayed in the same Democritan way. And similarly unconventional artists such as Jean-Étienne Liotard, Joseph Ducreux, and Jean-Jacques Lequeu were among others whose self-portraits also made the same gesture in the following decades. So did the German sculptor, Franz-Xaver Messerschmidt, whose laughing smile was only one of a range of excessive emotions in which he portrayed himself. A Democritan grimace was a symbolic way of attacking current court mores—and the dully standardized facial regime that derived from them.

The progress of the white-tooth smile of sensibility in the artistic repertoire was, however, more than an idiosyncratic specialism associated with a

Fig. 5.1 Quentin de La Tour, *Self-portrait*

clique of odd-ball artists. It had also become evident in the type of genre paintings that Jean-Baptiste Greuze had popularized. As we have seen, Greuze had come onto the scene in the late 1750s and early 1760s, just as the smile of sensibility was radiating outwards from the novels of Richardson and Rousseau, and when the *comédie larmoyante* on the stage was evolving into the bourgeois drama. At the same time, the heavy influence of Charles Le Brun's rules concerning the expression of emotion in history painting were being revised. Artists, connoisseurs, and the emergent grouping of art critics—men like Étienne de La Font de Saint-Yenne and *Encyclopédiste* Denis Diderot—criticized Le Brun's templates of expression as ponderous, artificial, stiff, and lacking nuance. Real emotions were normally, it was pointed out, complex and mixed and thus fell within the interstices or even wholly outside Le Brun's expressive taxonomy. Descartes's physiology, from which Le Brun had developed his ideas, was no longer taken seriously in Enlightenment Europe either. The pressing concern was to develop styles of expression which made room for the emergent nerve theory associated with ideas of sensibility. No wonder, then, that the *Conférence sur l'expression* seemed little help as regards something as complex and multifaceted as the smile.

The fact that in 1759 the distinguished connoisseur and artistic patron, the comte de Caylus, established a competitive prize within the Royal Academy of Painting for the best effort at the portrayal of an 'expressive head' (*tête d'expression*) showed how widespread concern had become. It was as though young artists needed to be given incentives to become capable of depicting in the painting of the human face what had come to be called (partly, it must be admitted, under Le Brun's influence) '*physionomie*'—that is, the look of the face, embodying a nuanced array of natural emotions which was too subtle for Le Brun's rather clunky expressive range. Revealingly, in the early years of the prize Caylus preferred to steer clear of the 'strong passions' (*passions fortes*) which had been Le Brun's concern, and to focus the competition instead on 'gentle passions'. These *passions douces*, which included affliction, gentleness, compassion, attention, and gaiety, were precisely the emotions best attuned to the ups and downs of sociability in the Parisian public sphere.

A more daring approach to the representation of facial expression was evident in Quentin de La Tour's portrait of the notorious singer and Opéra celebrity, Sophie Arnould (unfortunately lost, though surviving in engravings), as she appeared in the 1766 opera-ballet, *Zelindor*. La Tour may well have been drawing on Carmontelle's 1760 gouache portrait of Arnould singing the part of Thisbe in Francoeur and Rebel's opera, *Pyrame et Thisbe*, which showed the actress with expressive eyes turned upwards towards the heavens, a gesture at which, as we have seen, Raphael, Reni, Le Brun, Greuze, and many others had all tried their hand. La Tour reproduced the upward eye gesture, but added the singer's open mouth revealing her teeth. It appears to have been the La Tour (rather than the Carmontelle) image that the great sculptor Jean-Antoine Houdon utilized in making a portrait bust of the singer in 1774, allegedly as Iphigénie in Gluck's opera *Iphigénie en Tauride*, in which she had just enjoyed one of the most brilliant successes of her career. Her teeth are clearly on display (Fig. 5.2). The bust was shown publicly at the 1775 Salon, along with Houdon's sculpture of Gluck, and then passed straight into the possession of the sitter.

Sophie Arnould had a string of lovers drawn from the *haut gratin* of the French aristocracy—but this hardly made her respectable. On the contrary, in fact. This and the fact that she was a professional singer meant that the

Fig. 5.2 Jean-Antoine Houdon, *Sophie Arnould* (1775)

exposure of her teeth still just about fell within the traditional categories for whom artistic decorum permitted an open mouth. Also, she was acting an identity rather than embodying one. The fact that most artistic depictions of individuals shown smiling in this way in the years leading up to the Revolution did not have a recognizable identity also made them less shocking. In the 1787 Salon, for example, Jean-Antoine Houdon exhibited his 'Head of a young girl, in plaster' (according to the label) which also showed a young woman's smile with teeth on full display (Fig. 5.3). Houdon had chosen not to disclose that the 'young girl' was in fact his new wife, Marie-Ange Langlois, and the bust appears to have stayed within the family. Madame Vigée Le Brun paid for her audacity at the same exhibition, attracting critics who walked untroubled past Houdon's apparently generic bust. It is also worth noting that the subjects in the canvases of Jean-Baptiste Greuze shown displaying their emotions were also anonymous, purportedly

Fig. 5.3 Jean-Antoine Houdon, *Head of a Young Girl (Madame Houdon)* (1787)

universal figures (a mother, a bride, a fiancée, etc.) in much the same way. The fact that his paintings fell more within the category of genre painting than portraiture helped them to escape the critical wrath that Madame Vigée Le Brun's 1787 self-portrait attracted.

Madame Vigée Le Brun was something of a fashion-crazy eccentric, a trend-setter, and a courter of controversy. Revealingly, however, although she painted over thirty portraits of Queen Marie-Antoinette, she never allowed the glimpse of a royal tooth to show. But then, as we have seen, the queen typified a court culture that still resisted the smile of sensibility. The artist only managed to shock the artistically strait-laced when she represented the queen in the *en chemise* fashion; some critics thought that the portrait showed the queen in her underwear.

The latter point is revealing in another way too. In the past, identity in portraits had often tended to be conveyed through the clothing and accoutrements of the figure represented and not solely through physical resemblance. The 1787 Madame Vigée Le Brun self-portrait broke with this, as her clothing was indeterminately exotic, and the painter portrayed herself essentially as a young mother (albeit one with a twinkle in her eye). This was a point that was later (in 1792) strongly approved by the art theorist Pierre-Charles Levesque. French artists, he maintained, 'have themselves made a nature which lies'. The Vigée Le Brun self-portrait showed that 'they are returning to the path of the true, and consequently of the good in all genres'. The triumph of the smile was a triumph for natural virtue. Levesque made an interesting further point when he went on to state that it was by dint of this truth to life 'that the public has recently seen with so much pleasure the painting of Madame Le Brun and her daughter'. For the implication was that the public was a more reliable judge than aristocratic dabblers, connoisseurs, and art critics: the public opinion that Enlightenment thinkers hailed as the apotheosis of human reason extended to matters of taste. Following this logic to its culmination, those who thought otherwise were sectional, prejudiced, and anti-democratic in their attitudes.

Over the course of the late Enlightenment, this tension about the source of artistic quality had played out around the nature of the portrait, which had become the main means by which many painters made a living. They often resented the increasing tendency of their sitters to expect them to produce a characterization that suited them, rather than being in accordance with academic criteria. The sitters, gripped in a wave of sensibility, expected that sensibility to reflect back from their portraits. This kind of approach evidently prepared the ground for the Vigée Le Brun revolution.

Madame Vigée Le Brun and others followed further down the track indicated in the 1787 portrait. The smiling display of teeth became something of a signature gesture in her work. It was there not only in the subjects noted above: despite the raised hackles in the 1787 Salon, she had portrayed the smile in self-portraits in 1781 and 1782 and in her portrait of the duchesse de Polignac in 1783. Further examples would follow (the actor Paisiello in 1790, Emma Hamilton in 1791–2, Madame de Stael in 1808, for example). Other artists also grasped the freedom now on offer: Jacques-Louis David featured teeth in his portrait of Madame de Sériziat in 1795, for example (Fig. 5.4); Gérard in his Madame Barbier-Walbonne in 1796; and Ingres in a 'Portrait of a Woman' in 1806. Very much through the actions of Madame Vigée Le Brun, smile revolutionary, the open-mouthed smile was added to the repertoire of approved expressions in a portrait in Western

Fig. 5.4 Jacques-Louis David, *Madame de Sériziat* (1795)

art. No other painted smile—not even the *Mona Lisa*—would ever trigger such sharp cultural shock-waves.

Yet Madame Vigée Le Brun was not the only smile revolutionary in this pre-1789 moment. At the same time, if from a very different domain, there came into the public eye one Nicolas Dubois de Chémant, whom later generations would hail as the inventor of porcelain dentures. His white dentures proposed a white-tooth smile that was far from beautiful in the Vigée Le Brun manner, but which was just as striking in its way.

The idea for what he called 'mineral paste teeth' had hit Dubois de Chémant powerfully, he later recounted, when he was still reeling from an evening in the presence of a woman with powerful halitosis caused by her dentures. False teeth themselves were of course nothing new—indeed we find examples from the time of the pharaohs. During the Renaissance, virtuoso surgeons such as Ambroise Paré had dreamed up all sorts of fancy mouth-ware. Yet it was the advent of scientific dentistry in the work of Pierre Fauchard which accelerated interest in false teeth. Fauchard had developed a battery of tried-and-tested dental apparatuses, including a spring-loaded full denture set.

These and similar dental contraptions had their problems. Although dentures might help mastication and maintain the plumpness of the cheeks, they very rarely seemed to look, or indeed to smell, good. For, as Dubois de Chémant had learnt from bitter intimate experience, food became lodged in the threads or wires holding the false teeth in place, and produced a powerfully malodorous as well as visually disconcerting effect. For those without the full denture set, there was also a problem of colour conformity with existing teeth.

In the manufacture of false teeth, during the Enlightenment preference tended to be given to bones taken from animals and carved into the shape of teeth. Hippopotamus jaw was regarded as best in terms of whiteness, resistance to discoloration, and consistency, but ox, ivory, and walrus tusk were also employed, as was wood (though only by backwoodsmen like George Washington). Even Fauchard's spring-loaded denture sets were not problem-free either. Wearers needed quite strong jaw muscles to force their mouth shut, so that the mouth in fact often lolled unattractively open. Spring-loaded dentures also had the unfortunate habit of leaping dramatically from the owner's mouth at unguarded moments, adding to the quotidian dramas of salon life.

Informed sources held that artificial teeth became malodorous and visually repulsive so swiftly that they really had to be changed annually. Dubois de Chémant imagined an opera house filled with 500 individuals all wearing putrefying hippopotamus dentures—equivalent in fact, he calculated, to a whole hippopotamus. The cumulated stench, he held, would pose a serious public health risk. Furthermore, it came to be suspected that transplanted teeth, especially those culled from hospitals, morgues, cemeteries, and prostitute reformatories would spread disease. The gradual dissolution of such implants, Dubois de Chémant maintained, 'occasioned by the fermentation which results from the heat of the mouth, can inoculate the distemper of the person out of whose mouth they were taken'. He cited the celebrated English surgeon John Hunter in support of the assertion that artificial teeth often 'contained a venereal or scrofulous virulency'. Transplanted syphilis was a threat to all who dared to place the teeth of others in their mouths.

Tooth transplantation had become a surprisingly popular technology deployed to counter tooth loss. Fauchard had recommended removing a person's diseased tooth, cleaning it, filling it, and then restoring it in place in the client's mouth. This capacity of the mouth to adapt to reinsertion (actually quite limited in fact) expanded into the practice of taking another's teeth and putting them in place of missing teeth. In 1685, the first author in England to publish on the noble art of tooth-pulling had suggested that dog, sheep, goat, and baboon teeth might all be used for this purpose. These proposals seem happily not to have been followed up, but discarded human teeth did offer the basis for a market. Dentists advertised for teeth, and might have collections of literally thousands in their possession. The brother of the French actor Talma was a dentist in practice in London in the 1780s and wrote back to Paris asking his brother to procure several hundred teeth from the city's hospitals. Teeth yanked from battlefield corpses would prove another, and particularly buoyant sector of supply. 'Waterloo Teeth' and teeth extracted from corpses on American Civil War battlefields would be notorious in this respect throughout the nineteenth century.

Recourse was also had to extracting live teeth from the living poor to provide for the rich. A shiny white tooth could be whisked out of the mouths of poor Savoyard urchins from the streets of Paris and placed in the gaping gum-sockets of bourgeois mouths. The practice was ethically questionable, a point that the English caricaturist Thomas Rowlandson evoked in a 1787 print on the subject, with a little London chimney-sweep doing duty as an infant Savoyard (Fig. 5.5). It was also acknowledged to have potential medical and aesthetic as well as ethical drawbacks. Such teeth did not always take, and even if they did, they tended to discolour.

Against this background, one starts to see the attractiveness of Dubois de Chémant's 'mineral' teeth. We know that experiments to find a substitute for human and animal teeth had already started in Paris in the mid 1780s. Dubois experimented with a technique which had been trialled a decade or more previously by an apothecary at Saint-Germain-en-Laye called Alexis Duchâteau. One of the biggest technical problems which Duchâteau and then Dubois encountered was that the firing of dentures caused uneven shrinkage which made fit-to-mouth problematic and painful. There were also difficulties relating to colour retention, surface cracking, and excessive brittleness. Dubois experimented with hard-paste porcelain which was just being developed in France following the discovery of kaolin in the Limousin in the late 1760s. He decided to go direct to the royal manufactory at

Fig. 5.5 Thomas Rowlandson, *Transplantation of Teeth* (1787)

Sèvres, France's premier producer of high-quality porcelain goods. Sèvres workmen proposed to him that he should take wax impressions of the inside of a client's mouth and then make a model in plaster of Paris. They also helped him to create a little furnace within the premises of the manufactory, on which he undertook a series of trials so as to get the best, most lifelike colours, the most resilient paste and the most convincing appearance.

In 1788, Dubois de Chémant was ready to go public with a new product. He approached for their approval the Royal Society of Medicine, the Academy of Sciences, and the Paris Medical Faculty. These bodies praised his false teeth for their solidity, convenience, salubriousness, and beauty. The latter quality was an unexpected compliment, but the range of advantages conformed neatly with the advertising puffs at this time of dentists as well as similar producers of semi-luxury commodities such as razor manufacturers, herniary truss-makers, and wig-makers. (Indeed some denture-makers were soon claiming that dentures would soon be as widespread among the population as wigs.) Certificates in the bag, Dubois set

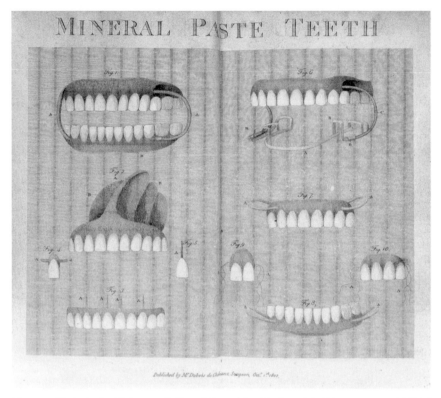

Fig. 5.6 Dubois de Chémant, 'Mineral Paste Teeth', from his *Dissertation on Artificial Teeth in General* (1797)

about publicizing his wares. His *Dissertation sur les avantages des nouvelles dents et râteliers artificiels, incorruptibles et sans odeur* ('Dissertation on the Advantages of the New Incorruptible and Odourless False Teeth and Dentures') appeared in 1788 (Fig. 5.6). Their appeal to both the useful (*l'utile*) and the agreeable (*agréable*) ticked the right Enlightenment boxes, as a later 82-year-old poet enthusiast was to proclaim:

> E'en helpless infants, whilst we press
> The cradle, sprouts the pearly tooth,
> And faithful to its trust remains
> Throughout the holiday of youth.
> But years advance, and teeth decay,
> Thus mystic nature has decreed,
> CHEMANT then brings a second set,
> Long live CHEMANT, our friend in need.

Well vers'd in wisdom's lore, he makes
The *utile* and *dulce* meet,
It's his the highest pitch of art
To blend the useful and the sweet.
When time has stripp'd our armory bare,
New grinders and new cutters gives;
CHEMANT steps in with subtle heed;
With his we laugh, with his we feed,
Long live CHEMANT, our friend in need.

Dubois de Chemant's publicity pitch stressed their natural look. This was very much the approach taken at this time by the cosmetics industry too, as we have seen. Dubois's confidence in the dentures was such that he wore them himself, thus becoming his own walking, talking, and smiling advertisement. He set up business in the ultra-fashionable Palais-Royal in central Paris. Owned by the duc d'Orléans, the Palais-Royal had become the acme of Parisian public sociability and the Mecca of the city's international tourist trade. Porcelain dentures were thus in their element at the heart of the Parisian public sphere. And it was here, moreover, in the Palais-Royal, that on 12 July 1789 the young lawyer and journalist Camille Desmoulins stood on a coffee-house table and famously called his fellow-Parisians to arms, as King Louis XVI threatened to surround the city and impose counter-revolution. Two days later, the Bastille fell, and with it collapsed the Bourbon absolute monarchy. The Palais-Royal was the point of confluence between a Parisian Smile Revolution at its apogee and a radical political and social transformation in which the smile would, paradoxically, end up being politically suspect.

Smiles under suspicion

In 1789, the adage of the Enlightenment dramatist, Marmontel, that 'the smile of the people is worth more than the favour of kings' seemed like a prophecy that was coming true. The Revolution brought a spontaneous smile of joy to the lips of French men and women. It seemed the apposite gesture to welcome in a new epoch in human history, and a perfect response to a movement that bade to transform the social, economic, and political order in the interests of the French nation as a whole. On the day following the fall of the Bastille, for example, when the triumph of the revolutionary cause seemed certain, 'all eyes were wet with tears', one observer noted, and 'intoxicated sentiment was everywhere'. A day or two later another observer noted how people, mixing 'smiles and sobs' ('*ris et pleurs*'), displayed 'a character of happiness and sensibility that no words could express'. Wherever one looked, a journalist observed, one saw Parisians, full of 'gaiety and joy' at the overthrow of the *Ancien Régime* and the new era ushered in by the Rights of Man. Royal diktat no longer supplied an appropriate template for expression and representation. Nature, progress, sensibility, civilized values—and good dentistry of course—had prevailed over Divine Right absolutism, and seemed to be bidding to make the smile an icon of radical transformation.

The root-and-branch destruction of the *Ancien Régime* and all its works was accompanied by a sense that the mission of social and personal improvement mapped out in the Enlightenment had reached an apotheosis. Sovereignty was now embodied not in the person of the monarch but in the abstract entity of the nation. A new society, with a new politics grounded in the Rights of Man, would make possible the regeneration of humanity. A 'new man'—such was the term used—worthy of these epochal changes could well thus wear on his face a smile that was both a symbol of its faith in the natural fellowship of humanity and pious hope for future happiness of all. The gaiety which Parisians had been progressively recovering over the eighteenth century now seemed the order of the day.

There seemed every hope that there would be a mutual reinforcement between the Smile Revolution and the social and political revolution ushered in during 1789. The Rights of Man and the Citizen approved by the National Assembly on 26 August of that year did not actually use the phrasing of the 1776 American Declaration of Independence, in which, 'life, liberty and the pursuit of happiness' were marked out as fundamental guides to social organization and individual action. But the thrust of the document was much the same. 'Happiness is a new idea in Europe', declared one ardent revolutionary, and the wide expectation was that happiness could be better guaranteed in France than in a United States that had drawn back from radical social transformation by maintaining the institution of slavery. The American Declaration of Independence, one speaker in the National Assembly condescendingly noted, had set 'a great example in the new hemisphere'; but it was now up to the French to address the whole of humanity.

The achievements of the French Revolution in the cause of social justice and harmony were so considerable that they do not require elucidation. Besides the Rights of Man, the abolition of feudalism (and after 1794 that of slavery), the establishment of the liberal freedoms, equality before the law, the career open to talent, and so on, all attest strongly in this sense. Smile Revolution and political revolution seemed to be part of the same project. Yet this happy conjunction was not to last. If the political revolution had started with a smile, that smile was soon under pressure, and gaiety passed quickly off the agenda. Indeed, the smile soon became a bone of political contention. An early straw in the wind was a decree passed by the National Assembly in June 1789 that stipulated that there was to be no laughter in its debates. The rule stayed in place even though the assembly's records show its transgression more than 400 times in the next two years of its existence (the first occasion taking place less than forty-eight hours after the rule was introduced). It seemed important that the representatives of the nation should conduct themselves with gravity and dignity and with the general demeanour of virtuous Roman republicans that they had come to admire in David's epic neo-classical paintings.

The ban on public laughter in the National Assembly did not of course rule out the smile, since the smile did not, according to the conduct books, involve any noise or bodily motion. Indeed in the new political culture now ushered in, what the journalist Joseph Cérutti called 'a smiling physiognomy' still seemed to many an agreeably democratic statement. Many writers and journalists sought to accommodate the new politics with the traditional spirit of French, and especially Parisian, gaiety. Cérutti thought that 'being always laughing and cheerful' was a national characteristic so that 'a truly patriotic gaiety' was not a contradiction in terms. The revolutionary journalist Antoine-Joseph Gorsas similarly tried to fashion out of the 'serene and tempered gaiety' of the French what he called 'patriotic laughter'. One should be 'calm, frank, open', but one's face should be 'on the "Fine Weather" side of the barometer of gaiety'.

Yet many revolutionaries regarded this epochal process as deserving of a more reasoned and serious approach. Within the political elite at least, preference tended to be given less to the politeness of the Parisian public sphere and more to the kind of stately gestures that Jacques-Louis David's paintings had illustrated. Jutting jaws, outstretched arms, and stiff upper lips were preferred to tremulous smiles. David's huge unfinished painting (of which only drafts and sketches survive) recording the Tennis-Court Oath of

1789, when the embryonic National Assembly had vowed to resist dissolution by the king, showed all the deputies in heroic gestural mode, their faces sternly serene, stoically determined.

With *passions fortes* prevailing over the *passions douces* that had been stimulated by Enlightenment sociability, the smile seemed to be becoming *démodé*, and it passed on to the defensive. 'This nation, so gay, so witty, so ready to laugh', commented one pamphleteer in 1789, 'is susceptible to gravity, reflectiveness and noble enthusiasm... Hitherto the nation has joked because it has been a crime to reason, because it has been allowed only to joke, and forbidden to learn and to concern itself with the common weal.' From this perspective, humour, jokiness, and a smiling demeanour were so many infantile maladies out of which the nation needed to grow.

What was increasingly on show in public life was not the open, gentle, civilized gesture of the Parisian Smile Revolution. Now, the smile was increasingly displaced by the harsh, combative, spiteful laughter of sarcastic depreciation. The smile of sensibility had been all about moderation; but now 'moderation' was becoming a dirty word. In the revolutionary lexicon, a 'moderate' was a 'false friend of the people, enemy of the constitution', who was increasingly under suspicion.

'France isn't laughing any more', noted the counter-revolutionary journalist Antoine de Rivarol. Yet the opposite was true, certainly in Paris. Indeed Rivarol, an ardent supporter of the beleaguered Louis XVI, was a hyperactive participant in what one pamphleteer called the 'laughter wars' that characterized the opening years of the Revolution. Spokesmen for the noble and ecclesiastical orders whose privileges had been swept away in the revolutionary maelstrom utilized the freedom of the press enshrined in the 1789 Rights of Man to attack all aspects of the revolutionary cause. Royalist and overtly counter-revolutionary printing presses and newspapers—not least the populist *Actes des apôtres* ('The Acts of the Apostles') for which Rivarol wrote—deployed sarcasm and satire about all aspects of change: revolutionary politicians, revolutionary laws, revolutionary vocabulary, revolutionary diction, revolutionary anything, and everything was grist to the humour mill. The barbs of the *Actes des apôtres* infuriated revolutionaries, not least because the newspaper's 100 per-cent oppositionism was often genuinely funny and attracted a broad audience. In this context, humour seemed a weapon of counter-revolutionary propaganda. Laughter, as one pamphleteer put it, appeared to be becoming 'the sign of counter-Revolution'.

Many revolutionaries regarded this mocking pro-aristocratic laughter, diffused through the printing presses, as out of place once war was declared with much of Continental Europe in April 1792. In the years between 1792 and 1794, the Revolution found itself in an exceptionally fragile situation, as war threatened the whole revolutionary project and triggered the Terror, the violently repressive regime run by the Committee of Public Safety of the Convention (France's national assembly between 1792 and 1795). Such a grave situation seemed to rule out even a benign sardonic smile as an appropriate gesture. Symptomatically, one of the first things that the national assembly had done on the overthrow of Louis XVI on 10 August 1792 and the subsequent declaration of a republic was to close down pro-monarchist counter-revolutionary newspapers and publishing houses. Aristocratic and counter-revolutionary laughter was no longer tolerable in print, or indeed anywhere else.

Yet aggressive laughter was not quite so easily disposed of in the new republic. In fact, the aristocratic mocking, *de haut en bas* humour of the counter-revolutionary press was already being matched by the full-throated plebeian humour generated by the radical popular movement in Paris. As cartoonists showed, the laughter of plebeian radicals, or *sans-culottes*, was meant to take the smile off the face of the aristocracy (Fig. 5.7). This trend

Fig. 5.7 *'Maudite Révolution'/'Ah l'bon decret'* (1789–90)

had been started by print journalists like Jean-Paul Marat and Camille Des-moulins in 1789, but the arch-exponent of this kind of humour was the famously foul-mouthed *Le Père Duchesne* newspaper run by the radical Parisian politician Jacques-René Hébert. Hébert assumed the identity of a crude and excessive but fiercely patriotic *sans-culotte*, dedicated to the Revolution, eager to destroy counter-revolution wherever it was to be found, and always on the qui-vive for signs of weakness and treachery within the political class.

Hébert sought out enemies even amongst his peers—especially, it seemed, his smiling peers. On 7 October 1793, Gorsas, political pamphlet-eer, journalist, and latterly member of the Convention was sentenced to death by the Revolutionary Tribunal that had been established in March of that year to deal summarily with counter-revolutionaries. A tumbril con-veyed him to the Place de la Révolution (today Place de la Concorde) to be executed by the guillotine that had been created to administer capital punishment for counter-revolutionary offences. He showed great stoicism on the scaffold, declaring his innocence—and he even managed a faint smile. The scaffold smile admitted defeat in his self-assigned project of accommodating 'serene and tempered gaiety' and 'patriotic laughter'. It was a defeat, and a smile, at which the *Père Duchesne* did not refrain from sneering: 'The bugger had got drunk so as to appear brave before the blade. Fuck it! The National Razor soon cut short his comic banter.'

Gorsas had not been executed for smiling of course. But reaction to his execution smile was a symbolic marker of a new and chilly seriousness that had enveloped political and social life since the happily smiling days of the early Revolution. Smiles had once been about openness and transparency. The smile of sensibility had even had a progressive and egalitarian edge to it. But now smiles were suspect. 'Face too jolly to be accounted a true republican', was the gaoler's lapidary and telling comment on a political suspect brought to the Sainte-Pélagie prison.

In the opinion of the youthful politician Louis-Antoine Saint-Just, a member of the Committee of Public Safety and an ally of its most prom-inent figure, Maximilien Robespierre, a smile signified dissimulation rather than transparency: 'dissimulation smiles, innocence grieves'. It thus had to be systematically distrusted. Saint-Just was reappropriating arguments over the artificiality of the smile that had been targeted at the phony, smirking smile that had been apparent at the royal court prior to 1789. But now it was aberrant plebeians as well as degenerate *petits-maîtres* who were the target. Couthon, Robespierre and Saint-Just's close ally on the Committee of

Public Safety, was of a similar opinion: 'all good citizens', he opined, 'must be physiognomists'. But they should be scrutinizing external appearances not for character and identity but for political persuasion. Sincere views had to be hunted down through and in spite of outward appearances. Individuals needed to display an alert vigilance in regard to rooting out criminal and counter-revolutionary intentions which hid themselves from view. Symptomatically, the Parisian municipality strictly forbade carnival taking place, and it was not just the crude popular fun that was now regarded as indecent but also the customary donning of masks at carnival times. Masks which feigned republican sincerity were what counter-revolutionaries wore in order to avoid their true colours becoming self-evident.

The distrust shown towards the smile appeared to be vindicated by the fact that the scaffold smile was becoming an emblem of political resistance. The tumbril journey and the climb to the scaffold provided a quotidian drama to which Parisians were ever alert. Many individuals broke down altogether, presenting an appalling tableau. This was the case with Madame du Barry, Louis XV's final mistress, for example. Her teeth chattering in fright, she 'cried as I have never seen anyone cry', noted the public executioner Henri Sanson. Hysterically imploring bystanders to rescue her, she yelled so loudly that she could be heard on the other side of the river Seine. What was altogether more impressive was the number of individuals who showed calm and sang-froid in the face of death. Executioner Sanson stood in awe of the large group of magistrates from the Parisian and provincial parlements sent to the guillotine in early 1794: 'there were no tears, no moans, no reproaches, no useless gestures. They died with the serene pride of the Romans who waited on their seats for the Gauls.' One of their number, Malesherbes, a friend of the *philosophes* during the Enlightenment, but who had taken on the defence in the king's trial out of a sense of moral duty, presented an even more imposing image: he died 'with the smiling steadfastness of a sage and the calm that comes from a conscience at ease with itself'.

It was indeed the victims' smile that executioner Sanson found the most disconcerting aspect of his duties. When he appeared in revolutionary gaols, he found that many prisoners, thinking it might be them next for the scaffold, 'smiled at me; and these smiles [he continued] had a singular effect on me. I could become accustomed to the horror that my presence occasioned, but it was altogether more difficult to take to the guillotine individuals ready to thank me for doing so.' The best of the men, he recorded, either went to their fate imposingly stoical like Malesherbes and his peers, or else laughing in the face of doom, like the merchant who after quaffing a glass of white wine and a dish of oysters 'went off to the guillotine as others would go to their wedding'. Yet it was the benign steadfastness of many of the politically prominent women whom he conducted to the scaffold that he found more moving still. They deployed the smile in the way that Richardson and Rousseau had taught them, but now with a stoical twist. There might be tears, but there were also smiles through, over, and beyond those tears.

The comte de Beugnot, who spent time as a prisoner in the Parisian gaols, though avoiding the guillotine, found the reaction of these women enormously moving:

> They treated misfortune like a naughty child at whom one could only laugh; and so they laughed very openly at the divinity of Marat, the priestliness of Robespierre, the magisterial character of Fouquier [the public prosecutor attached to the Revolutionary Tribunal]. And they seemed to say to all this bloody group of crawlers: you can kill us when you want, but you will never stop us being loveable . . .

Beugnot had seen Manon Philpon, better known as Madame Roland, go off to the guillotine in October 1793 with a sublime smile on her face. Roland was almost exactly the same age as Madame Vigée Le Brun (who would live nearly half a century longer). Like her, she had had her '*Nouvelle Héloise* moment'—in her case it was in the mid 1770s when she was twenty-one years old. 'Even were it to drive me mad', she later recalled, 'I would want no other book.' It offered 'the sustenance that was mine alone and the interpreter of feelings that I had before I read him, but that he alone was able to explain to me'. Rousseau's character Julie pointed out to her a thrilling pathway to living life to the full as loving wife, nurturing mother—and passionate lover. Fittingly, she went to the scaffold devoutly channelling Julie, while also evoking one of her cherished republican heroes from Plutarch. The butt of blood-curdling verbal assaults on her way to the guillotine, she 'listened with a disdainful smile'. Her final words, 'Oh liberty! What crimes are committed in thy name!' were uttered with 'a bitter smile'. For a woman who had sought to live out her private life in devout imitation of Rousseau's 'Nouvelle Héloise', what more apt description could there be for her final moments than the phrase that Rousseau had used to describe Julie's death-bed scene: 'smiles on the mouth, and tears in the eyes'?

Madame Roland was far from exceptional. It was as though a generation of Rousseau-lovers and Julie-imitators took this moment to deploy the smile as a transcendent symbol of their humanity—as, of course, Rousseau had meant it. At the sublime courage of Charlotte Corday, Marat's assassin, executioner Sanson bowed in respect. Similarly Lucile Desmoulins (in sharp contrast to her husband, the radical journalist and statesman Camille) was radiant with smiles. Madame Elisabeth, the king's sister, had her 'always sweet smile' on display throughout her trial and the procedures leading to her execution. In this, for Sanson, 'she resembled a saint come down from heaven'. Their lives on the line, such individuals allowed the guillotine moment to be the scene of the expression of character and of authentic individual identity. And the gesture that they deployed powerfully to produce this effect was the smile of sensibility fashioned during the Enlightenment and now given a heightened, stoical twist.

Thus, at the height of the Terror, revolutionary political life was not only caught in a pincer movement between open-throated populist radicalism and the sneeringly raucous humour of counter-revolutionary reaction. It was also finding the smile being appropriated as an apposite gesture of resistance by those adjudged to be counter-revolutionaries. Oddly, unexpectedly, surprisingly, in view of its earlier history and associations, the smile had changed political sides. It was no longer an icon of a unitary and egalitarian Revolutionary culture. The latter had become too deadly serious to accommodate much in the way of smiles. Instead, the smile had become a shared emblem in the freemasonry of political victimhood, a 'weapon of the weak', in the sense that the scholar James Scott has defined the expression, namely, a hidden transcript by which the powerless symbolically critiqued and cocked a snook at the powerful. The revolutionaries prided themselves on their stoical commitment to the national cause, and now gallingly found the arms of stoicism turned against them in the face of the guillotine's blade.

The revolutionaries in power reacted to this reversal in the meaning of the smile by stiffening into even greater levels of humourless, unsmiling seriousness. Symptomatic in this respect was the format of official festivities. Revolutionary culture was ceaselessly celebratory of its own deeds. Key dates such as 14 July and 10 August were noted moments of official rejoicing, while the deaths of leading figures in the Revolution such as Mirabeau and Marat also occasioned huge and elaborate ceremonies of remembrance. The ceremonials became more and more numerous as time went on, and more and more serious at the same time. The first celebration of the fall of the Bastille, on 14 July 1790, had involved great popular involvement and excitement: 'we must drive out the last breaths of despotism by our singing, our dancing and our laughter', claimed one journalist. Such cheerful popular allegresse became thinner on the ground as time went on. Festivities under the Terror tended to have strictly didactic aims, as though festive celebration was mainly an opportunity to moralize the population into political correctness and virtue through orchestrated and often heavy-handed allegorical displays. The people of Paris—who had been incorporated into earlier celebrations in line with the pre-1789 tradition of Parisian collective gaiety—were reduced to the role of spectator or walk-on part rather than participant, notably when the artist Jacques-Louis David became official pageant-master. Despite the revolutionary cult of transparency, many of these festivals felt desperately artificial.

The high seriousness that David sought to instil in revolutionary festivals had two sources. First, it transmitted the messages of the neo-classicism with which he had been associated under the Ancien Régime, and notably the idea that art should be a public and improving force within society. Secondly, it echoed the temperament and ideological stance of David's political mentor, Maximilien Robespierre, 'the Incorruptible', as he was styled, who prided himself on his grave demeanour. Long after the Terror, his sister Charlotte claimed that he always had a smile on his face, and his 1791 portrait as a deputy certainly indicates a slight up-turn of the mouth. Yet Robespierre was widely held by his revolutionary peers never to have been seen smiling or laughing. A severe facial tic gave his face the appearance of a twisted grimace, especially under stress. Curiously, David's own case was similar: a tumour around his lip gave his face an asymmetrically swollen look and he wisely eschewed smiling. The grim twins of revolutionary seriousness found it seemingly physically impossible to break into a smile.

Robespierre had at least taken out of the French Smile Revolution a greater concern for oral hygiene. That is, he possessed a toothbrush, talismanic technology of the Smile Revolution. His fellow deputy in the Convention, Barras, recounted how he had visited Robespierre when the Terror was at its height, in an attempt to get him to support moderation. He found him brushing his teeth. He noted that as Robespierre cleaned his teeth, he insouciantly spat out mouth-rinsing water at the feet of his fellow-deputy. The gesture conveyed, in Barras's account, a lack of civility on Robespierre's part and an overload of contempt for individuals he regarded as his inferiors rather than his fraternal equals. But there is also a hint of the public display of private functions that had characterized the Bourbon court: Robespierre was thus displaying manners that were both reprehensibly Bourbon and irredeemably bestial and uncivilized.

Notwithstanding Robespierre's oral hygiene, the Smile Revolution now seemed very far away. The Committee of Public Safety tended to characterize its opponents to left and right as unscrupulous and unserious dilettantes with a propensity to unseemly laughter. This was certainly the case with the radical journalist Hébert, who had been so eager to laugh and sneer at Gorsas's dying smile. Hébert himself would be guillotined for his radical political excesses six months later, in April 1794, when the Terror was at its height. Police spies noted with disgust how he conducted himself 'like the weediest of little women' (*femmelettes*). Much the same trajectory was evident for others who had a reputation for unseriousness. Robespierre's fellow Committee of Public Safety member Hérault de Séchelles, for example, was tried and executed at this time too. 'Hérault was serious within the Convention', Robespierre's ally Saint-Just stated; 'elsewhere he played the buffoon, and would laugh incessantly to cover up the fact that he never said anything'. The idea of laughter as camouflage for treasonous intentions also floated around the removal and execution of Robespierre's former school friend, the radical journalist, Camille Desmoulins, who went to the scaffold whingeing that he was being punished for causing people to laugh at his opponents. Robespierre's greatest rival, the rumbustious and hard-living Georges Danton, was executed alongside Desmoulins. He ranted wildly in prison the night before his execution, poking crude fun at Robespierre's allegedly virginal seriousness. He told fellow-prisoner Thomas Paine that he would go 'gaily to execution' and a drawing of him on his way to the guillotine shows him smiling a grim black and seemingly toothless smile. He would be cracking jokes with his fellow victims at the steps of the guillotine. It was as though only those who were destined for death could allow themselves the luxury of a smile.

Lavaterian twilight

The overthrow of Robespierre's Committee of Public Safety on 9 Thermidor Year II (27 July 1794) brought a breather in the advance of this relentlessly unsmiling political culture. There was a generalized retreat from Terror, and the further dismantling of the *sans-culotte* movement in

Paris. The Thermidorian and Directorial regimes (1794–9) saw a reinstitution of civil society and a hedonistic free-for-all among the wealthy classes who could now flaunt rather than hide their wealth and enjoy themselves without feeling guilty. But there was no going back to the Smile Revolution. In 1789 the smile had seemed a unifying and democratic gesture, and had had cultural edge, socially progressive aims, and political intent. In contrast, the mid and late 1790s saw the smile becoming viewed as either overtly counter-revolutionary or else as irrelevant to cultural and political debates. Although smiles in private caused no problem, the public smiling mouth had failed to become the icon of the new political era. In the strong dramas that played out in the 1790s, within revolutionary politics and indeed, under Napoleon from 1799 onwards, a smile of sensibility rarely seemed an apposite public gesture.

The cultural impact of the smile of sensibility since Richardson and Rousseau had been grounded in the conviction that this facial expression expressed the essence of character and was an icon of personal identity. From the mid 1790s onwards, in contrast, there was a recrudescence of the conviction that expressions were usually misleading, and indeed often deliberately so. Sincere views had to be hunted down through and in spite of overt outward appearances, as Couthon, Saint-Just and Robespierre had all urged. The smile seemed the human gesture most likely to mislead and to deceive. It could simply no longer be trusted.

Perhaps the most formidable assault on the capacity of the smile to reveal natural character and virtue at this time was not political in character but purportedly scientific. Physiognomy was in the process of resurrection. By the middle of the eighteenth century, under the influence of Charles Le Brun's works on the expression of the passions, the term 'physionomie' (or 'phisionomie') had been used to describe the transient look of a face. This was in fact a variant of its original meaning within the science of physiognomy, which since Antiquity had tended to judge character by facial conformation rather than fleeting expression. The vestiges of ancient physiognomy had been almost entirely written off in the Enlightenment as archaic and arrant nonsense. 'Will a man be less wise for having small eyes and a large mouth?', had asked the great naturalist Buffon, with studied sarcasm. Quite out of the blue, however, this seemingly defunct and anachronistic form of knowledge enjoyed an unlikely revival in European culture, with major negative consequences for the smile. This was very largely the work of the Swiss pastor, Johann Caspar Lavater.

Lavater's influence was immense. He died in 1801, by which time he had become one of the most famous individuals in Europe, receiving visits in Zurich from kings and princes, Grand Tourists, and travellers from every nation. Already by 1810, what contemporaries referred to as a 'physiognomical frenzy' had produced fifty-six editions of his *Physiognomical Fragments* (which had appeared in 1778) in all the major European languages, in everything from expensive and profusely illustrated infolios down to portable pocketbook editions. In France, for example, 1806 witnessed the appearance in France of both a handy *Lavater portatif* and a lavish ten-volumed collector's set of his works edited by Jacques-Louis Moreau de la Sarthe.

Lavater conjoined spiritual with scientific claims. He held that the human face was 'the extract of creation, the summary and centre of all excellences', and a reflection of the divine. The physiognomist's labours thus amounted to detecting and glorying in the hand of God. By understanding the alphabet of nature, one could both appreciate God's goodness and contribute to social harmony. But the physiognomist also detected order and regularity in nature which could be approached mathematically. Lavater thus downgraded the importance of passing expression in favour of the more stable and unchanging features of the body. Thus although in his publications, Lavater borrowed illustrations from Charles Le Brun's expressive gallery, he had little time for facial expression, which he wrote off as mere 'pathognomy', which he maintained misled rather then enlightened. He completely rejected Le Brun's system of the passions, and what he regarded as his over-emphasis on the face in movement. He denied that the eye-brows—for Le Brun, the prime and most sensitive measurable index of the passions of the soul—constituted a reliable physiognomic aide.

Symptomatically, Lavater thought that teeth had more to say about character than smiles. 'Clean, white and well-arranged teeth . . . [show] a sweet and polished mind and a good and honest heart', he maintained. It was not the case, he maintained, that people with bad teeth could not in some cases be estimable in their way. But, generally speaking, bad teeth revealed 'either sickness or else some melange of moral imperfection'. Ironically, his approach shows the influence of the Smile Revolution, in that he valorized the display of healthy white teeth. But lurking behind the smile of sensibility that might reveal them he glimpsed only 'the mirror of the courtier and the worldly-wise'. Despite its more positive connotations, Lavater held, the smile was fundamentally 'one of the elements of scorn, derision, disdain and irony'. Overall such mobile gestures offered less certainty about character and identity than the bone structure of the face

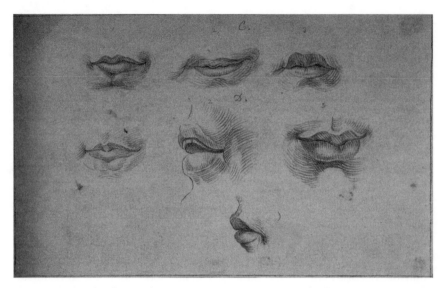

Fig. 5.8 Mouths, from Johann Caspar Lavater, *Essai sur la physiognomonie* (1806)

and head, which he regarded as 'the only genuine form of predestination' (a formulation which highlighted the theological aspects of his thinking). Lavater prized the morphology of teeth, lips, and eyes. In the world according to Lavater, noses, and ears said far more about character than the dynamics of the smile or the glance (Fig. 5.8).

For Lavater, physiognomic analysis required the face to be more like a still life than a *tableau vivant* of the passions. It was not the transient look of the face but the stability of its underlying features that was the guide. Where his Enlightenment predecessors had valorized mobility and energy in face and body, Lavater's preference was for what the great anatomist-surgeon Xavier Bichat called, at roughly the same time, 'the silence of the organs'. Analysis was done more accurately on the dead rather than the living and the sleeping rather than the waking individual. Lavater utilized technologies to get through to and to celebrate this physiognomic essence. He adopted the fashion of taking waxen images and death masks, turning the technique into a means of evaluating the character of the deceased. 'Death stops the agitations to which the body is prey while it is united to the soul', and on these grounds was welcomed by the master physiognomist. He also prized the silhouette as an additional analytical procedure. The technique had become popular in the 1760s as a party game in which facial expression could evidently find no place. Craniometry—that is, the calibration of the skull—also played a key role within the Lavaterian repertoire.

The face was consequently less important than hitherto, less the raw data from which knowledge was formed. According to canons of Lavaterian physiognomy, character could best be read scientifically in the blank-eyed, physiognomically rigid, closed-mouth (or deaths-head) stare (Fig. 5.9). The smile was a simple irrelevance in terms of judging character. It could not be

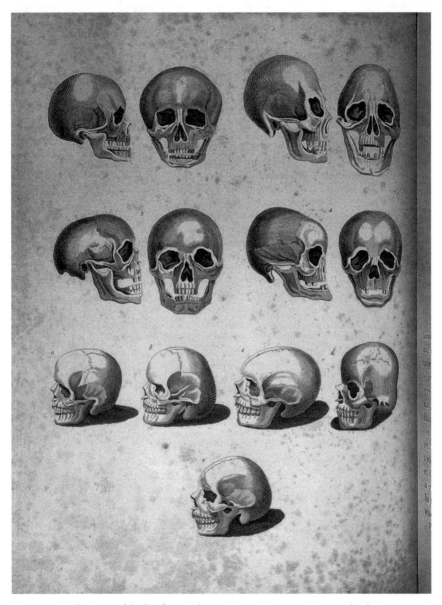

Fig. 5.9 Collection of skulls, from Johann Caspar Lavater, *Essai sur la physiognomonie* (1806)

taken seriously as a guide to character or as an expression of identity. Indeed, in the physiognomic technologies which Lavater prized most, a smile was simply invisible. It had lost the *raison d'être* it had acquired in the Smile Revolution.

The smile of sensibility had been an egalitarian gesture, and a kind of gestural down-payment on a humane and progressive future. But Lavater's techniques of measurement reintroduced moral and human hierarchy into facial conformation. His interest in the emergent discipline of craniometry helped garner scientific credentials. By the late 1780s and 1790s, scholars such as Peter Camper and Johann Blumenberg who were influenced by Lavater (and who in return influenced him) were laying down the principles of a racial science whose sombre legacy would cast a shadow over the nineteenth and twentieth centuries. He, Camper, and Blumenbach together popularized the division of the human species into racial types, for example; Blumenbach's Caucasian, American, Mongol, Ethiopian, Malay, and African categorization was particularly long-lasting. In their sliding scale of human worth, Caucasians came out on top, Africans ('Ethiopians') at the bottom. Social hierarchy also entered the Lavaterian frame: moral weaknesses were systematically more detectable on the heads of the popular classes. There was a sexual prioritization too: Lavater professed himself mystified by women ('I fled from them even when very young and I have never been in love'). On most of his calibrations he still thought that females were necessarily inferior. Despite these biases, the scientific credentials of Lavater's physiognomy were given an extra boost by their adoption among the disciples of alienist Phillippe Pinel within the emergent science of psychiatry.

There was an inherent politics in Lavaterian theory, then, and it was a depressing one. The determinism of the body limited the scope of human freedom. Human beings were only 'free like a bird in a cage', confined and constrained by their God-given bodies. Man 'has a circle of activity and sensibility, beyond which he cannot escape. Just as the human body has contours which mark its limits, so each mind has its sphere in which it moves; but this sphere is invariably determined.' This was a theory that evidently fitted well in the move away from revolutionary values in the late 1790s. In this deterministic Lavaterian universe, the smile had no role to play, no place to occupy. It could tell the world nothing. It could lie. A full circle had been turned. The Smile Revolution was over.

6

Beyond the Smile Revolution

In 1811, the English satirist, Thomas Rowlandson produced a coloured engraving, 'A French Dentist Shewing a Specimen of his Artificial Teeth and False Palates' (Fig. 6.1). Under the heading 'Mineral Teeth', we read:

> Monsieur de Charmant from Paris engages to affix from one tooth to a whole set without pain. Monsieur Dubois can also affix an artificial palate or a glass eye. He also distils.

As so often with Rowlandson, generalized social satire has its specific targets. Behind 'Monsieur de Charmant', a.k.a. 'Monsieur Dubois', whose dentures

Fig. 6.1 Thomas Rowlandson, 'A French Dentist Shewing a Specimen of his Artificial Teeth and False Palates' (1811)

make such a laughably comic impact on the English physiognomy, we easily detect the presence of Nicolas Dubois de Chémant. Our Parisian denture-maker was now an *émigré*, who since the days of the Revolutionary Terror had been based in London. The star of the engraving is the magnificent set of his dentures which, as was his wont, he dazzlingly displays in his own mouth as well as his buxom client's.

Rowlandson's sarcastic image provides us with an indication of the gloomy direction of travel for the smile in the 1790s and early 1800s. Indeed, the lives and career disasters of the once putative harbingers of the Smile Revolution—Dubois de Chémant and Madame Vigée Le Brun—have exemplary value in this respect. Both fled Paris, leaving the Smile Revolution far behind, and becoming *émigrés* from revolutionary France.

False harbingers

The French Revolution had started promisingly for Dubois de Chémant. In September 1791, under the terms of national legislation introduced by the national assembly, he had obtained government permission to manufacture and retail, for a period of fifteen years, his 'odourless dentures made of incorruptible paste'. Yet the business climate was deteriorating fast in Paris in ways that inhibited any progress with his new product. The high cost of Dubois's dentures—which may have been as much as 1,000 livres, three time a workers' annual salary—put them out of reach of all but the social elite. The time was impropitious for the long-term success of an expensive new product aimed at the upper echelons of Parisian society. Those echelons were in a state of turmoil. As the Revolution took a more radical turn, individuals eschewed dressing up and flaunting their fidelity to fashion, and indeed there was a tendency toward a drab dressing down, so as to avoid being ostentatious or conspicuous. Grand Tourists with tooth problems were now in short supply. Paris was becoming denuded of its wealthy elite, as many of the beneficiaries of the culture of the royal court left France altogether so as to remove themselves from the political upheavals under way.

Dubois moved his Parisian premises from the Palais-Royal and set up on the still just about fashionable Quai Conti opposite the Île de la Cité on the Left Bank. But times were fraught and he decided to branch out. He consequently established a sister company in the same year in London, based in premises in Frith Street in Soho. On 11 May 1791, he obtained an English patent for the porcelain paste with which he would create his line of dentures. In a way, by setting up in London, Dubois was merely pursuing his client base. Soho was full of French men and women who had been driven into emigrating by the turn of events in France. One-fifth of the community of emigrants who had fled revolutionary France to establish themselves in London lived here in fact, in a neighbourhood which was already highly Francophone due to infusions of Huguenot exiles since the seventeenth century. We know at least one of Dubois's clients, moreover: Arthur-Richard Dillon, the high-living aristocratic archbishop of Narbonne before the Revolution who had fled to London in the early 1790s. On his death in 1806, Dillon was buried in Saint Pancras cemetery. And in 2006, during excavations associated with the building of the Eurostar terminal at Saint Pancras, his remains were discovered with a set of a moderately pristine Dubois de Chémant's dentures still in his mouth (Fig. 6.2).

Revolutionary Paris provided an even worse cultural climate for false teeth, once the Convention went to war with most of Europe in April 1792. This was Dubois's *coup de grâce*. On 22 August 1792—less than a fortnight after the overthrow of Louis XVI and with Allied troops advancing towards the capital—we find Dubois making an unsolicited gift to the Convention of one of his horses for the war effort. But this was his last Parisian roll of the dice. He cracked shortly afterwards, fleeing the country in late 1792 in the aftermath of the September Massacres—the brutal massacre of political prisoners and many common felons in the Parisian prisons, sparked by

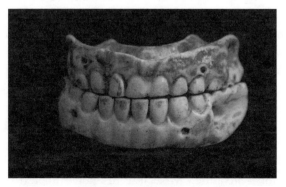

Fig. 6.2 The Dentures of archbishop Dillon

anxiety for the Revolution's military survival. The Terror had even less time for dentures than for white-tooth smiles.

Dubois de Chémant had made himself a political suspect by having a sales outlet in England. His emigration to London put him completely beyond the pale, especially from February 1793, when France and England went to war. The stain of Anglophilia meant that Dubois was *persona non grata* in France for at least as long as the Terror lasted and/or until war ended. In 1797 he decided to obtain English nationality (becoming, along with the fathers of Isambard Brunel and Augustus Pugin, one of a tiny minority of the French *émigré* community to take this step). This faithful pupil of Sèvres craftsmen was, later in the decade, turning to the equally famous Wedgwood business to provide him with the finest-quality pastes. The man who promised to bring smiles to the mouths of millions of toothless Frenchmen and women was pursuing the business of smiles in England rather than France— but with mixed effects. In his homeland, the smile that was the main selling point of his product had become politically suspect.

The proud boast that dentures would soon be as widespread as wigs was, moreover, already horribly dated. Wigs were under attack even in the 1780s for setting artificiality above a natural look. They were well on the way to oblivion by 1815, when, with the Napoleonic Wars over, most French *émigrés* returned to their homeland, leaving archbishop Dillon and his dentures back in London. Dentures, for all their art, never acquired the gilded future predicted for them, and they would retain only a niche presence in French society throughout the nineteenth century. In 1816, Dubois claimed to have sold over 12,000 full dentures in the previous decade (in 1797, the year in which he was naturalized, the number had stood at 3,000). By the 1840s, half a million dentures were being exported from Paris by the heirs of Dubois and his rivals, so the industry must have continued to exist and prosper within the city. Indeed, mineral teeth were widely known as 'dents de Paris'.

By that time Dubois de Chémant's originality in inventing porcelain false teeth was generally acknowledged. From 1804, his publicity was even carrying an endorsement by Edward Jenner, the discoverer of smallpox vaccination. Even though the Paris-based Italian dentist da Fonzi devised individual porcelain teeth in 1809, which in theory gave greater flexibility and practicality than Dubois's denture sets, they were rarely cited in the subsequent professional literature. 'Mineral teeth', noted English surgeon-dentist Joseph Murphy in 1811 categorically, 'were invented by M. De Chemant who in addition to being the inventor is as yet unrivalled in the art of constructing and adapting them.'

Yet criticisms soon built up. Writing in 1802, Joseph Fox thought Dubois de Chémant's dentures rather unnatural, and he mocked their manufacturer's pseudo-science. He stated, 'Considerable latitude must be given when we place the partial statements of an author possessing much vivacity and disposed to regard his own invention as meriting a decided preference.' Later in the century, John Gray, the author of a book entitled *Preservation of the Teeth*, nodded agreement:

> The things called mineral, or Jews' teeth, are now plentifully manufactured of porcelain; but they always look what they are and can never be mistaken for teeth . . . and by acting as a whetstone on any of the natural teeth soon wear them away.

We should probably not underestimate the importance of the design faults in Dubois de Chémant's porcelain teeth which his rivals highlighted—and which his clients must to some degree have suffered: the problems of fit, with all the pain and discomfort which that caused; the abrasive effect on opposing teeth; the click-clacking in speech as the upper set moved against the lower; and the decidedly off-putting noise of grinding porcelain while chewing. The weight of the full-set was also a factor which caused discomfort and likely embarrassment in some mouths. The contraption was far from well-suited to the revolutionary role claimed for it.

As Rowlandson's 1811 cartoon mercilessly emphasized, moreover, the appearance of Dubois's false teeth could be startlingly grotesque. Indeed, the joke links back to the Rabelaisian humour of the early modern period, and highlights the fact that the Old Regime of Teeth had really never gone away. The cult of sensibility and the rise of dental surgery had been a Paris-based luxury that left unaffected the vast majority of the French population (as well as just about all of the rest of Europe). What was different, from the beginning of the nineteenth century onwards, was that the benefit of dentistry that Parisian elites had enjoyed in the last decades of the *Ancien Régime* was progressively withdrawn from even those social groups.

There was in addition a striking Francophobia about Rowlandson's cartoon which linked back to English pre-revolutionary grumpiness about the French propensity to smile. Dubois de Chémant had had his career concluded in Paris in the 1790s because of his business links to London. But in England, he would always be the butt of English Francophobic humour.

Fig. 6.3 Thomas Rowlandson, 'Six Stages of Mending a Face' (1792)

Indeed, Rowlandson appears to have targeted Dubois de Chémant as early as 1792. In his cartoon, 'Six Stages of Mending a Face' (Fig. 6.3), he had satirized the claims of false eyelashes, wig, cosmetics and a full denture set in transforming an ululating old harridan (top right), into the smiliest young miss, who seductively dares to reveal her egregiously glossy white teeth.

Rowlandson dedicated the cartoon to Sarah Lady Archer, one of London's fast set, notorious for her gambling habits, but the final metamorphosis bears a more than passing resemblance in fact to Madame Vigée Le Brun, the second harbinger of the Smile Revolution on the eve of 1789. Her provocative open-mouthed smile (Fig. 0.1) which also featured overflowing hair and tilted head as well as white teeth, may well have been witnessed by Rowlandson who was in Paris in 1787. That smile had had the effect of opening the door to the depiction of the smile in academic portraiture, as we have seen. Yet in the event Madame Vigée Le Brun's smile failed to sweep all before it, a point that was affected by her personal fortunes after 1789.

As we have suggested, the new smile had been viewed in the late 1780s as a gesture which explicitly and daringly challenged the manners of the royal court and the cultural establishment. Though well-connected at court, where she was Queen Marie-Antoinette's favourite portraitist, Vigée Le Brun was widely viewed as a bourgeois parvenue, and she retained an air of bohemian eccentricity in the capital's public sphere. Yet in the autumn of 1789, almost as soon as the Revolution had got under way, she left France in disgust, an early emigrant from a political culture she found distasteful. From the time of the declaration of war in 1792, she and fellow *émigrés* would be marked out as traitors to the nation. Indeed, touring Europe throughout the 1790s and the early years of the next century bad-mouthing the revolutionary activities of her compatriots, Vigée Le Brun could be written off as an out-and-out *émigrée* reactionary. Her 1787 smile, we have suggested, was a gesture aimed against the stiffness of the culture of the royal court. But it would henceforth be reimagined as the dying, nostalgic cadence of an aristocratic *douceur de vivre* swept brutally aside by revolutionary high seriousness—and by the Terror. The broader context was a shift from gaiety to hard-nosed sarcasm. 'In previous times', recorded Madame de Genlis, the duc d'Orléans's former mistress, 'light and lively gaiety was full of natural and naïve charm; now it is in general sly, grim-acing, cruel or stupid.'

We see a similar rewriting of the history of the smile of sensibility in the changed opinions of Jacques-Louis David, who claimed that prior to 1789 his heart had not been in the portrayal of individuals with a certain look, or 'physionomie'. 'I seasoned [them] with a modern sauce, as people then used to say', he noted. 'I darkened the eyebrows just a little, I lightened the cheekbones, I opened the mouth slightly [*sic*], and finally I gave them what the moderns call "expression", and what I now call "grimace".' In this caustic and selective remembering (by a man with a twisted lip, of course), the smile of sensibility could be written off as a nauseatingly aristocratic grimace. The notion that the smile of sensibility had been a marker of individual identity and even an emblem of an enlightened and democratic sociability seemed very far away indeed.

Gothic grimaces

Madame Vigée Le Brun's smile had showcased the open mouth as seductive and attractive. But while revolutionary politics downgraded the political and cultural significance of the smile, Lavaterian physiognomy ruled out the very idea of a smile as a guide to character or as a key component of individual identity. For Lavater, the open mouth was if anything a *memento mori*. Furthermore, in the artistic culture which emerged in the 1790s, smiles were dismissed out of hand as mere grimaces, while the open mouth was also starting to be seen in an even more unsettling light, as the Gothic style came to give it a sinister, long-lasting twist.

The Gothic style had emerged first in mid eighteenth-century England. Horace Walpole's antiquarian reconstruction in his home in Strawberry Hill outside London from mid century onwards was an early manifestation. But the main vector of the style for the rest of the century was prose fiction. Walpole's *The Castle of Otranto: A Gothic Story* (1764) established the main features of the genre: ramped-up prose, suspense and horror, crumbly castles and other exotic locations, subterranean passages, suffocating and perverse sexuality, maidens in distress, and so on. William Beckford's *Vathek*, which in fact he wrote in French in 1782, and which was published either side of the Channel in 1786–7, was a further addition to the genre, with added orientalist flavouring. Matthew ('Monk') Lewis's *The Monk* (1796) and Anne Racliffe's *The Mysteries of Udolpho* (1797) were others in the genre to make an impact.

The Gothic had started to attract attention in France even before the Revolution, highlighting a new and different sensibility as regards the smile. French literary works started to indicate smiles that were 'chilling', 'ogre-like', 'frightful' and 'had nothing good about' them. These particular examples were in fact drawn from Beckford's *Vathek*, but a hot-house sensibility was evident in some native French works too. Joseph de Loaisel de Tréogate's popular tear-jerker, *Dolbreuse* (1783), for example, replayed Richardson and Rousseau's death-bed scenes with Gothic top notes. As the central character set about cremating his beloved wife at the end of the novel, 'at that very moment the face of my dead wife seemed to be lit up by a celestial light. I saw her complexion become animated, [and] her mouth smile at me . . .'—indeed a Gothic gesture.

A great many French men and women had reacted with amused distaste to the English Gothic texts before the Revolution, but the context for their reception changed radically in the late 1790s. The notorious marquis de Sade played with the genre in the 1790s, notably in his pornographic novels, particularly *Justine, ou les malheurs de la vertu* (1791) and *La Nouvelle Justine* (1799), which were also at the same time a black, parodic pastiche of the novels of sensibility of Richardson and Rousseau. Sade offered a cogent explanation for the sudden change of fortunes of the Gothic genre and the *roman noir* in France, and also for the flight from realism in novels published in the late 1790s. In his view, reality had simply out-done fiction, particularly in Paris: 'There was hardly a soul alive who did not experience more adversity in four or five years than the most famous novelist in all literature could have depicted in a century.' The Gothic was thus 'the necessary fruit of the revolutionary tremors that shook the whole of Europe'. In the 'age of iron' consequent on the Terror, conventional fiction would have been insipid, Sade maintained. In order to attract interest and attention, 'it was necessary to appeal to hell for help in composing titles of interest and for finding chimeras in the landscape'. Writing in the early nineteenth century, Charles Nodier, champion of Romanticism and practitioner of the Gothic tale, proposed a similar argument: 'People who had made history', he wrote, 'would not take anything less than strong emotions and the triumph of Good over Evil.' For individuals who had lived through the Terror and who 'could still smell gunpowder and blood, emotions were required akin to those that the return to order had weaned them off'.

Nodier's latter remark was made in the introduction he wrote in the early 1840s to a volume of the collected dramas of René-Charles Guilbert de Pixérécourt, whose *Victor, ou l'enfant du forêt* (1798) is usually credited as the first modern melodrama in France. Pixérécourt would write around one hundred such plays over the first half of the nineteenth century, providing a format that was the basis of this highly popular genre. In some ways, the melodrama was (with the addition of music) a continuator of the tradition of *comédie larmoyante* and bourgeois drama. But it was very much more emotionally charged than either of these two *Ancien Régime* genres. The kind of smile that had lingered on the lips in regard to these was far too insipid for the melodrama, which was characterized by strong emotions, extreme pathos, psychological extremes, morbid sexuality, and, of course, Virtue triumphing over Vice. Adding a spice of terror was the adoption of the characteristic locations of the Gothic novel (dungeons, castles, ruins, convents, dark forests, wild landscapes, etc.).

Melodrama thus bolstered the impact that the Gothic *roman noir* was making on French audiences from the late 1790s onwards. The two genres also seeped into and shaped the ways in which the Revolution and in particular the Terror were remembered by post-1794 generations. Sensationalist and anti-Jacobin histories pulled in much the same direction. Notable in this respect were post-Terror captivity narratives such as

Honoré-Jean Riouffe's highly popular *Mémoires d'un détenu* ('A Prisoner's Memoirs' (1794)), which offered a purportedly truthful account of prison life under the Terror. Furthermore, the Gothic smile from beyond the grave of the heroine in Loaisel de Tréogate's popular *Dolbreuse* (1783) echoed creepily in the animated debates in the late 1790s over whether the heads of those guillotined under the Terror expressed facial emotions even after being severed from the body. The story was told that when the executioner, holding up to the crowd the severed head of Charlotte Corday, Marat's assassin, slapped its face, the face blushed at the indignity. This sparked a learned and highly academic (if ghoulish) discussion, which continued through the latter part of the decade, over when the actual moment of death had occurred. One author claimed to have been present at an attempt to sew a victim's head back on, an experiment which he alleged had produced some facial twitchings—which eerily prefigured Mary Shelley's famously Gothic Frankenstein.

It would not prove difficult to find mouths (if not quite smiles) in the Revolution that were, to use the descriptors in *Vathek*, chilling, ogre-like, frightful and that had nothing good about them. Some of the cruellest forms of popular black humour in the Revolution focused on the mutilation of the mouths and faces of the Revolution's victims. An early example of popular violence meted out in the aftermath of the storming of the Bastille, for example, was the parading on the end of a pike of the head of the distinguished administrator Foulon, his mouth stuffed with straw as punishment for his alleged remark that if the poor were hungry they should eat straw—an image captured by the artist Anne-Louis Girodet (Fig. 6.4).

Also symptomatic of the invasion of the Gothic into the texture of the revolutionary experience and its subsequent recollection are the fates of some of Madame Vigée Le Brun's sitters around the time in the 1780s when she had painted and then presented her Salon self-portrait. Of these, the duchesse de Polignac died tragically young, probably of consumption, in Austria in 1793. Before her death, Polignac heard the news of the execution of her patron and bosom friend, Marie-Antoinette, Vigée Le Brun's favoured sitter. The queen was in fact horribly humiliated in the Revolutionary Tribunal, where to charges of treason against her, were added accusations of incestuous relations with her son—who was another of Vigée Le Brun's sitters. Her son would continue to be incarcerated in the Temple Prison in Paris, where he was subject to appalling treatment by his gaolers and would die in 1795, probably of tubercular illness. Madame du

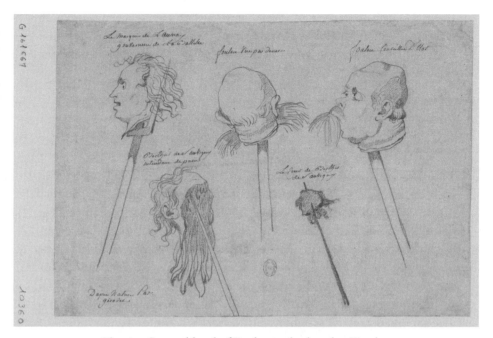

Fig. 6.4 Severed head of Foulon and others by Girodet

Barry, another Vigée Le Brun 1787 sitter, also died at the guillotine, ranting hysterically at the crowd.

The fate of the princesse de Lamballe, intimate friend of Queen Marie-Antoinette, whom Madame Vigée Le Brun had portrayed on several occasions in the 1780s, was ghastlier still. In the September Massacres of 1792, she was located by a vengeful crowd in the La Force prison, decapitated, and her head paraded around the streets of the city and taken to the Temple prison and waved threateningly on the end of a pike outside the windows of the imprisoned queen. The chronicler Louis-Sébastien Mercier records that the crowd cut off her pudenda and placed them around her lips on the severed head in a kind of perverse moustache. This final grisly, Gothic detail is unverifiable. But it is certainly the case that the tale circulated widely and with obsessive morbidity not only in Paris, but throughout Europe in the late 1790s and indeed across the nineteenth century.

Much the same was true of the death of Robespierre, who was taken to the guillotine on 28 July 1794 to the boos and hisses of Parisian crowds which the previous day had been in his thrall. In the mêlée surrounding his arrest, he had attempted to shoot himself, but had succeeded only in blowing a hole in the lower part of his jaw. His trial took place with him keeping his face together with a capacious bandage. As he stepped up to the executioner's blade, however,

> One of the guillotine crew brutally snatched away the bandage that held his poor broken jaw together. He let out a howl...He could for an instant be seen pale, hideous, his mouth wide open and his teeth falling to the ground...there was a heavy thud...

This macabre episode would be much recounted and gleefully elaborated upon in histories of the Revolution throughout the nineteenth century (more modern historians tend to be more circumspect with the detail, or more squeamish, and certainly less Gothic). The animal shriek had established Robespierre's subhuman bestiality at a stroke. For many of those throughout the nineteenth century who contemplated the French Revolution, this was a fitting end for a tyrannical and bestial monster, pointing a moral, adorning a tale. What lingered in the mind was not Robespierre's well-groomed smile of sensibility of his sister Charlotte's recollection, but rather the gaping, Gothic black hole where once a smile might have been. By reducing Robespierre to a kind of degree zero of humanity, suffused by the sheer animality proclaimed by that final, bestial, open-mouth howl, the nineteenth century would live with a monstrous, ideologically hyper-charged, and nightmare vision of what revolutions were all about.

A long distance had been travelled, in a very short time, from the 1787 smile of Madame Vigée Le Brun to Gothic accounts, memories, and recollections of the violent disfigurement of the mouth in the Terror. The distance travelled symbolized the end of the Parisian Smile Revolution.

Disappearing dentistry...

Parisian dentists experienced extremely severe difficulties during the 1790s and beyond. Although the Revolutionary assemblies set out to improve the organization of all aspects of medical education and training, white-tooth smiles were not top of the legislators' agenda. Indeed, for reasons which will be apparent, they were rather close to the bottom. By the turn of the nineteenth century, French scientific dentistry, once the wonder of Europe, was living off its dwindling capital. The result was that post-Revolutionary

France was in real danger of returning to the Old Regime of Teeth, where tooth loss and hideous tooth decay were accepted fatalistically. With the erstwhile technicians of the white-toothed smile in complete disarray, dentistry threatened to become one of surgery's lost arts.

The revolutionary assemblies had taken no time at all in showing determination to destroy the much-criticized medical hierarchy of the *Ancien Régime*. The universities that produced physicians were closed down and then radically reconstructed, notably by bringing into the teaching of medicine the kinds of practical skills for which Parisian surgeons had become famous. From 4 December 1794, three new 'schools of health' (*écoles de santé*) were created at Paris, Montpellier, and Strasbourg, merging the mission of the old surgical colleges with that of medical faculties. The 'birth of the clinic'—the emergence of modern scientific medicine—was in gestation. But the brilliant future for French medicine and surgery that was opening up failed to find a niche for dentistry.

Dentistry as a legally endorsed professional vocation had gone down in flames alongside other pre-revolutionary medical trades. Two pieces of legislation—the Loi d'Allarde of 2 March and Loi Le Chapelier of 17 June 1791—abolished all existing corporate bodies, from guilds through to surgical colleges and communities and their dependent subgroups of 'experts'. The Loi d'Allarde established the principle of an individual's freedom 'to engage in trade and to embrace any calling that he wishes'. Any individual could now apply for a *patente*—that is, the right to practise a trade, even a medically related one such as dentistry.

A report on medical organization at the start of the Revolution noted, with detectable glee, that 'with the abolition of the communities of surgeons, it is clear that oculists, lithotomists and dentists will have no future existence'. The medical establishment was evidently too grand to accommodate such lowly figures. An emphasis on the unitary nature of scientific medicine downgraded the very notion of specialization for nearly a century. Revealingly, dentistry was not recognized as a subject on the syllabus of the new *écoles de santé*. In 1800, the Parisian dentist Louis Laforgue made a personal appeal to Minister of the Interior Lucien Bonaparte to reorganize the teaching and practice of dentistry in France. Dental care was becoming, he pleaded, 'the apanage of the empiric, of the charlatan, and of any vendor of dental remedies who can garner the confidence of the sick'. Quacks were killing people as efficiently as the Napoleonic Wars, he stated (not necessarily with the greatest tact in a letter to Napoleon's brother).

When enduring reform of medical practice eventually came, in 1802, the state created two basic forms of practitioner. At the apex were doctors trained at the *écoles de santé*, which now used hands-on surgical-type teaching; while at the bottom were an ill-assorted generic group of 'health officers' (*officiers de santé*). The only subgroup given legal existence outside this two-level framework were midwives. This shuffling of the institutional pack meant that elite *Ancien Régime* surgeons were lifted into the upper group of physicians, whereas the lowlier form of surgeons, barbers, and the like were conflated with the *officiers de santé*. In the view of the veteran medical legislator, Michel-Augustin Thouret, the contrast was between 'transcendent and superior' practitioners and 'the everyday and commonplace'. Those individuals with prior dental training, along with post-1699 'experts' such as lithotomists and oculists, were henceforth lost in the undifferentiated mass formed by these largely undistinguishable and indeed undistinguished lowly practitioners. And because of the *patente*, as Laforgue had complained, trained dentists now competed in an open market on grounds of legal equality with individuals who merely paid for the licence.

In 1807, Edme-Michel Miel, who became a distinguished dental practitioner down to his death on the barricades in the 1830 Revolution, specifically petitioned the Minister of the Interior to set up a doctorate so that he could practise in the manner of the old *chirurgiens-dentistes* of the *Ancien Régime*. The ministry informed him there was no longer any intermediary level of this sort. He could practise dentistry but was not allowed any properly surgical practice. The profession definitively ruled out the kinds of expertise that had been practised before 1789. The progress of medical science was such that 'in order to treat part [of the human body] one must necessarily possess fundamental knowledge of all'. Determined efforts in the 1820s and then the late 1840s to secure national legislation to defend dentistry from the machinations of anyone who held the *patente* were unavailing.

The scientific capital that eighteenth-century dentists had siphoned off from their high-flying surgical colleagues now dwindled and disappeared. The subject lost its scientific edge. The commercial dimension of writings on dentistry, already increasingly evident in the last years of the *Ancien Régime*, became more pronounced. The lack of legal and institutional protection meant that the specialism would simply not attract good candidates in the future. French mouths were thus henceforward almost as unprotected and as uncared-for as in the pre-Fauchardian days of *le Grand Thomas* and his ilk.

A vestige of France's one-time hegemony in mouth care did remain and even strengthen in the nineteenth century, and that was the production of the paraphernalia of daily mouth care, particularly toothbrushes, powders, and mouthwashes. These were the kind of semi-luxury *articles de Paris* that tended to sell well on national and international markets. The medical faculties were severe in regard to authorizations, but the new government patent office (the *Institut national de la propriété industrielle*) and the Ministry of the Interior less so. From the turn of the century, inventors in their droves started patenting products relating to tooth maintenance and mouth care as well as general health. Alongside eaux de cologne, cosmetic creams and powders, hair-oils, wig-glues, anti-wrinkle creams, and the like were rouges, lipsticks, tooth-whiteners, mouthwashes, tooth-powders and pastes, and so on. There were new denture recipes too (although Jacques-Pierre's Brousson's adoption of crushed sea-shells does not seem to have got off the ground), and new denture glues too. Toothbrush designs also received a boost: the first toothbrush patent was delivered on 14 December 1818 to one Jacques-Pierre Naudin, an inhabitant of Paris. (Another would follow in 1819.) Soon the area around Beauvais to the north of Paris would become one of the most productive toothbrush manufacturers in Europe, with a large export market.

The commercial buoyancy of Parisian tooth-care commodities was a poor substitute, however, for the loss of the international hegemony in dentistry that Paris had enjoyed in the previous century. Napoleon I had had his teeth looked after by an offshoot of eighteenth-century dentistry, namely, Dubois-Foucou, Louis XVI's dentist, who had been a rival to and critic of denture-maker Dubois de Chémant. But by mid century, Napoleon III would turn to North American dental expertise for his own and his family's mouth care in the shape of the Philadelphia-trained Thomas Evans. This highlighted how far the prestige and competence of French dentistry had fallen. Indeed, whereas the French had supplied dentists to the crowned heads and ruling elites of Europe before 1789, from the 1840s it would be Americans who took their place. And it was the United States of America that emerged, by the middle of the nineteenth century, as the new product champion of dental science. Leading-edge dentistry had crossed the Atlantic, and it would be the United States which, even as early as the 1830s and 1840s, was displaying all the avatars of professional dentistry (dental schools, professional organizations, learned journals, etc.). From then onwards, the United States would enjoy global pre-eminence in the field of dentistry. In France, in glaring contrast, it would not be until the very end of the nineteenth century—in 1892 in fact—that dentistry began to receive proper professional organization. Fauchard was forgotten. After 1786, *Le Chirurgien-dentiste* would have to wait until 1961 to have a further edition! For the next century and more, French dentistry would be playing catch-up with international competitors.

. . . Vanishing smiles

The effect of the French Revolution was thus to eradicate the professional infrastructure for effective mouth care that had been established over the course of the eighteenth century. In addition, the Revolution—and in particular the Terror—completely destroyed the positive cultural aura that hovered around the mouth.

Before the Revolution, the open-mouth, white-tooth smile—the smile of sensibility—had symbolized a new, optimistic, and progressive view of social and public intercourse and exchange. It was rooted in the cult of sensibility that emerged in the middle decades of the eighteenth century. What had started on the stage (in *comédies larmoyantes* and bourgeois dramas) and on the page (in novels by Richardson, Rousseau, and their followers) was transferred into the lives of men and women of the Parisian cultural and social elite, who responded eagerly to the promise of better teeth supplied by the ambitious and entrepreneurial group of Parisian dentists. A white-toothed smile offered a gauge of identity and moral worth. The new smile of sensibility may have started as a private accomplishment, but as we saw it also became, through the processes of smile contagion, a lubricant of Parisian sociability in the bourgeois public sphere and a vaunted emblem of Parisian gaiety. The exhibition of Madame Vigée Le Brun's famous 1787 portrait seemed to mark its definitive arrival within the canons of Western art but also as a legitimate public gesture. That gesture had a strong political aura too, for it seemed directly to oppose the unchanging tight-lipped facial regime that the Bourbon monarch still embodied.

Sadly, the optimistic Enlightenment view of human nature and the idea of human perfectibility came under pressure even from 1789 and looked hopelessly shop-worn in the light of the Terror. The mutilating violence of the turbulent years from 1792 to 1794 bade to wipe the smile of sensibility from French lips (even though, as we have seen, such a smile had a heroic half-life as a weapon of moral and political resistance). Smiles were now distrusted not only as weapons of dissimulation but also for the threat they carried of morphing into the laughter of sarcastic counter-revolutionaries or raucous radical sans-culottes, each of which threatened physical violence. The leitmotiv of Parisian gaiety had suffered an eclipse. For much of the nineteenth century, Parisians were viewed not as quintessentially gay and cheerful but as a threatening, dangerous, blood-thirsty, and cannabilistic mob of *classes dangereuses*, on which English caricaturist James Gillray provided a savagely ironic commentary (Fig. 0.5).

The reputation of the Parisian labouring classes as *classes dangereuses* would be strengthened by spasmodic bouts of revolutionary violence across the century in 1830, 1848, 1851, and 1870–1. The smile of sensibility was erased from public life and even from collective memory. It was replaced as an emblem of Parisian life with something very different and very unpleasant. Furthermore, it was not only those who opposed or distanced themselves from the Revolution who rejected the smile of sensibility. Even those who carried forward something of the revolutionary message into the nineteenth century did so too. Napoleon, who consolidated many revolutionary gains (while destroying many others), adopted a stiff and unbending public persona. He was certainly known to unbend: when Chateaubriand first met him around 1800, he thought his smile 'affecting and beautiful'. And we know that Napoleon took care to ensure it stayed that way. His daily toilette was impeccable, and included cleaning his teeth with a toothbrush. Indeed, the Wellcome Collection in London possesses one of his toothbrushes, with his initials inscribed upon it (Fig. 6.5).

It is not clear how much good toothbrushing did for Napoleon. Sir Henry Bunbury, the army officer who was tasked to inform Napoleon in 1815 of his deportation to Saint-Helena, recorded that 'his teeth are bad and dirty and he shows them very little'. On Saint-Helena they would soon be falling out. More important than these minutiae of Napoleon's private life is the fact that the smile, while retaining its traditional role as a private gesture, lost its status as a collective and public act during his reign. The Napoleonic regime's self-presentation continued in the neo-classical idiom, but with a Roman-imperial rather than Roman-republican face. Jacques-Louis David, who had shifted seemingly quite unproblematically from a fixation on Robespierre to one on Napoleon, set the tone of his regime's propaganda. Napoleonic gestures were epic and theatrical. Smiling was the last thing one would imagine Napoleon doing in public. And the Vigée

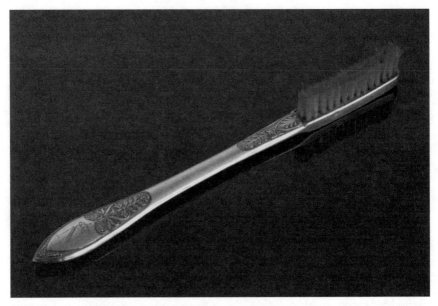

Fig. 6.5 Napoleon's toothbrush

Le Brun smile tended henceforward to be said to reveal an aristocratic *douceur de vivre* characteristic of the *Ancien Régime*—even if at the time it had been anything but.

Napoleon's successors did nothing to change the situation. When in 1815 the Bourbon dynasty returned in the form of Louis XVIII (Louis XVI's brother and heir), it was famously said 'to have learnt nothing and forgotten nothing'. This predisposition extended to the reimposition of many of the stiff court protocols established by Louis XIV. Ceremonial rituals still had little time for a smile. It would not be until much later, even well into the twentieth century, that the white-tooth smile would be adopted by French political figures.

Resistance to the public smile was grounded in notions of masculinity that, as we have seen, had started to develop in the late eighteenth century. The serious demeanour of men was further marked out in vestimentary ways from the early nineteenth century onwards by what has been called 'the great masculine renunciation'—the replacement of decorative and colourful dress by dark business suits. In a dark suit, smiles seemed frivolous and unmasculine. As a corollary, the Rousseau-influenced ideology of 'separate spheres' bade to push women out of public life and to confine them within a world of family, domesticity, and private virtues.

One upshot of the tectonic shifts in the gender regime from this period onwards was that the smile was not only increasingly erased from public life, but it was also increasingly gendered female. The beautiful smile had always been associated with women in Western culture of course but, as we have seen, the Enlightenment smile of sensibility had been a cross-gender gesture grounded in the informal institutions of Enlightenment sociability. When irate English tourists got hot under the collar about the French habit of endlessly smiling at them their irritation was even more targeted at men than women. In the Parisian public sphere before the Revolution, smiling was a norm for the French, and not simply for French women. Yet by 1789, there were clear early indications of a shift in gender roles and behaviours. Medical opinion, for example, was already tending to view women as more sensitive (and indeed hysterical) than men. The development of 'separate spheres' ideology and the emergence of new tougher versions of masculinity seemed to confirm the notion that men who smiled were effeminate. Thus the decades around the turn of the century witnessed a kind of feminization of smiling, under the pressure of slow but wide-ranging changes in gender differentiation.

These influences played out gloomily in painting and portraiture too. Madame Vigée Le Brun really had broken once and for all the decorous artistic conventions that forbade the open-mouth smile to all but the poor, the insane, and the emotionally hyper-aroused. As we have seen, other artists in her wake took advantage of this new-found freedom. But looking over the nineteenth century as a whole it is striking how rarely that freedom was taken up. Indeed the old conventions about the restriction of smiling that the Vigée Le Brun smile had bade to replace seem to have resurfaced. It was only in the last decades of the nineteenth century that painters would on any grand scale start to depict white-tooth smiles in their portraiture. The sombre, unsmiling, and often drab mood of nineteenth-century public life was still only a poor backdrop for radiant smiles.

There had been a blissful moment in 1789, when the French Revolution had seemed to be on the point of adopting as the symbol of its transforma-tive impact the new smile that had been forged in Paris in the late eighteenth century. That smile seemed an emblem of a fairer and happier society that was in the making. It was not to be. But in setting the Paris Smile Revolution into perspective, it is worth stressing how unusual that moment and that conjunction of factors really were. First of all, while other Western societies enjoyed a cult of sensibility in the eighteenth century, very few had an indigenously generated political revolution—and none experienced the brilliant emergence of dentistry in France, and indeed Paris in particular. If there was going to be a 'Smile Revolution' anywhere it was going to be in Paris. Secondly, despite the interlinkages between the miscellaneous developments that we have explored in this book, the range of phenomena which combined to produce the Smile Revolution was very extensive. Involved in the process were surgical and scientific advances; significant social, economic, and political developments; and also changing notions of emotion, expressive behaviour, selfhood, and gender. Each inevitably followed different trajectories and particular rhythms of development. It was thus perhaps less surprising that the Smile Revolution didn't last—was indeed as transient and evanescent as the smile itself—than that it happened at all.

The smile had been erased from public life long even before 1800. Yet though gone it would hardly be forgotten. From the Revolutionary decade onwards, the smile was increasingly strongly gendered. In the long term, men in dark suits would keep teeth and smiles out of their public repertoire, making the benign, white-tooth smile a quintessentially female attribute, best indulged in the domestic calm of the home. The smile has fought its way back into public life and into the behaviour of men as well as women, particularly from the mid twentieth century. Yet it lacks that sense of clear-eyed democratic promise that the smile enjoyed in public life on the cusp on the revolutionary changes brought about from 1789. The smile has 'caught up', so to speak, with democracy, then. But it has done so in ways that only underline how specific the Smile Revolution in eighteenth-century Paris really was.

Postscript

Towards the Twentieth-Century
Smile Revolution

The Smile Revolution of late eighteenth-century France had proved a false dawn—or a damp squib. It would not be until the twentieth century that the smile made what has proved to be a spectacular comeback. This was initially a slow process, but the twentieth-century Smile Revolution was complete by the middle decades of the century. As with its predecessor in the eighteenth century, it was a complex phenomenon which involved social and cultural as well as scientific and technological changes. France was not in the vanguard of change as it had been earlier. Now, particularly in the later stages, the USA led the way.

The virtual prohibition on the use of the white-tooth smile in western portraiture had been ended by Madame Vigée Le Brun in 1787. The smile did thereafter feature in portraits, as we have suggested, but it was still very much a minority taste. And it remained very heavily gendered. Women might occasionally be shown with a white-tooth smile, but this was still invariably seen as an unbecoming gesture for males. In France, no artistic movement embraced white teeth as wholeheartedly as, for example, the Pre-Raphaelites in England. Artistic modernism which generally shunned naturalism and figurative portrayal did not reserve much of a niche for the smile. Oddly, the artistic movements which did highlight the open mouth in their art, following in the wake of Edvard Munch's *The Scream* (1893), were the expressionists, Dadaists, and Surrealists. For them, the open mouth and the display of teeth were more likely to be linked to the grimace, the Democritan smile of mockery, or the gaping Gothic hole.

Fig 7.1   Franz-Xaver Winterhalter, *Queen Victoria* (1843)

England's Queen Victoria was famously 'not amused', and her official portraits are certainly very glum. In fact, in 1843, she commissioned the German court artist Franz-Xaver Winterhalter to paint an intimate portrait of her to present as a special gift to her new husband, Prince Albert (Fig. 7.1). She chose to be represented in reclining fashion, smiling charmingly, and displaying her teeth. This probably makes her the first European monarch to wear the Vigée Le Brun smile in a portrait. Yet the circumstances of the commission were significant. Victoria made the painting a personal gift to Albert, and hung it in their private suite. It was never seen publicly in her lifetime. Winterhalter also painted a number of famously glamorous portraits of Napoleon's III's empress Eugénie which were publicly displayed. We know that the princess enjoyed the services of the emperor's personal dentist, Thomas Evans. But it was no longer a question of having healthy and beautiful teeth, but rather of the propriety of showing them in a public setting. And Empress Eugénie kept her mouth as firmly shut in public as did Queen Victoria, and as did her successors until well into the following century.

Only right at the very end of the nineteenth century, were teeth and smiles timidly finding their way more evidently into painted portraits.

Interestingly, it seems to have been female artists, such as Berthe Morisot and Mary Cassatt, who gave a lead in this. The pace of change was initially slower in regard to photographic portraiture. Strangely perhaps, given the new medium's more naturalistic, even documentary potential, white teeth failed to establish themselves in photography in the nineteenth century. There were technical reasons for this. For all of the nineteenth century, and especially during the early days, posing times were long (thirty minutes at first). In the 1860s and 1870s, sitters frequently wore neck-braces, arm-bands, and waist-restrainers to ensure stillness. Even when the exposure time was reduced to a minute or less, this still removed the possibility of anything like instantaneousness or spontaneity in capturing identities. The possibility of a wide smile morphing into a smirk or a rictus was still present. Thoughtful-ness, character, and demureness were about the best that nineteenth-century photography could manage in the quest for emotional variation.

Yet more important than these technical issues in explaining reticence in photographing smiles was the cultural capital that painting still enjoyed as a mode of representation. In deference, photographers tended to reproduce rather than to challenge or replace the most traditional conventions in painting they could find. In terms of formality, respectability, and *gravitas*, photographers thus outdid painters, who were starting to branch out. Photographic studios were equipped like an artist's studio, and portraits highlighted statuary, Greek columns, drapes, luxuriant furniture, tassels, exotic clothes, very much on the model of painting. In this context, the smile was perhaps most evident in erotic and pornographic photography, but in these genres facial expression tended to be incidental. Then again, Darwin's image of a 'smiling ape' in his *Expression of the Emotions* in 1872 which we highlighted earlier had to be retouched—for there was no other trustworthy method available for a human (let alone an ape) to supply a genuine-looking and sincere smile. Somehow that did not seem a problem in an age which appeared to have given up on the smile.

What really gave the smile a boost around the turn of the twentieth century was improved camera technology. A range of innovations from the 1880s to around 1900 changed the staid and static traditions of photo-graphy. Gelatin dry plates produced a faster result than had hitherto been imaginable, and made it possible for normal photography to encompass bodies in motion for the first time. As a consequence, the mobile and expressive face became a real possibility as a subject. Moreover, the new cameras could be mass-produced, were cheap, and could be adapted to being hand-held. This brought them well within the compass of enthusiastic amateurs.

Yet if snapshot technology was ready and in place so as to allow a complete transformation in the ways individuals presented themselves for being photographed, it took a surprising amount of time for more informal posing styles to settle in. Aesthetic and cultural conventions still acted as a brake on innovation. The most technically bold innovators with the snapshot camera tended to be outliers, such as Jacques-Henri Lartigue, who adored photographing friends and relatives sliding down bannisters, jumping in the air, diving in the water, falling off bicycles, and so on. But Lartigue was still an unknown at this stage of his life and had no influence. Outside such rare bright spots, static, grave, and inexpressive seriousness still continued to predominate. Moreover, the development of police and forensic photography in the 1880s and 1890s reinforced this tendency. Paris police chief Alphonse Bertillon devised a highly specific form of identification photography which would prove enduringly influential. Drawing on the current scientific claims of racial anthropology and degeneration theory (which still registered the influence of Lavaterian physiognomy), Bertillon's facial technology aspired to capture an individual's true essence (Fig. 7.2). The police mug-shot never lied, it seemed. Nor did it smile.

In the event, the emergence of new cultural models was needed to stimulate change. In the eighteenth century, the cult of sensibility had acted as a trigger: people wanted to cry and smile like their novelistic heroes and heroines. In the early twentieth century, new media took this path-breaking emulative role. Of prime importance was film and the associated medium of studio photography. More even than novels, film encouraged processes of identification with the lifestyle and self-presentation of celebrity or fantasy figures. Before the First World War, film studios in Hollywood started to make the posed images of their stars into media outputs with mass appeal. The smile was gradually becoming a key feature of this new medium, which boomed in the inter-war years, when the close-up came into its own. It still tended to be women who specialized in the full-on, teeth-displaying smile, most men preferring a wry, characterful closed-mouth approach. But white glossy teeth—which could moreover be retouched to produce hyper-perfection—eventually became strongly pervasive within visual culture for men as well as women.

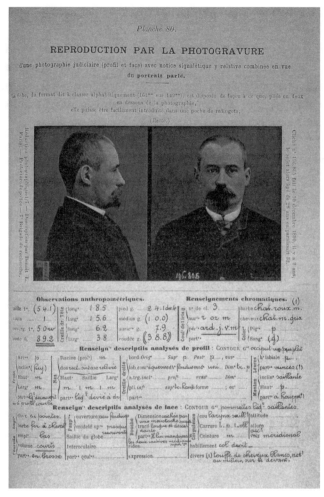

Fig. 7.2 Alphonse Bertillon, Personal Dossier

Where film-stars led the way, private individuals followed, particularly in the inter-war period. Even some politicians began to go with the flow (though the ones who traded most in charisma such as Hitler, Mussolini, Lenin, and Stalin preferred a mysterious, facially immobile gravity). By the beginning of the Second World War, the practice of saying 'cheese' in front of camera had begun. The display of teeth in photography was becoming the norm for those who watched films as much as for those who starred in them.

Particularly after 1945, visual advertising and popular psychology joined film media as drivers of change. Businesses in the West—and most of all in the USA, the wealthiest society in the world—spent enormous and increasing amounts of money on advertising, realizing the importance of visual triggers in promoting sales. Seemingly a smile could sell anything. This included oneself, especially if one followed the precepts of self-help psychology. Mid-West farm-boy Dale Carnegie made himself into a millionaire with his enormously influential *How to Win Friends and Influence People*. This had first appeared in 1936, but the 1940s and 1950s would see its heyday in the USA and the infiltration of its messages down the social scale and across the world. Smiling was one of Carnegie's key ways to get people to like you; and liking you was the first step towards you influencing them (and you probably selling them something too). Public figures and ordinary individuals now did not shrink from presenting their personalities in ways that in the past would have been hermetically private (though symptomatic of how far France was behind, the twentieth century's most notorious public figure, Charles de Gaulle, was simply never known to smile in public—and not much in private either). The smile increasingly beamed down from advertising hoardings and simultaneously, through television, it infiltrated private homes as well, lodging itself securely in collective dreams and nightmares.

The desirability of the perfect white-tooth smile offered a tremendous entrepreneurial niche for commercialized dentistry. Dentistry had professionalized precociously in the USA in the nineteenth century, and for most of the following century America led the way. Good, healthy but above all attractive teeth and smiles, it was insinuated, offered a pathway to riches, rewards, and happiness for dental clients. It certainly brought wealth to more than a few entrepreneurial dentists. US dentistry was a world leader that other nations were soon bidding to emulate. Increasingly cosmeticized—as regards uniformity, symmetry, evenness, and preternatural whiteness—American teeth and smiles constituted a far from negligible sector of US soft power, particularly in the post-Cold War era.

The triumph of the twentieth-century Smile Revolution stimulated a postmodernist response in the early 1960s to the emergent Smile Revolution. Andy Warhol's ironically flat depiction in 1962 of thirty-two Campbell's (soon-to-be-iconic) soup cans satirized art practice and taste as much as it did the mindless replicability of advertising images. Warhol added an extra twist in his Marilyn Monroe dyptych, also in 1962 (Fig. 7.3). A witty commentary on the times, the work highlighted how the smile of this highly individualistic and charismatic film star was just as replicable as a

Fig. 7.3 Andy Warhol, *Marilyn Monroe, Dyptych* (detail) (1962)

can of soup. Oddly, the absent feature in this sort-of-portrait was any sense of the sitter. The artwork simultaneously celebrated both the celebrity of banality and the banality of celebrity—and the mythic ubiquity of the smile.

Western modernity shrugged off Warhol's implicit critique of its practices, and the start of the twenty-first century sees the place of the smile in modern culture largely unchallenged. The gesture seems as ubiquitous as ever, as widely accepted as having a place within modern life—and quite as banal. The end of the twentieth century did witness the emergence of some social practices which either complicated the appearance of the smile (piercing, tattooing, mouth jewellery, metallic teeth, and other dental protheses) or even its visibility (notably the Muslim veil). Yet it would seem recklessly implausible to argue that these changes signal the end of the modern world's love-affair with the white-toothed smile. Indeed, they may even enhance its appeal. At the time of writing, the smile seems here to stay. But of course Madame Vigée Le Brun and denture-maker Dubois de Chémant probably thought much the same in the late 1780s.

NOTES

ABBREVIATIONS

AB   Archives de la Bastille
AN   Archives Nationales (Paris)
ARTFL The ARTFL/Frantext Database (*)
BIUM Bibliothèque Inter-Universitaire de Médecine(**)
BNF   Bibliothèque Nationale de France
DDAD *Dents, dentistes et art dentaire: histoire, pratiques et représentations*, ed. Franck Collard and Evelyne Samama (Paris, 2012)
ET   Étude (notarial practice)
MC   Minutier Central
n.d.   no date
n.p.   no pagination
INPI   Institut national de la propriété industrielle

(*) The ARTFL/Frantext Database contains over 3,500 French language texts, ranging from the twelfth century to the present. It is particularly strong in canonical works of French literature and culture. It is accessible at: <artfl-project.uchicago.edu/>. The ARTFL website also includes the 'Dictionnaires d'autrefois' resource, which contains French-language dictionaries from the sixteenth century to the present (accessible at: <artfl-project.uchicago.edu/content/dictionnaires-dautrefois>) and Diderot's *Encyclopédie* (accessible at: <encyclopedie.uchicago.edu/>).

(**) The Bibliothèque Inter-Universitaire de Médecine website contains an enormous number of medical texts, mainly in French. Particularly useful is the Bibliothèque medica@. The site address is: <www.bium.univ-paris5.fr/histmed/medica.htm>. Located under 'Odontologie' are over one hundred historical dentistry texts. There are also commentaries on many of the key texts for the eighteenth and early nineteenth century in the 'Sources de l'odontologie' section, at <www.bium.univ-paris5.fr/histmed/medica/odonto.htm>.

INTRODUCTION

1 **displayed a self-portrait at the Paris Salon**: [Moufle d'Angerville], *Mémoires secrets*, xxvi (18 September 1787), pp. 351–2. The passage is reproduced in Bernardette Fort, *Les Salons des 'Mémoires secrets', 1767–87* (Paris, 1999), p. 321. See Ch. 5 for a fuller discussion of this incident.

3 **The list of books devoted to its history is extremely short**: Angus Trumble, *A Brief History of the Smile* (New York, 2004) is the best general work, and it contains a very serviceable bibliography. Short visual coverages of the face and smile include Marina Vaizey, *Smile* (London, 2002) and Alexander Sturgis, *Faces* (London, 2005). These draw on the resources of the British Museum and the National Portrait Gallery respectively. On the *Mona Lisa*, see esp. Donald Sassoon, *Mona Lisa: The History of the World's Most Famous Painting* (London, 2001). There is a much more copious literature on laughter, on which I will be drawing. An excellent collection on a closely related subject is *DDAD*.

The great *Encyclopédie*: See Denis Diderot and Jean d'Alembert (eds.), *Encyclopédie, ou Dictionnaire raisonné des sciences, des arts et des métiers*, 17 vols. + 11 vols. of plates (Paris, 1751–72). See ARTFL for this; and for dictionary definitions, ARTFL, 'Dictionnaires d'autrefois'.

deterred artists from the Renaissance onwards from seeking to try: see the discussion relating to photography, esp. pp. 179–80 herein. Sitters for painted portraits faced similar problems. Édouard Pommier, *Théories du portrait de la Renaissance aux Lumières* (Paris, 1998) provides a useful discussion of the value and problematics of truth-to-life in portraits. See too A. Niderst, 'La ressemblance au XVIIe siècle' in J. M. Bailbe (ed.), *Le Portrait* (Rouen, 1987). The issues are further discussed in Richard Brilliant, *Portraiture* (London 1991); Shearer West, *Portraiture* (Oxford, 2004); and Joanna Woodall, 'Introduction: Facing the Subject', in Woodall (ed.), *Portraiture: Facing the Subject* (Manchester, 1997).

4 As the psychologist Paul Ekman has shown in our own day: Ekman has gained a leading position in this domain. I have drawn especially on his *Telling Lies: Clues to Deceit in the Marketplace, Politics and Marriage* (New York, 1985); Paul Ekman and Wallace V. Friesen, 'Felt, False and Miserable Smiles', *Journal of Nonverbal Behavior*, 6 (1982); Paul Ekman and Willibald Ruch, 'The Expressive Pattern of Laughter', in A. W. Kaszniak (ed.), *Emotion Qualia and Consciousness* (Tokyo, 2001). A critique of Ekman's 'anti-culturalist' approach is offered in Robert J. Barrett and Mary Katsikitis, 'Foreign Faces: A Voyage to the Land of Eepica', in Mary Katsikitis, *The Human Face: Measurement and Meaning* (Boston, 2003). See too Vicky Bruce, *Recognising Faces* (Hillsdale, NJ, 1988); and Vicky Bruce and Andy Young, *In the Eye of the Beholder: The Science of Face Perception* (Oxford, 1998).

the 'Duchenne smile': see François Delaporte, *Anatomy of the Passions* (Stanford, 2008); François Delaporte et al. (eds.), *La Fabrique du visage: de la physiognomonie antique à la première greffe* (Turnhout, Belgium, 2010); M. Gervais and D. S. Wilson, 'The Evolution and Function of Laughter and Humor: A Synthetic Approach', *Quarterly Review of Biology*, 80 (2005: especially useful); and Paul Ekman, Richard J. Davidson, Wallace V. Friesen, 'The Duchenne Smile: Emotional Expression and Brain Physiology II', *Journal of Personality and Social Psychology*, 58 (1990).

Present-day studies of smiling and laughing: besides some discussion of early infant development in the works by Ekman and Bruce cited earlier, see also M. K. Rothbart, 'Emotional Development: Changes in Reactivity and Self-regulation', in Paul Ekman and R. J. Davidson (eds.), *The Nature of Emotion: Fundamental Questions* (Oxford, 1994) and Pierre Rousseau, 'Les Premièrs Expressions du visage du bébé à la naissance', Delaporte et al., *La Fabrique du visage*, pp. 159ff.

5 the play-face of a number of great apes: in this discussion, I have drawn heavily on the discussion by Marina Davila Ross, Michael J. Owren, and Elke Zimmermann, 'Reconstructing the Evolution of Laughter in Great Apes and Humans', *Current Biology*, 19 (2009).

Darwin noted this convergence . . . in 1872: Charles Darwin, *The Expression of the Emotions in Man and Animals* (1872), ed. Paul Ekman (London, 1999). The smiling ape is at p. 135.

reaffirmed in the Renaissance by Rabelais: 'rire est le propre de l'homme': François Rabelais, *Gargantua* (1534), 'Avis aux lecteurs'. He was adapting a phrase from Aristotle: 'man is the only animal that can laugh'.

7 post-dated the play-face: it has been suggested that this development may have taken place between 4 and 2 million years ago.

feedback loop: on smiling and 'emotional contagion' generally, besides the works cited earlier (p. 4 herein), see Elaine Hatfield, John L. Cacioppo, and Richard L. Rapson,

'Emotional Contagion', *Current Directions in Psychological Sciences*, 2 (1993); and James Fowler and Nicholas Christakis, 'Dynamic Spread of Happiness in a Large Social Network: Longitudinal Analysis over 20 Years in the Framingham Heart Study', *British Medical Journal* (December 2008 [a2338]). For smiling and sales techniques, see S. Douglas Pugh, 'Service with a Smile: Emotional Contagion in the Service Encounter', *Academy of Management Journal*, 44 (2001).

8 **what the historian, William Reddy, has labelled 'emotives'**: William M. Reddy, *The Navigation of Feeling: A Framework for the History of the Emotions* (Cambridge, 2001).

the American anthropologist Clifford Geertz: Clifford Geertz, 'Thick Description: Toward an Interpretive Theory of Culture', in Geertz, *The Interpretation of Cultures: Selected Essays* (New York, 1973).

9 **cheesy grin**: saying the word 'cheese' so as to give a smiling effect seems to date back to the 1940s.

were particularly bad in the late eighteenth century: for an overview which highlights sugar as the main 'villain of caries etiology' in the *longue durée*, see Luis Pezo Lanfranco and Sabine Eggers, 'Caries through Time: An Anthropological Overview', in Ming-yu Li (ed.), *Contemporary Approach to Dental Caries* (published online, 2012). Some specific examples include: Philip A. Evans and Kevin Wooldridge, *Saint Pancras Burial Ground Excavations for Saint Pancras International, the London Terminus of High Speed 1 (2002–3)* (London, 2011), esp. 127ff.; D. K. Whittaker and T. Molleson, 'Caries Prevalence in the Dentition of a Late Eighteenth-century Population', *Archives of Oral Biology*, 41 (1996); K. W. Alt, 'Practical Dentistry in the Eighteenth Century: Historical Grave Findings from Saint-Hippolyte, Le Grand Sacconex', *Schweizer Monatschrift für Zahnmedizin* (1993); David Henderson et al., 'Archaeological Evidence for Eighteenth-century Medical Practice in the Old Town of Edinburgh', *Proceedings of the Society of Antiquaries of Scotland*, 126 (1996); K. Rönnbäck, 'From Extreme Luxury to Everyday Commodity: Sugar in Sweden, Seventeenth to Twentieth Century', *Göteborg Papers in Economic History*, 11 (2001); and Z. Palubackaite et al., 'Dental Status of Napoleon's Great Army (1812): Mass Burial of Soldiers in Vilnius', *International Journal of Osteoarchaeology*, 16 (2006).

CHAPTER 1

16 **Hyacinthe Rigaud's famous state portrait of Louis XIV**: there is a brief but excellent discussion of this painting in Michael Levey, *Painting and Sculpture in France, 1700–1800* (London, 1971), p. 4. The portrait plays with the notion of the king's two bodies—one biological, one eternal—discussed in the classic Ernst Kantorowicz, *The King's Two Bodies: A Study in Medieval Political Theology* (Princeton, NJ, 1957).

17 **sculpted legs . . . the finest he ever saw**: the duc de Saint-Simon, cited in Dirk Van Der Cruysse, *Le Portrait dans les Mémoires du duc de Saint-Simon* (Paris, 1971), p. 168. For Louis as dancer, see Régine Astier, 'Louis XIV, *Premier Danseur*', in David L. Rubin (ed.), *Sun King: The Ascendancy of French Culture during the Reign of Louis XIV* (London, 1992).

'Teeth, Sire?', replied the Cardinal, 'Ah! Who does have any?': Saint-Simon, *Mémoires*, Grands Écrivains de France edn, 43 vols. (Paris, 1879–1928), xxv, p.182.

18 **'Individuals who keep all their teeth healthy . . . rare'**: Pierre Fauchard, *Le Chirurgien-dentiste, ou traité des dents*, 2 vols. (Paris, 1728), Preface, n.p. On Fauchard, see later, esp. Ch. 3.

demographic crises . . . which struck early modern Europe: see esp. Marcel Lachivier, *Les Années de misère: la famine au temps du Grand Roi* (Paris, 1991).

'**often toothache is so bad...prefers to have the tooth pulled out**': Jacques Guillemeau, *La Chirurgie française* (1594), cited in Georges Dagen, *Documents pour servir à l'histoire de l'art dentaire en France, principalement à Paris* (Paris, 1925), p. 48. See Micheline Ruel-Kellerman, '"Douleur des dents": du vécu au commentaire. De Vésale à Fauchard', in DADD.

19 **accoutrements of timelessness**: on this theme see esp. Jean-Marie Apostolidès, *Le Roi machine: spectacle et politique au temps de Louis XIV* (Paris, 1981) and Peter Burke, *The Fabrication of Louis XIV* (Cambridge, 1992).

two teeth already present in his mouth: for everything relating to Louis XIV's health and bodily condition, see Stanis Perez, *La Santé de Louis XIV: une bio-histoire du roi-soleil* (Paris, 2007): see pp. 31–2 for the birth teeth. This work supplants earlier accounts of the king's health, the best of which is Michelle Caroly, *Le Corps du roi soleil: grandeurs et misères de sa majesté Louis XIV* (Paris, 1990). For royal teeth, see too Colin Jones, 'The King's Two Teeth', *History Workshop*, 65 (2008).

Dutch anti-French pamphleteers... War of Spanish Succession (1701–14): Burke, *The Fabrication of Louis XIV*, pp. 135–49 and 211–12; Perez, *La Santé de Louis XIV*, p. 366.

'**the king's teeth are poor by nature**': *Journal de santé de Louis XIV*, ed. Stanis Perez (Grenoble, 2004), pp. 199–200. See Perez, *La Santé de Louis XIV*, pp. 73–6, 187.

another witness observed: Perez, *La Santé de Louis XIV*, p. 187.

forty such individuals: [Jean Pinson de La Martinière], *Estat de la France, comme elle estoit gouvernée en l'An MDCXLVIII* (Paris, 1970 [1649]), pp. 85–6. For the 'royal medical household', see Laurence Brockliss and Colin Jones, *The Medical World of Early Modern France* (Oxford, 1997), esp. pp. 241ff.; and Alexandre Lunel, *La Maison médicale du roi: le pouvoir royal et les professions de santé (XVIe–XVIIIe siècles)* (Paris, 2008).

20 **the *Lever* and the *Coucher***: on court protocol and etiquette, see Jean-François Solnon, *La Cour de France* (Paris, 1987), pp. 356ff.; and Frédérique Laferme-Falguières, *Les Courtisans: une société de spectacle sous l'ancien régime* (Paris, 2007).

washing the mouth out: as recommended, for example, in the limited number of texts dedicated to mouth care such as Urbain Hémard, *Recherche sur la vraye anathomie des dents, nature et propriété d'icelles* (Lyon, 1581); Bernardin Martin, *Dissertation sur les dents* (Paris, 1679); and Sieur de Fleurimont, *Moyens de se conserver les dents belles et bonnes* (Paris, 1682). On these early texts, see BIUM.

rosemary or some other aromatic plant: *Journal de santé de Louis XIV*, pp. 226–7; Pierre Dionis, *Cours d'opérations de chirurgie démontrées au Jardin royal* (Paris, 1708), p. 418.

bloodlettings... which physicians inflicted on the royal body: see the good overall accounts in both Perez, *La Santé de Louis XIV*; and Caroly, *Le Corps du roi soleil*.

the Galenic theory of the bodily humours: See Ch. 2, pp. 65–6 herein.

'**the large quantity of confitures... snacks**': Perez, *La Santé de Louis XIV*, pp. 186–7. Martin, *Dissertation sur les dents* and similar texts were only fitfully aware of the noxious effects of sticky foodstuffs on the teeth. Toothache remedies routinely included honey.

Since the Middle Ages... of any sort: Brockliss and Jones, *The Medical World*, esp. chs. 2, 3.

21 **a surgeon's subsequent capacity for... operational procedures**: Dionis, *Cours d'opérations*, p. 417.

'**operators for the teeth**': general histories of dentistry provide broad, Europe-wide overviews of this group. See e.g. Walter Hoffman-Axthelm, *History of Dentistry* (Chicago, 1981); Malvin E. Ring, *Dentistry: An Illustrated History* (New York, 1985); Michel Dechaume and Pierre Huard, *Histoire illustrée de l'art dentaire: stomatologie et odontologie*

(Paris, 1971); and Dagen, *Documents pour servir à l'histoire de l'art dentaire*. See too Roger King, *The Making of the Dentiste, c.1650–1760* (Aldershot, 1998).

the remaining teeth on the upper right side of Louis's jaw: the episode is covered in *Journal de santé*, p. 225; see Perez, *La Santé de Louis XIV*, pp. 73–6; King, *Making of the Dentiste*, pp. 68–70; and, more generally, Toby Gelfand, *Professionalizing Modern Medicine: Paris Surgeons and Medical Science and Institutions in the Eighteenth Century* (Westport, CT, 1984), p. 34.

22 **'... I want to be cured as though I were a peasant'**: cited in Perez, *La Santé de Louis XIV*, p. 83n.

not uncommon to pull out one's own teeth: example in Philip Riedler, *La Figure du patient au XVIIIe siècle* (Geneva, 2010), p. 147.

Saint Apollonia was particularly sought after: see Véronique Boucherat, 'Une dent contre elle: l'iconographie du martyre et du personnage de sainte Apolline à la fin du moyen âge', in DDAD: focused on Spain but of broader interest.

the earliest French surgical work specifically devoted to the teeth: Hémard, *Recherche*, p. 60; *Recueil et suite de remèdes faciles et domestiques recueillis par Madame Fouquet*, 6th edn (Amsterdam, 1704), pp. 266, 338–9. This edition is particularly full.

cris de Paris: Vincent Milliot, *Les Cris de Paris ou le peuple travesti: les représentations des petits métiers parisiens (XVIe–XVIIIe siècles)* (Paris, 1995). See too Laurent Vissière, 'Des cris pour rire? Dérision et auto-dérision dans les cris de Paris (XIIIe–XVIe siècles)', in Elisabeth Crouzet-Pavan and Jacques Verger (eds.), *La Dérision au moyen âge: de la pratique sociale au rituel politique* (Paris, 2007).

23 **Rabelaisian orifice**: the classic study of the author of *Gargantua* and *Pantagruel* is Mikhail Bakhtin, *Rabelais and his World* (Bloomington, IN, 1984). For a brief but pertinent critique, see Aron Gurevich, 'Bakhtin and his Theory of Carnival' in Jan Bremmer and Herman Roodeburg (eds.), *A Cultural History of Humour from Antiquity to the Present* (Cambridge, 1997). See too Georges Minois, *Histoire du rire et de la déraison* (Paris, 2000); Daniel Ménager, *La Renaissance et le rire* (Paris, 1995); and Carol Clark, '"The Onely-languag'd Men of All the World": Rabelais and the Art of the Mountebank', *Modern Language Review*, 74 (1979). The quote from Gargantua is here given in the English of the Urquart and Mottet translation, *The Works of Rabelais* (London, n.d.), p. 80.

24 **Italian troupes of players ... from the Wars of Religion onwards**: M. A. Katrizky, 'Was *Commedia dell'Arte* Performed by Mountebanks? *Album Amicorum* Illustrations and Thomas Platter's Description of 1598', and Jonathan Marks, 'The Charlatans of the Pont-Neuf', both in special issue, ed. Katrizky, 'The Commedia' Dell'Arte', *Theatre Research International*, 23 (1998).

orviétan: see esp. Claude-Stéphen Le Paulmier, *L'Orviétan: histoire d'une famille de charlatans du Pont-Neuf aux XVIIe et XVIIIe siècles* (Paris, 1893); David Gentilcore, '"Sole Secret of the Orviétan": Charlatans and Medical Secrets in Early Modern Italy', *Medical History*, 38 (1994).

'to lie like a tooth-puller': the phrase appears in the Dictionary of the Académie française from 1694. See ARTFL, *Dictionnaires d'autrefois*.

Lieutenant-Général de Police ... with wide-ranging powers over public order: for a general history of the institution, biased towards the late eighteenth century, see Vincent Milliot, *Un Policier des Lumières: suivi de 'Mémoires de J. C. P. Lenoir'* (Paris, 2011).

without needing to pass through the normal procedures of training and certification: see esp. Jean Verdier, *La Jurisprudence de la médecine en France*, 2 vols. (Alençon, 1762–3), i, p. 497 and ii, pp. 75ff. On licensing in general, see too Brockliss and Jones, *The Medical World*, pp. 238ff.

25 *artisans suivant la cour*: for this system, see Verdier, *Jurisprudence de la médecine*, ii,
   pp. 144ff. Registers of the *Prévôté de l'hôtel du roi*, at AN V3/191–8, give details of
   these individuals over most of the seventeenth and eighteenth centuries. See Brockliss
   and Jones, *Medical World*, pp. 628–9.

   a royal grant of the privilege of retailing approved medical treatments: Verdier,
   Jurisprudence de la médicine, ii, pp. 144ff., and Brockliss and Jones, *Medical World*, esp.
   pp. 627–9.

   Pont-Neuf: Edouard Fournier, *Histoire du Pont-Neuf* (Paris, 1862); Michel Sélimonte,
   Le Pont-Neuf et ses charlatans (Paris, 1980). See Joel Coste, 'Théâtre et Pont-Neuf.
   Charlatans et arracheurs de dents à Paris, 1580–1620', in DADD; and Robert
   M. Isherwood, 'The Singing Culture of the Pont-Neuf', in Robert M. Isherwood,
   Farce and Fantasy: Popular Entertainment in Eighteenth-century Paris (Oxford, 1986), ch. 1.
   For Paris generally in the late seventeenth century, see Colin Jones, *Paris: Biography of a
   City* (London, 2004); René Pillorget, *Paris sous les premiers Bourbons, 1594–1660* (1988);
   Georges Dethan, *Paris au temps de Louis XIV* (Paris, 1990); and Leon Bernard, *The
   Emerging City: Paris in the Age of Louis XIV* (Durham, NC, 1970).

26 **One late seventeenth-century visitor**: [Jean-Paul Marana], *Lettre d'un Sicilien à un de
   ses amis*, ed. Valentin Dufour (Paris, 1883), p. 57.

   Tabarin: Sara Beam, *Laughing Matters: Farce and the Making of Absolutism in France*
   (Ithaca, NY, 2007), esp. pp. 147–50, 168–72.

   It was characteristic of such figures...both elite and popular: see Tabarin,
   Oeuvres complètes, ed. Gustave Aventin (Paris, 1858). See too Molière, 'L'Amour médecin', 'Le Malade imaginaire', etc.

28 **'Mazarinades'**: the Carmelina episode is recounted in *Agréable récit de ce qui s'est passé
   aux dernières barricades de Paris* (Paris, 1649), p. 13. Carmelina, Contugi and another
   operator called Cormier also appear in another Mazarinade, *Le Ministre d'Estat flambé, en
   vers burlesques* (Paris, 1649), p. 11. For Barry, see Dancourt, *L'Opérateur Barry* (1700).

   Surgeon Bernardin Martin...worse than that of a peasant: Martin, *Dissertation
   sur les dents*, p. 62. See BIUM.

29 **Castiglione's *Il Libro del cortegiano***: I have used the edition, Baldesar Castiglione, *The
   Book of the Courtier: The Singleton Translation* (London, 2002). See C. H. Clough,
   'Francis I and the Courtiers of Castiglione's Courtier', *European Studies Review*, 8
   (1978); and Peter Burke, *The Fortunes of 'The Courtier'* (Oxford, 1995). For courtesy
   in general, and its transformation into civility and politeness, the seminal texts are still
   Norbert Elias's *The Court Society*, ed. Stephen Mennell (Dublin, 2006); and his *The
   Civilizing Process* (Oxford, 1994). See also Roger Chartier, 'From Texts to Manners:
   A Concept and its Books: *Civilité* between Aristocratic Distinction and Popular Appro-
   priation', in Norbert Elias, *The Cultural Uses of Print in Early Modern France* (Princeton,
   1987); and Jacques Revel et al., 'Forms of Privatization' in Roger Chartier (ed.), *A
   History of Private Life*, III: *Passions of the Renaissance* (London, 1989).

   'after the fashion of fools...the inept or buffoons': Castiglione, *Book of the
   Courtier*, p. 106.

   what was deemed laughable: see the excellent discussion in Quentin Skinner,
   'Hobbes and the Classical Theory of Laughter', in Quentin Skinner, *Visions of Politics*,
   iii: *Hobbes and Civil Science* (Cambridge, 2002). Of course, Rabelais himself was con-
   tributing to these debates. See Gregory David de Rocher, *Rabelais's Laughers and Joubert's
   'Traité du Ris'* (Alabama, 1979). See too Michael A. Screech and R. Calder, 'Some
   Renaissance Attitudes to Laughter', in Anthony H. T. Levi (ed.), *Humanism in France at
   the End of the Middle Ages and in the Early Renaissance* (Manchester, 1970).

   nibbling of a sheep: cited in Ménager, *La Renaissance et le rire*, p. 174.

30 *'sourire'* or *'souris'*: the evolving dictionary definitions can be followed in ARTFL, *Dictionnaires d'autrefois*.

Traité du ris: Laurent Joubert, *Traité du ris, contenant son essance, ses causes, et mervelheus essais, curieusement recherchés, raisonnés et observés* (Paris, 1579). See the English translation and discussion of the work: Laurent Joubert, *Treatise on Laughter*, ed. and trans. Gregory David de Rocher (Alabama, 1980). The Joubert quotation in the French text is on p. 20. See also Colin Jones, 'Laughing over Boundaries', *Transactions of the Royal Historical Society*, 21 (2011).

In the dedication of his volume . . . delightful picture of the laughing face: the quotation on the smiling face is in the unpaginated dedication at the front of the volume; for the negative depiction of laughter, see pp. 160–1.

31 **a social taxonomy of laughter**: see Dominique Bertrand, *Dire le rire à l'âge classique: représenter pour mieux contrôler* (Aix-en-Provence, 1995), p. 71. For the animal comparisons, see Joubert, *Traité du ris*, p. 221. See too Marin Cureau de La Chambre, *Charactères des passions* (Paris, 1663). On this point, see Skinner, 'Hobbes and the Classical Theory of Laughter', esp. pp. 146, 156–7, 162–3.

32 **'laughter varies according to social rank'**: Bertrand, *Dire le rire*, p. 71; René Demoris, 'Le Langage du corps et l'expression des passions de Félibien à Diderot', in J. P. Guillerm (ed.), *Mots et couleurs* (Lille, 1986), p. 11; Adrien de Montluc de Cramail, *Discours académique du rire* (Paris, 1630), p. 35; Jean-Jacques Courtine and Georges Vigarello, 'La Physiognomonie de l'homme impudique', in Olivier Burgelin and Philippe Perrot (eds.), *Parure, pudeur et étiquette* (Paris, 1987: esp. for the vagina equation); Jean Verdon, *Rire au moyen âge* (Paris, 2001), p. 69 (for the *Roman de la Rose*); Ménager, *La Renaissance et le rire*, p. 188; and Bertrand, *Dire le rire*, p. 161 (Henri Étienne).

The English philosopher Thomas Hobbes . . . the misfortunes of others: Skinner, 'Hobbes and the Classical Theory of Laughter'; the quotation is at p. 142; Cureau de La Chambre, *Charactères des passions*, pp. 231–2.

33 **Erasmus's pedagogical best-seller, *De civilitate morum puerilium***: see Chartier, 'From Texts to Manners', pp. 76ff.; H. de La Fontaine Verwey, 'The First "Book of Etiquette" for Children, Erasmus' *De civilitate morum puerilium*', *Quaerendo*, 1 (1971).

Bibliothèque bleue: See Lise Andries, *La Bibliothèque bleue au XVIIIe siècle: une tradition éditoriale* (Oxford, 1989).

Jean-Baptiste de La Salle: De La Salle's pedagogic texts are available in numerous editions (e.g. *Oeuvres* (Rome, 1993)), but there is a surprising dearth of good historical studies of the saint. See Yves Poutet, *Saint Jean-Baptiste de La Salle: un saint au XVIIe siècle* (Paris, 1992); and Chartier, 'From Texts to Manners', pp. 88ff.

'The wise man . . . is hardly heard laughing at all': see the edition of Erasmus, *La Civilité puérile*, bilingual edition, ed. Alcide Bonneau (Paris, 1877), p. 23.

34 *Nouveau Traité . . . parmi les honnestes gens*: The first edition was published in Brussels in 1671. I have used the Amsterdam 1679 edition. The quotation comes from the 'Premier Avertissement', n.p. See too Kamal Farid, *Antoine de Courtin (1622–85): étude critique* (1969).

'he imitate a great Prince . . . rules of decorum': Courtin, *Nouveau Traité*, p. 115.

Counter-Reformation Catholic Church proved keen to join the fight: Minois, *Histoire du rire*, esp. ch. 9 ('Fini de rire').

35 **The carnivalesque in all its forms was now under attack**: Beam, *Laughing Matters*, pp. 125ff., including attacks on festive societies. See Minois, *Histoire du rire*, pp. 288ff.

Jesus had never laughed in the Bible: see J. Le Goff, 'Jésus, a-t-il-ri?', *L'Histoire*, 158 (1992); Minois, *Histoire du rire*, pp. 103ff.

Jean–Baptiste Thiers, *Traité des jeux*: its full title is *Traitéx des jeux et des divertissements qui peuvent être permis, ou qui doivent être défendus aux chrétiens selon les règles de l'Église et le sentiment des Pères* (Paris, 1686). See Minois, *Histoire du rire*, p. 303. See incidentally, Courtin, *Nouveau Traité*, pp. 150ff. Thiers's better-known work, *Traité des superstitions* (1679) was an equally hard-hitting attack on vestiges of paganism, in line with the post-Tridentine assault on the perceived excesses of popular culture.

36 **bishop Bossuet of Meaux joined the fray**: *Maximes et réflexions sur la comédie* (1694); *Politique tirée des propres paroles de l'écriture sainte*, A. Philolenko ed. (Paris, 2003), pp. 81–2. See Minois, *Histoire du rire*, pp. 321ff.

Cardinal Richelieu: Richelieu, *Testament politique*, ed. Françoise Hildesheimer (Paris, 1995), pp. 214, 197 (and see pp. 195–8, 248).

the king had rarely smiled: Madame de Motteville, cited in Perez, *La Santé de Louis XIV*, p. 66, n.4. Visconti, cited in Jérôme Duindam, *Vienna and Versailles: The Courts of Europe's Dynastic Rivals, 1550–1750* (Cambridge, 2003), p. 164.

37 **'a serious appearance and look'**: Georges Giraud (ed.), *Mémoires du curé de Versailles François Hébert (1686–1704)* (Paris, 1927), p. 40.

the post of court fool proved: Maurice Lever, *Le Sceptre et la marotte: histoire des fous de cour* (Paris, 1983), esp. pp. 238ff.

'It's a strange business, making persons of quality laugh': Molière, *Critique de l'École des femmes* (1663).

as toothless as her spouse: see her complaints about her articulacy, since 'la prononciation s'en est allée avec les dents' ('my pronunciation disappeared with my teeth'), cited in Roger King, *The Making of the Dentiste, c.1650–1760* (Aldershot, 1998), p. 164.

'Old Wrinkly': translating 'vieille ratatinée'. It was the Princesse Palatine, the mother of the duc d'Orléans. 'Old Rubbish', 'Old Witch', and 'Old Dregs' (*vieille ordure, vieille sorcière, vieille ripopée*) were other of her choice expressions for Maintenon. *Lettres de madame la duchesse d'Orléans, née Princesse Palatine*, ed. Olivier Amiel (Paris, 1981), pp. 26, 52, 244, etc.

38 **Norbert Elias**: see note page 29 herein.

anal fistula: Toby Gelfand, *Professionalizing Modern Medicine*, p. 34; *Journal de santé de Louis XIV*, pp. 76–9; Perez, *La Santé de Louis XIV*, pp. 76–89.

'very fashionable': Dionis, *Cours d'opérations*, p. 281.

'the court's ape': De La Bruyère, 'De la ville', in id. *Les Caractères* (Paris, 1696), p. 302.

39 **'the words courteous and courtesy . . .', noted Father Bouhours in 1675**: [Dominique Bouhours], *Remarques nouvelles sur la langue française* (Paris 1675), p. 36; Courtin, *Nouveau Traité de la civilité*, 'Avertissement', n.p.

Some writers still believed . . . to make a gentleman: see Nicolas Faret, *L'Honneste Homme, ou l'Art de plaire à la cour* (Paris, 1630), Introduction (n.p.). For anti-court discourses, see later, pp. 95–6 herein.

One of Courtin's allies: [Bouhours], *Remarques nouvelles*, p. 33.

risus sardonicus: there is a good discussion of this in Ménager, *La Renaissance et le rire*, pp. 57ff.

40 **'a smile full of grace and majesty'**: these examples are culled from ARTFL/Frantext.

'hard and polished': La Bruyère, 'De la cour', pp. 311, 308. La Bruyère was punning with the word '*poli*', which can mean both 'polished' and 'polite'.

41 face-whitening creams: see Patricia Philippy, *Painting Women: Cosmetics, Canvases and Early Modern Culture* (Baltimore, MD, 2006); Catherine Lanoë, *La Poudre et le fard: une histoire des cosmétiques de la Renaissance aux Lumières* (Paris, 2008).

the ancient tradition of physiognomy: see the discussions later at pp. 50–1 and 150–6 herein; Jean-Baptiste Morvan de Bellegarde, *Réflexions sur le ridicule*, 4th edn (Paris, 1699).

best advice going for courtiers: see Bernard, *Dire le rire* (including for La Rochefoucauld).

42 Madame de Sévigné . . . 'for some years, no one laughs any more': Madame de Sévigné, *Lettres*, Grands Ecrivains de France edn, 14 vols. (Paris, 1862–8), iv, p. 494 (18 June 1676).

CHAPTER 2

43 'the study sketches of Watteau . . . all over and pointing in all directions': Marcel Proust, *A la recherche du temps perdu*, i: *Du côté de chez Swann*, ed. Pierre Clarac and André Ferré, 3 vols. (Paris 1954), p. 240. The drawings shown in Fig. 2.1 were executed *c.*1716 and are located at the Louvre (which purchased them in 1858). 'Over-exhibited' in the nineteenth century, they were commented on by the Goncourt brothers in 1863, before being seen by Proust: Pierre Rosenberg and Louis-Antoine Prat, *Antoine Watteau, 1684–1721: catalogue raisonné des dessins*, 3 vols. (Paris, 1996), ii, pp. 806–7 for this drawing. See also François Moureau and Margaret Morgan Grasselli (eds.), *Antoine Watteau (1684–1721): le peintre, son temps et sa légende* (Paris, 1981). For further association between the Regency and the smile: Verdun-Louis Saulnier, *La Littérature du siècle philosophique*, 9th edn (Paris, 1970), p. 16: the Regency was 'un temps de critique souriante dans le goût de Shaftesbury et de Fontenelle'.

44 Paris was ready for change . . . the aura of failure hanging over its last few years: Colin Jones, *The Great Nation: France from Louis XV to Napoleon, 1715–99* (London, 2002), esp. ch. 2 (and, for Louis XV's initial popularity in Paris, pp. 38, 74). On the Regency's cultural impact, see Jay Caplan, *In the King's Wake: Post-Absolutist Culture in France* (Chicago 1999); Roland Mortier and Hervé Hasquin (eds.), *Etudes sur le XVIIIe siècle: 26: Topographie du plaisir sous la Régence* (Brussels, 1998); Denis Reynaud and Chantal Thomas (eds.), *Le Régent entre fable et histoire* (Paris, 2003). For eighteenth-century Paris more generally, see Colin Jones, *Paris: Biography of a City* (London, 2002); Jean Chagniot, *Nouvelle histoire de Paris: Paris au XVIIIe siècle* (Paris, 1988); and David Garrioch, *The Making of Revolutionary Paris* (London, 2002).

45 the Régiment de la Calotte: Antoine de Baecque, *Les Éclats du rire: la culture des rieurs au XVIIIe siècle* (Paris, 2000), ch. 1, 'Le Régiment de la Calotte, ou les stratégies aristocratiques du rire bel esprit (1702–52)'.

'. . . gaiety and fun under the Regency': Voltaire cited in Jean Meyer, *La Vie quotidienne des français au temps de la Régence* (Paris, 1979), p. 18.

Shaftesbury: I have used Comte de Shaftesbury, *Oeuvres*, ed. Françoise Badelon (Paris, 2002, following the 1769 Geneva edn): p. 381 ('possesses a moral sense'); p. 64 ('amicable collision'). See Vic Gatrell, *City of Laughter: Sex and Satire in Eighteenth-century London* (London, 2000), esp. pp. 163–71. For *jocositas* and *hilaritas*, see Georges Minois, *Histoire du rire et de la dérision* (Paris, 2002), p. 409.

46 *fête galante*: for Watteau, see esp. Julie-Anne Plax, *Watteau and the Cultural Politics of Eighteenth-century France* (Cambridge, 2000); and Thomas E. Crow, *Painters and Public Life in Eighteenth-century Paris* (London, 1985).

47 **the old ceremonial manuals . . . disinterred and applied intact**: Michel Antoine, *Louis XV* (Paris, 1989) pp. 162, 435. For court protocol over the century, see Frédérique Laferme-Falguières, *Les Courtisans: une société de spectacle sous l'ancien régime* (Paris, 2007).

48 **The artist Jean-Marc Nattier**: Xavier Salmon, *Jean-Marc Nattier, 1685–1766* (Versailles, 1999), pp. 26–8.

snooty and superior: the 'smirking air' evident in much French portraiture was commented on disapprovingly by Joseph Addison in the *Spectator* in 1711: Melissa Percival, *The Appearance of Character: Physiognomy and Facial Expression in Eighteenth-century France* (London, 1999), p. 86. In his 'Essai sur la peinture', Diderot was similarly enraged by such 'simpering'. See p. 129 herein.

Madame de Pompadour . . . in the ceremonial of the toilette: for Pompadour and her toilette, see Melissa Hyde, 'The Make-up of the Marquise: Boucher's Portrait of Pompadour at her Toilette', *Art Bulletin*, 82 (2000); Ewa Lajer-Burcharth, 'Pompadour's Touch: Difference in Representation', *Representations*, 73 (2001); and Alden Gordon and Teri Hensick, '"The Picture within the Picture": Boucher's 1750 Portrait of Madame de Pompadour Identified', *Apollo*, 480 (2002).

49 **Charles Le Brun**: Le Brun's work is analysed in Jennifer Montagu, *The Expression of the Passions: The Origin and Influence of Charles Le Brun's 'Conférence sur l'expression générale et particulière'* (London, 1994), a classic text. Besides Percival, *The Appearance of Character*, esp. chs. 2, 3; see too Stephanie Ross, 'Painting the Passions: Charles Le Brun's *Conférence sur l'expression'*, *Journal of the History of Ideas*, 45 (1984); Thomas Kirchner, *L'Expression des passions: Ausdruck als Darstellungsproblem in der französischen Kunst und Kunsttheorie des 17 und 18 Jahrhunderts* (Mainz, 1991); Louis Marin, 'Grammaire royale du visage', in *A visage découvert*, exhibition catalogue (Paris, 1992); and Paolo Bonvecchio, 'Il corpo come luogo dell'espressione', in Paola Giacomoni (ed.), *Immagini del corpo in età moderna* (Trento, 1994).

50 **the cryptic codes of physiognomy**: Martin Porter, *Windows of the Soul: The Art of Physiognomy in European Culture, 1470–1780* (Oxford, 2005) and Jean-Jacques Courtine and Claudine Haroche, *Histoire du visage: exprimer et taire ses émotions, XVIe–début XIXe siècle* (Paris, 1988).

The Scientific Revolution . . . making occult physiognomic lore seem out of date: for an overview, see John Henry, *The Scientific Revolution and the Origins of Modern Science* (Basingstoke, 2001). For Descartes and the soul, Montagu, *The Expression of the Passions*, pp. 17–19.

51 **'the motor of the face'**: *a visage découvert*, p. 9, and esp. the chapter by Louis Marin, 'Grammaire royale du visage'.

Rigaud's 1701 portrait . . . discussed in the previous chapter: see pp. 16–17 herein.

a striking gallery of faces . . . according to this Cartesian rationale: see Percival, *The Appearance of Character*, pp. 42, 120.

54 **to smile like Leonardo da Vinci's *Mona Lisa***: Donald Sassoon, *Mona Lisa: The History of the World's Most Famous Painting* (London, 2001). In fact it was not until the nineteenth century that the Mona Lisa really became acknowledged as an iconic ideal of beauty.

codes of civility and decorum: for Castiglione and the tradition of civility, see pp. 29–30 herein. For decorum as a prerequisite of French artistic conventions, see Édouard Pommier, *Théories du portrait: de la Renaissance aux Lumières* (Paris, 1998), esp. pp. 376ff. There are—of course—some well-known exceptions to this rule. But these really do seem to be exceptions to rules which were very systematically upheld. Confirmation to this line of argument is provided by Étienne Jollet, '"Cachez ces dents que je ne saurais voir": la représentation des dents dans les arts visuels en France au XVIIIe siècle', in DADD.

A Spanish peasant boy: more satirical paintings of crude peasant types are particularly evident in Dutch art in the sixteenth and seventeenth centuries. See Catherine Veron-Issad, 'Dents et soins dentaires dans la peinture néerlandaise du XVIIe siécle', in DADD. See also Guillaume Kientz, 'Cris, rires, rictus chez Caravage et les caravagesques'.

Caravaggio, Georges de la Tour, Velazquez, and others fitfully generate a sense of menace: Caravaggio's *I Cavadenti* is at Florence, the de La Tour at the Getty Museum, Los Angeles. See Kientz, 'Cris, rires, rictus'. For more cheerful singing, see Piero della Francesca, *Nativity*, in the National Gallery, London.

A further connotation of the open mouth in Western art is folly: Don Juan Calabazas, court jester, was painted by Velazquez in 1637–9. The work is held at the Prado Museum. For Dutch genre painting, besides Veron-Issad, 'Dents et soins den-taires', see Mariet Westermann, 'How Was Jan Steen Funny? Strategies and Functions of Comic Painting in the Seventeenth Century', in Jan Bremmer and Herman Roode-burg (eds.), *A Cultural History of Humour from Antiquity to the Present* (Cambridge, 1997). Hals's so-called *Laughing Cavalier* is in the Wallace Collection, London. Besides a painting by François Boucher depicting a boy with a carrot (in the Art Institute, Chicago), other childish open mouths include Hals (*Laughing Boy*), Murillo (*Boy Laughing, Laughing Child*), etc. Implied infantilism appears to be indicated in the case of negroes depicted smiling e.g. by Rubens.

57 **the Greek philosopher Democritus . . . a grin revealing his teeth**: Michel Mon-taigne, *Essais*, 2 vols. (Paris, 1992), i, ch. 50. Notable early modern depictions include those by Rubens (1603); Rembrandt (1669: Wallraf-Richartz-Museum and Fondation Corboud, Cologne); and Antoine Coypel (1692: Musée du Louvre). A surprising female Democritus appears to be indicated in Judith Leyster's self-portrait (1630). For Watteau, see Rosenberg and Prat, *Antoine Watteau*, iii, p. 1390–1. Generally for the eighteenth century, see Anne Richardot, 'Un philosophe au purgatoire des Lumières: Démocrite', *XVIIIe siècle. Numéro spécial: Le Rire* (Paris, 2000). See also discussions in Quentin Skinner, 'Hobbes and the Classical Theory of Laughter', in Quentin Skinner, *Visions of Politics*, iii: *Hobbes and Civil Science* (Cambridge, 2002), pp. 153ff.; Dominique Bertrand, *Dire le rire à l'âge classique: représenter pour mieux contrôler* (Aix-en-Provence, 1995), pp. 67–71; and Minois, *Histoire du rire*, pp. 49ff. Representations of Democritus sometimes overlap with those of Diogenes.

59 **images from the *Conférence***: Montagu, *The Expression of the Passions*, esp. pp. 85ff., and Percival, *The Appearance of Character*, esp. ch. 2.

the article on 'Passion' in Diderot's great *Encyclopédie*: *Encyclopédie*, xii, pp. 150–2. For associated images see vol. xx, Plates XXIV–VI (Pl. XXV includes 'le ris').

actor manuals are full of Lebrunian grace notes: Dene Barnett, *The Art of Gesture: The Practices and Principles of 18th-century Acting* (Heidelberg, 1987), and Shearer West, *The Image of the Actor: Verbal and Visual Representation in the Age of Garrick and Kemble* (New York, 1991), esp. pp. 91ff.

'one averts one's face . . . in the presence of the Great': La Bruyère, *Les Caractères* (Paris, 1696), 'Des ouvrages de l'esprit', p. 145.

Writing in the 1770s, Denis Diderot: see the account of the incident and its impact in Anne Vincent-Buffault, *Histoire des larmes (XVIIIe–XIXe siècles)* (Paris, 1986), pp. 66ff. For Voltaire's view, Marivaux, *Journaux et oeuvres diverses*, ed. Frédéric Deloffre and Michel Gilot (Paris, 1988), p. 617 and, for other reactions, p. 620. Montesquieu's opinion is recorded and discussed in Jean Ehrard, *L'Idée de la nature en France dans la première moitié du XVIIIe siècle* (1963), p. 277.

60 **'comédie larmoyante'**: Félix Gaiffe, *Le Drame en France au XVIIIe siècle* (Paris, 1910); Félix Gaiffe, *Le Rire et la scène française* (Paris, 1931), p. 135; Gustave Lanson, *Nivelle de La Chaussée et la comédie larmoyante* (Paris, 1903). The Voltaire citation is from Vincent-Buffault, *Histoire des larmes*, p. 68.

61 **'The theatre is deserted, when [his] comedies are being performed'**, Gaiffe, *Le Rire*, pp. 137ff.

'scrupulous exactness as regards decency' : Gaiffe, *Le Rire*, pp. 137ff.

'three comedies like that will kill tragedy altogether': Gaiffe, *Le Drame*, p. 160. See generally Scott S. Bryson, *The Chastised Stage: Bourgeois Drama and the Exercise of Power* (Stanford, CA, 1991), and David J. Denby, *Sentimental Narrative and the Social Order in France, 1760–1820* (Cambridge, 1994). The Mercier quotation is from his *Du théâtre* (Amsterdam, 1773), p. 103.

Louis XV detested *comédies larmoyantes*: Lanson, *Nivelle de La Chaussée*, p. 282.

62 **'the court's ape'**: La Bruyère, *Les Caractères*, 'De la ville', p. 302.

this soggy cascade of public tears: Collé is cited in Gaiffe, *Le Drame*, p. 295; Voltaire is cited in Vincent-Duffault, *Histoire des larmes*, p. 72; 'another author' is Bachaumont, cited from 1764 in Gaiffe, *Le Rire*, p. 138.

As for the play's genre . . . the characters seeking too zealously to be pathetic, Voltaire, *L'Écossaise*, Preface, n.p.

'sourire' in French literary works of the period: the examples are drawn from the ARTFL-Frantext data-base of canonical literary works. From 1650 to 1720, ten-year average frequencies are at 0.0001% and 0.00007%, with no occurrences between 1700 and 1710. There is a subsequent rise of between four- and sixfold in the 1740s. The ten-year frequencies between 1750 and 1789 are between 0.00021% (1750s, 1770s) and 0.00033% (1780s). The Google n-gram ('sourire', 1650–1800) shows a comparable rise in usage. The rise from 1750 is not quite as sharp but this is probably explicable in terms of it being a less literary sample than the ARTFL/Frantext corpus. See p. 185 herein.

63 **the great novels of the English author Samuel Richardson**: Richardson's *oeuvre* nourished the cult of sensibility in England and by ricochet across Europe. Two helpful introductory works to the study of the phenomenon are Janet Todd, *Sensibility: An Introduction* (London, 1986), and John Mullan, *Sentiment and Sociability: The Language of Feeling in the Eighteenth Century* (Oxford, 1988). Also focused on England is G. J. Barker-Benfield, *The Culture of Sensibility: Sex and Society in Eighteenth-century Britain* (Chicago, 1992)—though see G. S. Rousseau, 'Sensibility Reconsidered', *Medical History*, 39 (1995), pp. 375–7. For France, see esp. Anne C. Vila, *Enlightenment and Pathology: Sensibility in the Literature and Medicine of Eighteenth-century France* (Baltimore, MD, 1998) and Jessica Riskin, *Science in the Age of Sensibility: The Sentimental Empiricists of the French Enlightenment* (Chicago, 2002)—both are excellent on the scientific as well as literary and cultural aspects of the phenomenon.

'You cannot go into a house without finding a *Pamela*': Lynn Hunt, *Inventing Human Rights: A History* (New York, 2007), p. 42; and Daniel Mornet, 'Enseignements des bibliothèques privées, 1750–80', *Revue d'histoire littéraire de la France* (1910).

Diderot, the zealous apostle of bourgeois drama: the quotation is from his 'Éloge de Richardson', in Denis Diderot, *Contes et romans*, ed. Michel Delon (Paris, 2004), p. 900. The comparison with Moses, Homer, Sophocles, and Euripides can be found at p. 901.

64 **Jean-Jacques Rousseau's *Julie, ou la Nouvelle Héloïse***: the literature on Rousseau's novel is immense. In terms of links with Richardson over issues of sensibility, see Hunt, *Inventing Human Rights*, esp. ch. 1, 'Torrents of Emotion', pp. 35ff. For eighteenth-century letter-

writing, see Dena Goodman, *The Republic of Letters: A Cultural History of the French Enlightenment* (Ithaca, NY, 1994).

The English divine William Warburton . . . in his post-Regency days: Warburton was writing in 1748. See Michael Sonenscher, *Sans-culottes: An Eighteenth-century Emblem in the French Revolution* (Princeton, NJ, 2008), p. 72.

'Come, fellow men . . . ', Diderot exclaimed: Diderot, 'Éloge de Richardson', p. 900.

65 **The term 'sensibility'**: for the medical and scientific filiations of sensibility, see esp. Vila, *Enlightenment and Pathology* and Riskin, *Science in the Age of Sensibility*.

'What is sensibility? . . . the vivid effect on our soul of an infinity of delicate observations': in a letter to his lover Sophie Volland in 1760, cited in Riskin, *Science in the Age of Sensibility*, p. 1. See too Diderot, 'Éloge de Richardson', p. 898.

66 **the classical theory of laughter**: see p. 29.

philanthropy and *bienfaisance*: Catherine Duprat, *'Pour l'amour de l'humanité': le temps des philanthropes. La philanthropie parisienne des Lumières à la monarchie de Juillet* (Paris, 1993); and Emma Barker, *Greuze and the Painting of Sentiment* (Cambridge, 2005), ch. 7.

the plot of *Clarissa* at times reads like a contest of smiles: *Lettres anglaises*. Citations as follows: Letter 154, t. 1, p.481 ('misleading sweetness'); Letter 27, t. 1, p. 280 ('madman or a lunatic'); Letter 147, t. 3, p. 408 ('Old Satan and I'); Letter 304, t. vi, p. 79 ('tenderness and concern'); Letter 347, t. vi, p. 433 ('a sweet smile beamed joy'; and ff. for the deathbed scene in general). I have used ARTFL to compile this list.

67 **'gaiety was not constrained . . . and tears in the eyes'**: Rousseau, *La Nouvelle Héloise*, (1761, 6e partie), p. 319.

68 **a deluge of fan mail**: this section draws heavily on Robert Darnton. 'Readers Respond to Rousseau', in Robert Darnton, *The Great Cat Massacre and Other Episodes in French Cultural History* (New York, 1985). The quotations are from pp. 242–3.

69 **'I cry . . . I know that I am a man.'**: Louis-Sébastien Mercier, *Du théâtre* (Paris, 1773), p. 133.

twenty-first century psychologists: see Introduction, notes concerning pp. 4–5 herein.

70 **Julie's lover, Saint-Preux, chastises her for having her portrait painted**: *La Nouvelle Héloise* (1761, 2e partie), p. 401.

'the smile of the soul': for Voltaire, see p. 62 herein; Louis-Sébastien Mercier, *Mon Bonnet de nuit, suivi 'Du théâtre' et de textes critiques*, ed. Jean-Claude Bonnet (Paris, 1999), p. 1237.

'a beautiful individual will lack grace . . . without a smile': the quotation is from Voltaire.

71 **Sir *Charles Grandison***: the quotations are from the *Nouvelles lettres anglaises* (1755): Letter 31, p. 309 ('her first smile')'; Letter 98, p. 416 ('Each look of complaisance'); Letter 94, p. 372 ('the charming girl!'); Letter 2, pp. 12–13 ('her colouring'). List compiled with the help of ARTFL.

72 **the great natural historian Buffon**: Georges-Louis Leclerc, comte de Buffon, *Histoire naturelle, générale et particulière*, 44 vols. (Paris, 1749–1804), ii (1749), p. 527.

Greuze specialized in genre painting: see esp. Tom Crow, *Painters and Public Life*, esp. ch. 5; and Barker, *Greuze and the Painting of Sentiment*. Of the paintings, *L'Accordée de village* is at the Louvre; *La Piété filiale* at the State Hermitage Museum, Saint Petersburg; and *La Mère bien-aimée* in a private collection.

'to link together events in ways that would enable the writing of a novel'; Diderot, 'Éloge de Richardson', p. 898. Condillac's view is cited in René Demoris, 'Les Passions en peinture au XVIIIe siècle', in Christiane Mervaud and Sylvain Menant (eds.), *Le Siècle de Voltaire* (Oxford, 1987), p. 381.

Greuze's virtuosity: *Le Gâteau des rois* is held at the Musée Fabre, Montpellier. The comparison with Rubens's *Marie de Médici* is discussed in Percival, *The Appearance of Character*, pp. 59, 115. My interpretation differs from that of Percival. See also p. 133 herein.

CHAPTER 3

75 **Le Grand Thomas**: the life and times of *le Grand Thomas* are covered in Colin Jones, 'Pulling Teeth in Eighteenth-century Paris', *Past and Present*, 166 (2000), and A. Chevalier, 'Un charlatan du XVIIIe siècle: le Grand Thomas', *Mémoires de la Société de l'histoire de Paris et de l'Île-de-France*, 7 (1880). I have gone back to the sources cited by Chevalier and added to them. The micro-history of his life presented in this chapter is based on contemporary sources, most notably: *Avis salutaire au public* (Paris, 1729); *Harangue du Grand Thomas, opérateur pour les dents sur le Pont-Neuf en réjouissance de l'heureux accouchement de la reine et de la naissance du Dauphin* (Paris, 1729); *Désolation du festin du Grand Thomas* (Paris, 1729) (this and the previous two texts can be consulted at BN, Collection Clairambault 1159); *L'Ordre et la marche de l'entrée du Grand Thomas en habit de cérémonie* (Paris 1729: BN, Cabinet des Estampes, Collection Hennin, 57, 5066); *À Monsieur Thomas: des empyriques du siècle le plus illustre et le seul charitable* (Paris, 1736: this one-page undated handbill, with no place of publication, is reproduced in facsimile in Georges Dagen, *Documents pour servir à l'histoire de l'art dentaire en France* (Paris, 1925), p. 107); *Apothéose du Docteur Gros Thomas* (Paris, 1760: facsimile copy in *Le Chansonnier français: recueil de chansons, ariettes, vaudeveilles et autres couplets choisis. XIIe Recueil*, 2 vols. (reprint edn, Geneva, 1971), ii, pp. 117–22. Besides the two engravings shown here, see too *La Véritable Figure du superbe bonnet du Grand Thomas, opérateur sans-pareil*, BN, Collection Clairambault, 1159; and *Le Grand Thomas en son académie d'opérations* (Paris, ?1730: BN, Collection Hennin, 58, 13939). Thomas appears as a figure in the Pont-Neuf landscape in other engravings, for example *Vue particulière du Pont-Neuf, regardant vers le Pont Neuf*, as noted in Chevalier, 'Un charlatan', pp. 77–8.

a worthy heir: see pp. 24-8 herein.

76 **his consultation chamber**: Figure 3.2 also notes: 'Le Grand Thomas en son Hôtel Rue de Tournon donne aussi des Audiances [*sic*] au Public'.

77 **'... So stops my singing muse and all this peroration'**: *À Monsieur Thomas*.

In a play, Le Vaudeville: précis and extracts from the play, written by Panard, are drawn from [Parfaict], *Dictionnaires des théâtres de Paris*, 7 vols. (Paris, 1756), vi, p. 46.

The birth in 1729 of a Dauphin: on this episode, *Avis salutaire* is particularly helpful, and may be complemented by police reports on the set of incidents in Bibliothèque de l'Arsenal, Paris: AB, 10160; and by the account in Edmond J. F. Barbier, *Journal historique et anecdotique du règne de Louis XV*, ed. Arthur de la Villegille, 4 vols. (Paris, 1847–56), i, p. 297. *L'Impromptu du Pont Neuf* is given in full in *Histoire de l'auguste naissance de Monseigneur le Dauphin*, ed. Chevalier Daudet, 3 vols. (Paris, 1731). The play was popular and was revived in 1730 and 1736 in the presence of the duc de Lorraine: *Mémoires pour servir à l'histoire des spectacles de la Foire, par un Acteur romain*, 2 vols. (Paris, 1743), ii, pp. 56, 115, 224.

79 **'... The host spent the day seeing his windows being broken ...'**: the witness was the poet Alexis Piron: see his *Oeuvres*, ed. Édouard Fournier (Paris, 1870), letter xl, and also lxxi and lxxii.

'... a great deal of laughter from the crowd of people gathered round him': cited in Walter Hoffman-Axthelm, *Die Geschichte der Zahnkeilhunde* (Berlin, 1985), p. 223.

'...toothache seemed to approach, only to expire at his feet': Louis-Sébastien Mercier, *Le Tableau de Paris*, 12 vols. (Amsterdam, 1788), i, ch. 50, pp. 160–1.

An anonymous obituary poem for Thomas: *Apothéose*, p. 121.

the inventory of his possessions drawn up . . . after his death: AN, Châtelet de Paris Y15808. See also AN, MC ET/XCVII 361, 362 for documents relating to the succession. In Annik Pardailhé-Galabrun, *La Naissance de l'intime: 3000 foyers parisiens, XVIIe–XVIIIe siècles* (Paris, 1988), the author cites some 884 inventories whose contents she valued between 1727 and 1789. Only twelve (eight nobles or high magistrats, one financier, and three merchants) reached the 50,000 livres mark. Evidently this comparison is rough and ready in that it excludes real estate. But the general point remains: Thomas died owning considerable liquid assets.

80 embodied in the person of Pierre Fauchard: for general background on the emergence of dentistry, see the works cited in notes to p. 21. On Fauchard, see esp. André Besombes and Georges Dagen, *Pierre Fauchard, père de l'art dentaire moderne (1678–1761) et ses contemporains* (Paris, 1961); and Dagen, *Documents pour servir*. These are the main sources pillaged by general historians of dentistry, who invariably tell Fauchard's life in hagiographical mode. For a good account which places Fauchard in the broader context, see Roger King, *The Making of the Dentiste, 1650–1780* (London, 1999). King is excellent on technical aspects—he is a practising dentist himself. These sources provide nearly all the biographical details we have on Fauchard: they also draw strongly on Fauchard's own *Le Chirurgien-dentiste, ou traité des dents*, 2 vols. (Paris, 1728). There were further editions of the latter in 1746 and 1786 (the 1746 one slightly enlarged). See Julien Philippe, 'Le Chirurgien-dentiste ou traité des dents de Pierre Fauchard: une comparaison des trois éditions', *Actes de la Société française d'histoire de l'art dentaire*, 16 (2011). An English translation of Fauchard did not appear until the twentieth century: Pierre Fauchard, *The Surgeon Dentist, or Treatise on the Teeth*, trans. Lillian Lindsay (London, 1946). Although the term *dentiste* appears to be new, the sixteenth-century surgeon Ambroise Paré used the word '*dentateur*' ('dentator' in the original Latin): *Oeuvres*, 11th edn (Lyon, 1652), p. 393.

81 two post-Renaissance works . . . that were worth their salt: namely, Hémard and Martin, for whom see p. 188, n.20 herein. The following reference and quotations are in the unpaginated Preface to Fauchard's 1728 volume. See BIUM. For the medieval and early modern background, see DDAD (esp. articles by Danielle Jacquart, Susan Baddley, Franck Collard, Laurence Moulinier-Brogi, and Bertha Gutierrez Rodilla).

Cours d'opérations chirurgicales: see earlier, Ch. 1, p. 21 herein. See also René-Jacques Croissant de Garengeot, *Traité des opérations de chirurgie* (Paris 1720; numerous later editions in 1720s and 1730s); Guillaume Mauquest de La Motte, *Traité complet de chirurgie* (Paris, 1722). Fauchard is particularly severe on Garengeot in the second edition (1746) of his work.

82 the context of institutional squabbles: this can be followed in Toby Gelfand, *Professionalizing Modern Medicine: Paris Surgeons and Medical Science and Institutions in the Eighteenth Century* (Westport, CT, 1980), esp. chs. 1–3. For Dionis on Parisian surgery's excellent reputation, *Cours d'opérations*, Preface, n.p. For the world of surgery and medicine, see the synoptic overview supplied in Laurence Brockliss and Colin Jones, *The Medical World of Early Modern France* (Oxford, 1997), esp. chs. 3, 4.

83 'a good anatomical surgeon': Dionis, *Cours d'opérations*, Preface (n.p.).

Parisian master wigmakers: see the overview in Michael Kwass, 'Big Hair: A Wig History of Consumption in Eighteenth-century France', *American Historical Review*, 111 (2006). See Gelfand, *Professionalizing Modern Medicine*, p. 38.

Paris surgeons organized a new hierarchy within their own ranks: Gelfand, *Professionalizing Modern Medicine*, pp. 31ff.; Dagen, *Documents pour servir*, pp. 21ff. Note that the 1728 edition of Fauchard recorded that 'ce n'est que depuis peu que dans la ville de Paris on a ouvert les yeux sur cet abus' (unpaginated preface), whereas in the 1746 edition 'depuis peu' is replaced by the words 'environ 1700' (pp. xii–xiii). For herniotomists, see Liliane Pérez and Christelle Rabier, 'Self-machinery: Steel-trusses and the Management of Hernias in Early Modern Europe', *Technology and Culture*, 43 (2013).

84 **Fauchard's reponse . . . was to erect a theoretical distinction**: *Le Chirurgien-dentiste*, ii, pp. 192–3; Preface, unpaginated (for Carmelina: this appears not to have been the Frondeur Carmelina, see p. 28 herein, but his successor, often known as Carmelina Quarante).

   'Some say that they cure toothache . . . gnawing the tooth and causing pain': Fauchard, *Le Chirurgien-dentiste*, i, p. 123; for the following quotation, see ii, pp. 178–9. For the bell reference, see Fig 2.2, where such a bell is indeed shown.

   Fauchard was particularly scathing: Fauchard, *Le Chirurgien-dentiste*, ii, pp. 178–81.

85 **In the preliminary pages . . . of *Le Chirurgien–dentiste***: besides Parisian surgeons, medical luminaries testifying to Fauchard's qualities included Winslow, Silva, Hecquet, and Helvétius. Later editions carried these testimonials at the back of the book.

   gentlemanly science: this is a key concept in the historiography of early modern science. It was first discussed seriously in Simon Schaffer and Steve Shapin, *Leviathan and the Air-Pump: Hobbes, Boyle, and the Experimental Life* (Princeton, NJ, 1985).

87 **'The author also keeps fine sponges . . . the diseases of the mouth'**: Fauchard, *Le Chirurgien-dentiste* (2nd edn, 1746), pp. 368–9.

   A good marriage: the personal details of Fauchard's life can be followed in King, *The Making of the Dentiste*, pp. 98–9 and Dagen, *Pierre Fauchard, passim*.

88 **the pan–European Enlightenment**: Stephane Van Damme, *Paris, capitale philosophique de la Fronde à la Révolution* (Paris, 2005), and, for general background, David Garrioch, *The Making of Revolutionary Paris* (Berkeley, CA, 2002) and Colin Jones, *Paris: Biography of a City* (London, 2004), ch. 6, 'The Kingless Capital of the Enlightenment'.

   an optimistic general account of human progress: most classically outlined in d'Alembert's 'Preliminary Discourse' to the *Encyclopédie*, consultable at ARTFL, *Encyclopédie*. Useful general works on the Enlightenment from the perspective adopted here include Dena Goodman, *The Republic of Letters: A Cultural History of the French Enlightenment* (Ithaca, NY, 1994); Daniel Roche, *La France des Lumières* (Paris, 1993); and Dan Edelstein, *The Enlightenment: A Genealogy* (Chicago, 2010).

89 **'One must laugh at everything'**: Voltaire cited in M. H. Cotoni, 'Le rire, la plainte et le cri dans les dernières années de la correspondance de Voltaire' in C. Biondi et al. (eds.), *La Quête du bonheur et l'expression de la douleur dans la littérature et la pensée françaises* (Geneva, 1995), p. 462; and, for *perfidium ridens*, Liese Andries, 'État des recherches', 'Le Rire', special number, *XVIIIe siècle*, 32 (2002). For French gaiety, besides de Baecque, *Les Éclats du rire*, see Anne Richardot, *Le Rire des Lumières* (Paris, 2002), esp. pp. 129ff.

   literature of sensibility: see above, p. 63 herein. For Voltaire, see Goodman, *Republic of Letters*, p. 4.

   Shaftesbury's theories of morality and politeness: see pp. 45–6 herein.

90 **'Gaiety, activity, politeness and sociability'**: d'Holbach cited in David A. Bell, *The Cult of the Nation in France. Inventing Nationalism, 1680–1800* (Cambridge, MA, 2001), p. 147.

   'consists in being gay': Louis-Antoine Caraccioli, *Paris, le modèle des nations étrangères* (Paris, 1777), p. 317. For Paris as capital of philosophy and science, see Van Damme, *Paris, capitale philosophique*.

'**the home of laughter**': Caraccioli, *Paris, le modèle des nations étrangères, ou l'Europe française*, p. 295 (for beggars), p. 338; Joseph Cérutti cited in Antoine de Baecque, *Les Éclats du rire: la culture des rieurs au XVIIIe siècle* (Paris, 2000), p. 155; David Bindman, *Ape to Apollo: Aesthetics and the Idea of Race in the Eighteenth Century* (Ithaca, NY, 2002), p. 76 (for Kant and the French preference for 'smiling beauty'); Johann-Caspar Lavater, *L'Art de connaître les hommes par la physiognomonie*, ed. Jacques-Louis Moreau de la Sarthe, 10 vols. (Paris, 1806), iv, p. 47; Voltaire is cited in Anne Richardot, *Le Rire des Lumières* (Paris, 2002), p. 129.

'**revolution in people's ideas**': Mercier, *Tableau de Paris*, iv, p 264 ('revolution'); iv, pp. 1–7 ('very different').

91 **English tourists**: Tobias Smollett, *Travels through France and Italy*, ed. F. Felsenstein (Oxford, 1979), esp. Letters VI, VII. More generally, see Jeremy Black, *France and the Grand Tour* (Basingstoke, 2003), esp. ch. 2 ('Paris': Pulteney is cited at p. 25); John Lough, *France on the Eve of Revolution: British Travellers' Observations, 1763–1788* (London, 1987).

a law of gravity in England: Ange Goudar in 1779, cited in Josephine Grieder, *Anglomania in France, 1740–89: Fact, Fiction and Political Discourse* (Geneva, 1985), p. 61 (gravity), p. 62 (parapets). The Swiss visitor was Béat de Murault. He and John Andrews are cited in Anne S. Hargreaves, *White as Whales Bone: Dental Services in Early Modern England* (Leeds, 1998), p. 9.

Meetings and greetings at the royal court: see Colin Jones, 'Meeting, Greeting and Other "Little Customs of the Day" on the Streets in Pre-Revolutionary Paris', *Past and Present*, 2003, Supplement 4 (2009), esp. pp. 154–61.

92 **A public sphere had emerged of voluntaristic, informal groupings**: Jurgen Habermas, *The Structural Transformation of the Public Sphere: An Enquiry into a Category of Bourgeois Society* (Cambridge, MA, 1991); Roger Chartier, *The Cultural Origins of the French Revolution* (Durham, NC, 1991).

the growing commercialization of Parisian society in this period: Daniel Roche, *Le Peuple de Paris: essai sur la culture populaire au XVIIIe siècle* (Paris, 1981); Cissie Fairchilds, 'The Production and Marketing of Populuxe Goods in Eighteenth-century Paris', in John Brewer and Roy Porter (eds.), *Consumption and the World of Goods* (London, 1993); Colin Jones, 'The Great Chain of Buying: Medical Advertisement, the Bourgeois Public Sphere and the Origins of the French Revolution', *American Historical Review*, 101 (1996); and William H. Sewell, Jr, 'The Empire of Fashion and the Rise of Capitalism in Eighteenth-century France', *Past & Present*, 206 (2010). For the inner mechanisms of consumer demand in the period, see too Jan de Vries, *The Industrious Revolution: Consumer Behaviour and the Household Economy, 1650 to the Present* (Cambridge, 2008).

93 **Fashion reached well down the social scale**: besides the works cited above at p. 92 herein, see esp. Daniel Roche, *The Culture of Clothing: Dress and Fashion in the Ancien Régime* (Cambridge, 1994).

'**the theatre is no longer in the theatre**', **Mercier opined**: Mercier, *Le Tableau de Paris*, iv, p. 191.

'**not to offend peoples' eye and nose**': this was the Earl of Chesterfield: *Letters to his Son*, 3 vols. (London, 1774), ii, p. 82; Beaupréau, *Dissertation sur la propriété et la conservation des dents* (Paris, 1764), p. 15.

'**zones of emotional refuge**': William Reddy, *The Navigation of Feeling: A Framework for a History of Emotion* (Cambridge, 2001), p. 145.

94 **Emergent codes of *politesse***: for older forms of *honnêteté*, see p. 34 herein.

'**let us leave the condition of** *honnête homme* . . . **Virtue has nothing to do with it**': *Les Moeurs*, cited in Emmanuel Bury, *Littérature et politesse: l'invention de l'honnête homme, 1580–1750* (Paris, 1996), p. 200; and *Encyclopédie*, viii, p. 287.

95 *petit-maître:* Marivaux's *Le Petit-maître corrigé* (1734) is an example of the genre which is surveyed over the century in the introductory materials in Frédéric Deloffre (ed.), *Marivaux: le petit-maître corrigé* (Geneva, 1995). See too Richardot, *Le Rire des Lumières*, pp. 97ff. Barère is cited in André Monglond, *Le Pré-romantisme* (Paris, 1930), p. 334.

'**laughs are never true and caresses countefeit**': Mercier, *Le Tableau de Paris*, i, p. 310, and v, p. 297. For 'generalised corruption', Mercier, *Du théâtre*, p. 81; and Genlis, *Adèle et Théodore*, Letter 36, p. 282. For these and other references, see ARTFL.

Desirable and desired smiles: I am drawing here on ARTFL/Frantext. See pp. 62, 185 herein.

96 '**the smile of the people**': Mercier, *Le Tableau de Paris*, ii, p. 139.

'**Public opinion**' **was in gestation**: see esp. Chartier, *Cultural Origins*, pp. 20ff. The point about misleading translation is made by Keith Baker in his essay in Craig Calhoun (ed.), *Habermas and the Public Sphere* (London, 1992).

a sizeable fraction of the high nobility . . . within the Parisian public sphere: as is powerfully shown in Antoine Lilti, *Le Monde des salons: sociabilité et mondanité à Paris au XVIIIe siècle* (Paris, 2005).

'**taking up the shuttlecock when it falls from the racquet**': cited in Goodman, *Republic of Letters*, p. 110.

Mercier might vaunt Paris as the home of 'true politeness': *Tableau de Paris*, iv, p. 109 ('true politeness'); v, p. 245 ('speak of ordure').

97 '**What characterizes a civilized nation . . . People are careful to moderate them**': Claude-Henri Watelet, *L'Art de peindre* (Paris, 1770), p. 390. For Mercier, see p. 70 herein.

'**Having mentioned laughing**': Chesterfield, *Letters . . . to his Son*, 3 vols. (London, 1776), i, p. 372. For the 'mirth of the mob', see ii, p. 72.

CHAPTER 4

98 **the progressive loss of his teeth**: the saga may be followed progressively in Abbé Fernando Galiani and Louise d'Épinay, *Correspondance*, 4 vols. (Paris, 1992–5): see esp. the exchanges between them in 1770 and 1771. Madame d'Épinay then lost her own teeth in 1775.

a golden age of dentistry: for Marie-Antoinette, see Maurice Boutry, *Le Mariage de Marie-Antoinette* (Paris, 1904), p. 39. For Laverand, see also Pierre Baron, 'Dental Practice in Paris', in Christine Hillam (ed.), *Dental Practice at the End of the Eighteenth Century* (Amsterdam and New York, 2003), p. 130. On George Washington, Bernhard W. Weinberger, *An Introduction to the History of Dentistry in America*, 2 vols. (Saint-Louis, OH, 1948), ii, p. 171. For Casanova, see George S. Rousseau, 'The Consumption of Meat in an Age of Materialism', in Robert C. Leitz and Kevin L. Cope (eds.), *Imaging the Sciences: Expressions of New Knowledge in the 'Long' Eighteenth Century* (New York, 2004), p. 249.

99 **Grand Tourists**: Chesterfield, *Letters . . . to his Son*, 3 vols. (London, 1776), iii, pp. 73–4; O. Delphin (ed.), *Journal de Madame Cradock: Voyage en France (1783–6)*, p. 330.

Voltaire's 'smile of the soul': see p. 62 herein.

100 **a cadre of dental specialists**: there were 33 of them in 1761 according to Jèze, *Tableau de Paris* (Paris, 1761), p. 6; 36 in 1776 according to *État de médecine, chirurgie et pharmacie*

en Europe pour l'année 1776 (Paris, 1776); and 43 in 1777 according to *État de la médecine, chirurgie et pharmacie en Europe et principalement en France pour l'année 1777* (Paris, 1777).

the alleged wonder-drug orviétan: Claude-Stéphen Le Paulmier, *L'Orviétan: histoire d'une famille de charlatans du Pont-Neuf aux XVIIe et XVIIIe siècles* (Paris, 1893). See too p. 24 herein. For Étienne Bourdet, see Hillam (ed.), *Dental Practice in Europe*, pp. 117–18, 472. For the orviétan episode, see too AN V3 193 (19 May 1764). It is worthy of note that in the 1730s, the Pont-Neuf's *Grand Thomas* was referring to himself as a 'héros dentiste'.

101 **the position of 'inspector of operators'**: for the episode involving being 'inspector of operators' see Pierre Baron, 'Louis Lécluze 1711–92: acteur, auteur poissard, chirurgien-dentiste et entrepreneur de spectacle', Doctoral Thesis: Université de Paris-IV, 2008, p. 28.

Jean-Baptiste Ricci... exhibited exotic animals: see Baron, 'Dental Practice in Paris', pp. 141–3. For the request for exotic animals, AN, MC ET/XXIV 728 (20 September 1751). It seems unlikely that Ricci's demand for tigers from Africa was crowned with success.

no other city in Europe: see the various essays on France, Britain, the Netherlands, Hungary, and Germany in Hillam, *Dental Practice, passim*. The English were particularly recalcitrant to the charms of dentistry: see Colin Jones, 'French Dentists and English Teeth in the Long Eighteenth Century: A Tale of Two Cities and One Dentist', in Roberta Bivins and John V. Pickstone (eds.), *Medicine, Madness and Social History: Essays in Honour of Roy Porter* (Basingstoke, 2007).

strong scientific credentials: see Roger King, *The Making of the Dentiste in France, c.1650–1760* (Aldershot, 1998), esp. pp. 131–45; Robert Bunon, *Expériences et démonstrations faites à l'Hôpital de La Salpêtrière et à S. Côme en présence de l'Académie de Chirurgie* (Paris, 1746), p. 345.

Parisian surgery was even more markedly world-class: see esp. Toby Gelfand, *Professionalizing Modern Medicine: Paris Surgeons and Medical Science and Institutions in the Eighteenth Century* (Westport, CT, 1980), esp. pp. 9–10, 94–5; and Laurence Brockliss and Colin Jones, *The Medical World of Early Modern France* (Oxford, 1997), esp. ch. 9, 'The Rise of Surgery'.

102 **by publishing openly**: Pierre Fauchard, *Le Chirurgien-dentiste ou traité des dents*, 2 vols. (Paris, 1728), Preface, n.p.; Bunon, *Expériences et démonstrations*, 'Avertissement', n.p.

A new body of dental-surgical writing: all of the texts cited are individually discussed in the BIUM website.

Within a few years, Bourdet noted: [Étienne] Bourdet, *Recherches et observations sur toutes les parties de l'art du dentiste*, 2 vols. (Paris, 1746), i, p. vii; Jacques-René Duval, *The Dentiste de la Jeunesse, or the Way to Have Sound and Beautiful Teeth* (London, 1820), p. viii.

a number of serviceable works: these are covered in most conventional histories of dentistry. See too Carlos Gysel, *L'Histoire de l'orthodontie: ses origines, son archéologie et ses précurseurs* (Brussels, 1997), chs. 23–30. For the English, see Jones, 'French Dentists and English Teeth'.

103 **the range of activities in which a dentist could engage**: Pierre Dionis, *Cours d'opérations*, Preface, n.p., and p. 417; and Fauchard, *Le Chirurgien-dentiste*, i, Preface, n.p. See King, *The Making of the Dentiste*, p. 139–40.

five military campaigns: for Lécluze's life and work, see Baron, 'Louis Lécluze', *passim*.

the rhetorical style of natural science deployed by surgeons and physicians: see Baron, 'Louis Lecluze', p. 896. See Claude Mouton, *Essay d'Odontotechnie, ou dissertation sur les dents artificielles* (Paris, 1746), p. 42.

105 **the new dentistry was all about conservation**: see King, *The Making of the Dentiste*, pp. 138–9. On hygiene, see also James C. Riley, *The Eighteenth-century Campaign to Avoid Disease* (London, 1987); Brockliss and Jones, *The Medical World of Early Modern France*, 'The Invention of Hygiene', pp. 459ff.

106 **'conservation instead of destruction'**: Robert Bunon, *Expériences et démonstrations*, p. 9 ('Je veux conserver au lieu de détruire'); Fauchard, *Le Chirurgien-dentiste*, i, esp. Preface, n.p., and ch. 3.

general regimen: Fauchard, *Le Chirurgien-dentiste*, i, esp. ch. 3, 'Le régime et la conduite que l'on doit tenir pour conserver les dents', pp. pp. 41ff., 69.

Mercier could still remember le Grand Thomas touting his wares on the Pont-Neuf: Louis-Sébastien Mercier, *Tableau de Paris*, 12 vols., (Amsterdam, 1788), i, pp. 160–1; v, pp. 74–5. See pp. 75–80 herein for *le Grand Thomas*.

107 **a notable degree of plagiarism**: see Baron, 'Louis Lécluze', esp. pp. 866ff.

convenience now came politely wrapped: Fauchard, *Le Chirurgien-dentiste* (2nd edn, Paris, 1746), ii, p. 346.

bourgeois clients could feel at home: for Bourdet, see p. 99 herein. The information given is based on the post mortem inventories of the individuals involved in the Minutier Central at the Archives Nationales in Paris, AN MC ET/XL 303, 17 November 1751 (Claude Jacquier de Géraudly); AN MC ET/XCII, 19 August 1786 (Le Roy de la Faudignière); AN MC ET/IX 824, 16 October 1789 (Étienne Bourdet); and AN MC ET/XLI 848, 13 July 1819 (Jules Ricci). The relevant document for Claude Mouton is the post-mortem sale of his main property: AN MC ET/XXXIII 508, 8 April 1751. There is biographical information on several of these individuals in Baron, 'Dental Practice in Paris', pp. 132–8, 117–18, 141–3. For Greuze's 'Epiphany', see p. 72 herein.

109 **emergent nerve theory**: see pp. 65–6 herein. And for the particularly sensitive, see Lindsay B. Wilson, *Women and Medicine in the French Enlightenment: The Debate over 'Maladies des Femmes'* (Baltimore, MD, 1993).

the new dentist's armamentarium: Fauchard, *Le Chirurgien-dentiste*, i. p. 184; ii, for instrumentation; Louis Laforgue, *Dix-sept articles relatifs aux maladies des dents* (Paris, Year VIII [= 1800]), ii, p. 200. Laforgue was admitted as a dentist in 1785: see Baron, 'Dental Practice in Paris', pp. 128–9.

110 **By deferring extraction**: Fauchard, *Le Chirurgien-dentiste*; Anselme Jourdain, *Traités des maladies et des opérations réellement chirurgicales de la bouche*, 2 vols. (Paris, 1778), ii, pp. 4–5. For these client-based concerns (including the sofa), see esp. Fauchard, *Le Chirurgien-Dentiste*, esp. i, pp. 144ff. The sensibility quotation comes from Mahon, *Le Citoyen dentiste* (Paris, Year VI = 1798), pp. 186. Mahon practised in Paris from the 1790s and on pp. 182–6 paints a nostalgic image of pre-Revolution dentistry.

111 **'an intuitive sense of delicacy, tact, great skill and a real sensibility'**: for an update on Fauchard's advice (*Le Chirurgien-dentiste*, i, pp. 144ff.), see F. Maury, *Traité complet de l'art du dent, d'après l'état actuel des connaissances*, 3rd edn (Paris 1841)—including a tip about location on the second floor. For the floor position, see Dionis, *Cours d'opérations*, p. 425; and for the head under the arm, Louis Lécluze du Thilloy, *Nouveaux Éléments d'odontologie, contenant l'anatomie de la bouche ou la description de toutes les parties qui la composent et de leur usage* (Paris, 1754), pp. 124–5.

112 **to build up their client base . . . that had most money to spend**: the estimations are based on addresses given in Baron, 'Dental Practice in Paris', compared against those of the two 1776–7 works entitled *État de la médecine* (see pp. 202–3, n.100 herein). For the social

complexion of the neighbourhoods involved, see *Atlas de la Révolution française: XI. Paris*, ed. Emile Ducoudray, Raymonde Monnier, and Daniel Roche (Paris, 2000), p. 30.

Jean-Baptiste Ricci when he had a tooth problem: *Journal of My Life by Jacques-Louis Ménétra*, ed. Daniel Roche (New York, 1986), p. 21. For case-histories, see for example Fauchard, *Le Chirurgien-dentiste*, and for advertisements see note for p. 114 herein.

113 **archaeological evidence**: see the works cited in the note for p. 9 herein.

mal du siècle: Philip Riedler, *La Figure du patient au XVIIIe siècle* (Geneva, 2010), p. 97.

Isabelle de Charrière: cited in Riedler, *La Figure du patient*, p. 97.

smile anxieties: Ricci, *Réflexions sur la conservation des dents, les maladies qui les affectent et les Remèdes qui leur conviennent* (Reims, n.d.), p. 3.

114 **Print acted to bring together suppliers and clients**: for advertisements, see Colin Jones, 'The Great Chain of Buying: Medical Advertisement, the Bourgeois Public Sphere and the Origins of the French Revolution', *American Historical Review*, 101 (1996). See too Pierre Baron and Xavier Deltombe, 'Dental Products in France in the Eighteenth Century: Their Production, Distribution, Commercialisation', *Dental Historian*, 32 (1997). Significantly, of the dental works cited in the following paragraphs, only Bourdet and Hébert have been picked up as contributors to dental science in the BIUM website. Bourdet's work was entitled *Soins faciles pour la propreté de la bouche et pour la conservation des dents, suivi de l'art de soigner les pieds* (Lausanne, 1782).

115 **'Great Chain of Buying'**: Jones, 'Great Chain of Buying'.

'gives grace to their smile': Jean-Louis Colondre, *Essai sur les plus fréquentes maladies des dents et des moyens propres à les prévenir et à les guérir* (Geneva, 1791), pp. vii.

'the beauty of teeth is not a point of coquetry': Étienne Bourdet, *Soins faciles pour la propreté de la bouche et pour la conservation des dents* (Paris, 1759), p. vi; Anselme Jourdain, *L'Art de se conserver en santé* (Paris, Year IV [= 1796]), p. 275 (Jourdain was also the author of *Traité des maladies . . . de la bouche*, published in 1778).

116 **convenience, comfort, and good health**: Claude Géraudly, *L'Art de conserver les dents* (Paris, 1737), p. viii–ix. Michael Kwass makes a very similar case for wigs, which are also often seen as an emulative, trickle-down phenomenon: see his 'Ordering the World of Goods: Consumer Revolution and the Classification of Objects in Eighteenth-century France', *Representations*, 82 (2003); and Michael Kwass, 'Big Hair: A Wig History of Consumerism in Eighteenth-century France', *American Historical Review*, 111 (2006). For herniotomists, see Liliane Pérez and Christelle Rabier, 'Self-machinery: Steel-trusses and the Management of Hernias in Early Modern Europe', *Technology and Culture*, 54 (2013). For the editorial rhetoric, see Jones, 'Great Chain of Buying', esp. pp. 19–25.

an uphill, but patriotic struggle: for anxieties about children's teeth, see discussions in the *Encyclopédie*, as cited in Colin Jones, 'Bouches et dents dans l'*Encyclopédie*: une perspective sur l'anatomie et la chirurgie des Lumières', in Robert Morrissey and Philippe Roger (eds.), *L'Encyclopédie: du réseau au livre et du livre au réseau* (Paris, 2001), pp. 81–2; Louis Lécluze, *Eclaircissements essentiels pour parvenir à préserver les dents de la carie et à les conserver jusqu'à l'extrême vieillesse* (Paris, 1755), pp. 5, 20.

the issue of speech and enunciation: for the *Encyclopédie*, see Jones, 'Bouche et dents', *passim*. For Galiani, see p. 98 herein. Bourdet, *Recherches et observations*, ii, pp. 211–12.

117 **Loss of teeth . . . disenfranchisement from society and worse**: Lécluze, *Nouveaux Éléments*, pp 22–3; Honoré Gaillard Courtois, *Le Dentiste observateur* (Paris, 1775), pp. 44–5.

118 **Tooth conservation and beautification were held to start at home**: for the tongue-scraper (with illustration), see Lécluze, *Nouveaux éléments*, p. 217. For the toothbrush, see Sacha Bogopolsky, *La Brosse à dents ou l'histoire de la 'mal aimée'* (Paris, 1995), and Sacha Bogopolsky, *Itinéraire culturel et technologique de la brosse à dents* (Paris, 1999), esp. pp. 19–23. The author underestimates the broad use of the toothbrush in France over the eighteenth cemtury. See examples in Riedler, *La Figure du patient*, e.g. p. 53.

'**physicians of the self**': Jean A. Hébert, *Le Citoyen dentiste, ou l'art de seconder la nature pour se conserver les dents, et les entretenir propres* (Lyon 1778), p. 31.

might seem like professional suicide: interestingly, similar arguments about the relationship between self-help and professional support are evident as regards razors and shaving in Alun Withey, 'Shaving and Masculinity in Eighteenth-century Britain', *Journal of Eighteenth-century Studies*, 36 (2012). For France, see esp. Jean-Jacques Perret, *La Pogotonomie, ou l'art d'apprendre à se raser soi-méme* (Paris, 1769).

119 **the wherewithal of personal mouth care**: Géraudly, *L'Art de conserver les dents*, pp. 157–60. Many other dental works advertised either implicitly or explicitly. Explicit advertisements were often at the back of their books. See p. 87 herein. The Parisian newspaper-advertiser, the *Affiches de Paris*, was full of publicity for dental products. See Jones, 'Great Chain of Buying', pp. 27–30.

Two million pots of rouge were sold throughout France in 1781 alone: for *le fard* and cosmetics and rouge, Lanoë, *La Poudre et le fard*, esp. p.293.

a more substantial part of their income: Pierre Baron, 'Dental Practice in Selected Areas of France', in Hillam (ed.), *Dental Practice*, pp. 60–3; for Le Roy de la Faudignière's business, see pp. 132–8. For the stock revealed in post-mortem inventories: Le Roy de la Faudignière AN MC ET/XCII, 19 August 1786 (especially medicine bottles) and for Billard, AN MC ET/I 117, 4 June 1751. For false teeth and hippopotamus jaw, see p. 137 herein.

120 '**a satellite revolving round a whirlwind**': Mercier, *Tableau de Paris*, iv, p. 258.

121 **existing modes of behaviour at court**: for wigs, see Kwass, 'Big Hair'. For *le fard* and cosmetics and rouge, Lanoë, *La Poudre et le fard*, esp. p. 293.

crème de beauté: Martin, *Selling Beauty*, p. 123.

some movement away from Louis-Quatorzian models: Jean de Viguerie, 'Le Roi et le "public": l'exemple de Louis XV', *Revue historique*, 278 (1987). The courtier was the duc de Croy, cited in Colin Jones, *Madame de Pompadour: Images of a Mistress* (London, 2002), p. 51.

122 **a rare Enlightenment enthusiast for the beard**: J. A. D[ulaure], *Pogonologie, ou histoire philosophique de la barbe* (Constantinople and Paris, 1769), p. xi–xii.

Courtiers and *petits-maîtres*: see p. 95 herein.

Rousseau's strongly gendered writings: for Rousseau and gender, see esp. Dena Goodman, *The Republic of Letters: A Cultural History of the French Enlightenment* (Ithaca, NY, 1994); Joan Landes, *Women and the Public Sphere in the Age of Democratic Revolution* (Ithaca, NY, 1988).

new idealized forms of virility: for Winckelman, Édouard Pommier, 'La Vision de l'antiquité classique dans la France des Lumières et de la Révolution', *Revue de l'Art*, 83 (1989); Édouard Pommier, *Winckelmann: naissance de l'histoire de l'art* (Paris, 2003), and for David, Thomas E. Crow, *Painters and Public Life in Eighteenth-century Paris* (London, 1985). For neo-classicism generally, Guillaume Faroult, Christophe Leribault, and Guilhem Scherf (eds.), *L'Antiquité révée: innovations et résistances au XVIIIe siècle* (Paris, 2011).

123 **he placed his talents at the disposal of French republicanism**: see p. 150 herein.

institutional reorganization of medicine: Louis XV's support for the surgeons is highlighted esp. by Gelfand, *Professionalizing Modern Medicine*. See p. 82 herein.

new-style dentists in the court medical entourage: AN O1 63 (18 November 1719); 68 (14 January 1724). See also AN O1 79 (13 December 1735); and King, *The Making of the Dentiste*, pp. 183–4. Caperon was awarded prized lodging in the Louvre and property in the town of Versailles where he built a mansion; and he was ennobled in 1745: AN O1 80 (30 January 1740), 92 (1 March 1748), 94 (19 July 1750), 99 (12 February 1755). AN O1 89 (December 1745). Charles-Philippe Albert, duc de Luynes, *Mémoires sur la cour de Louis XV*, 17 vols. (Paris, 1908), viii, p. 303.

124 **some repositioning of the teeth**: see the anonymous 'Journal de police sous Louis XV (1742–3)', in Edmond-Jean-François Barbier, *Chronique de la Régence et du règne de Louis XV (1718–63)*, 8 vols. (Paris, 1857–66), p. 199. See Luynes, *Mémoires*, iv, 282–3.

Succeeding him in post was Mrs Cradock's Étienne Bourdet: for Bourdet, see *passim* and Baron, 'Dental Practice in Paris', pp. 117–18. He too was ennobled: AN O1 111 (November 1757). See AN O1 105 (5 December 1761). His postmortem inventory is at AN MC ET/IX/824 (19 October 1789). For Dubois-Foucou, see King, *The Making of the Dentiste*, p. 186; Baron, 'Dental Practice in Paris', p. 123. The purchase of reversion to the post is set out in a contract located at AN MC ET/IX/827 (27 March 1783).

Royal support for Parisian dentists: Luynes, *Mémoires*, viii., p. 303. Changes within the other posts within the royal medical household can be followed in successive annual editions of the *Almanach Royal*. See too AN MC ET/LXXXIX 596 (Mouton 'opérateur ordinaire du roi et son dentiste', 16 February 1761); AN MC ET/XL/303 (Géraudly's will, 17 November 1751); and, more generally, Jones, 'The King's Two Teeth', *passim*.

125 **growing weary of his mistress**: René Louis de Voyer de Paulmy, marquis d'Argenson, *Journal et mémoires*, ed. Edme J. B. Rathery (Paris, 1859–67), ii, p. 179.

supremely unconcerned about the state of his mouth: for the 1742 incident, see d'Argenson, *Journal et mémoires*, iii, p. 260. For Mme de Vintimille, see ii, p. 392; iv, p. 386. And for Louis XVI's leg and Artois's mouth, see Félix, comte d'Hezeques, *Souvenirs d'un page à la cour de Louis XVI* (Paris, 1873), pp. 6, 60.

particularly for their children: for Marie-Thérèse, Luynes, *Mémoires*, ix, p. 26; and for Madame Victoire, ix, pp. 11–12.

126 **'burials, deaths and surgical operations'**: such was the judgement of Louis's long-serving minister, the duc de Choiseul, *Mémoires*, ed. Jean-Pierre Guicciardi and Philippe Bonnet (Paris, 1987), pp. 192–3; for the *eau de Luce* incident, see Luynes, *Mémoires*, ii, p. 29.

127 **'Such things . . . are essential business in *ce pays-ci*'**: Vicomte de Reiset, *Joséphine de Savoie, comtesse de Provence* (Paris, 1913), pp. 58–9. The phrase, *ce pays-ci*, was classic insider jargon at Versailles for referring to the court.

The case of queen Marie-Antoinette confirmed this: Boutry, *Le Mariage de Marie-Antoinette*, p. 36; Chateaubriand, *Mémoires d'outre-tombe*, ed. Maurice Levaillant and Georges Moulinier, 2 vols. (Paris, 1951), i, p. 167.

sketched minutes after her execution: The French Senate contains a remarkable drawing, allegedly by Jacques-Louis David, of the queen's severed head.

CHAPTER 5

128 **Louis-Sébastien Mercier noted in his** *Tableau de Paris* **in 1781**: Louis-Sébastien Mercier, *Tableau de Paris*, 12 vols. (Amsterdam, 1788), v, p. 74. The first volumes of this work had been published in 1781.

the so-called 'Pre-Revolution': for a brief overview, see Colin Jones, *The Great Nation: France from Louis XV to Napoleon (1715–99)* (London, 2002), ch. 8. For mesmerism, see Robert Darnton; *Mesmerism and the End of the Enlightenment in France* (Cambridge, MA, 1968); and for ballooning, Marie Thébaud-Sorger, *L'Aérostation au temps des Lumières* (Rennes, 2009).

129 **In the Academy of Painting in the early 1780s**: the La Harpe episode is noted in the Vigée Le Brun memoirs: *Souvenirs*, 3 vols. (Paris, 2011), i, p. 36. See generally Melissa Percival, 'The Expressive Heads of Élisabeth Louise Vigée Le Brun', *Gazette des Beaux-Arts* (November 2001); and see p. 1 herein.

neo-classical aesthetics: Denis Diderot, *Salons*, ed. Jean Seznec, 4 vols. (Oxford, 1957–66), iii, p. 338; Carmontelle is cited in André Monglond, *Le Préromantisme* (Paris, 1930), p. 328. See p. 62 herein, for traditional views about open mouths in portraits.

130 **the 'smile of the soul'**: see p. 70 herein. Vigée Le Brun, *Souvenirs*, i, p. 22 (*Clarissa*); iii, p. 137 (pilgrimages).

his numerous subtly animated portraits: for La Tour, see Xavier Salmon, *Le Voleur d'âmes: Maurice Quentin de La Tour* (Paris, 2004), esp. 'L'Image de soi: auto-portraits et portraits', pp. 47ff. Although facial animation is a particular feature of La Tour's work, teeth are very rare in his portraits. See esp. the musician Manelli and Marguerite Lecomte (both 1753). Thanks to Mechtild Fend for drawing the latter to my attention.

in the guise of Democritus: see pp. 57–9 herein on this theme. An overview of the Democritus theme is given by Anne Richardot, 'Un philosophe au purgatoire des Lumières', *Dix-huitième siècle: numéro special, Le Rire*, 32 (2000). For Watteau as Democritus, see p. 58 herein. For La Mettrie, see the well-known engraving, *c.*1760, by Georg Friedrich Schmidt, that was much recopied. For Lequeu, Philippe Duboy, *Jean-Jacques Lequeu: une énigme* (Paris, 1977). And for Ducreux, Martial Guédron, *L'Art de la grimace: cinq siècles d'excès de visage* (Paris, 2011), pp. 121ff. (also excellent for the re-emergence of the grimace in French culture at this time). Messerschmidt's heads are analysed in Maraike Buckling (ed.), *The Fantastic Heads of Franz Xaver Messerschmidt* (Frankfurt, 2004): see esp. pp. 106–15, 'The Artist as He imagined Himself Laughing'. (In fact he seems to be smiling, but showing his teeth.)

131 **genre paintings**: see p. 72 herein. For the emergence of art criticism, see Richard Wrigley, *The Origins of French Art Criticism from the Ancien Régime to the Restoration* (Oxford, 1993); and Diderot, *Salons*. For views on Le Brun's shortcomings as regards the subtlety of emotional expression, see Melissa Percival, *The Appearance of Character: Physiognomy and Facial Expression in Eighteenth-century France* (London, 1999), esp. ch. 3; and Linda Walsh, 'The Expressive Face: Manifestations of Sensibility in Eighteenth-century French Art', *Art History*, 19 (1996). Percival and Walsh also discuss Caylus's *tête d'expression* competitions. For *passions douces*, Percival, *The Appearance of Character*, p. 104.

132 **Sophie Arnould**: for Sophie Arnould, see Colin Jones, 'French Crossings IV: Vagaries of Passion and Power in Enlightenment France', *Transactions of the Royal Historical Society*, 23 (2013). For the Arnould portrait, see Anne Poulet, Guilhem Scherf, and Ulrike Mathies, *Jean-Antoine Houdon, Sculptor of the Enlightenment* (Washington, DC, 2003), pp. 96–103 and, for Gluck, pp. 104–9.

expressive eyes turned upwards towards the heavens: see p. 72 herein.

133 **the traditional categories for whom artistic decorum permitted an open mouth**: see Vigée Le Brun's portrait of the Neapolitan composer Paisiello in 1791, also shown with his teeth exposed.

'Head of a young girl, in plaster': Poulet et al., *Jean-Antoine Houdon*, pp. 133–6. For Greuze, see p. 72 herein.

134 **a courter of controversy**: besides Vigée Le Brun's own *Souvenirs*, see the biographical analyses of Mary Sheriff, *The Exceptional Woman: Elisabeth Vigée Le Brun and the Cultural Politics of Art* (Chicago, 1996); and Angelica Goodden, *The Sweetness of Life: A Biography of Elisabeth-Louise Vigée Le Brun* (London, 1997). On the *chemise* episode, see Vigée Le Brun, *Souvenirs*, i, pp. 65–6, and Sheriff, *The Exceptional Woman*, pp. 143–5.

135 **Pierre-Charles Levesque**: from the *Encyclopédie méthodique. Beaux-Arts*, vol. 2, cited in Tony Halliday, *Facing the Public: Portraiture in the Aftermath of the French Revolution* (Manchester, 1999), p. 18.

resented the increasing tendency ... rather than being in accordance with academic criteria: for resentment over bourgeois clients' passion for portraits, see Halliday, *Facing the Public*, pp. 5ff. See p. 92 herein for the growth of the Parisian public sphere in the eighteenth century.

others followed further down the track indicated in the 1787 portrait: see the discussion of portraiture in the late 1790s in Halliday, *Facing the Public*.

136 **Nicolas Dubois de Chémant**: the main source for Dubois de Chémant's life is Georges Dagen, 'Dubois de Chémant', in Dagen, *Documents pour servir à l'histoire de l'art dentaire en France, principalement à Paris* (Paris, 1925), 'Nicolas Dubois de Chémant'. See too Pierre Baron, 'Dental Practice in Paris', in Christine Hillam (ed.), *Dental Practice in Europe at the End of the Eighteenth Century* (Amsterdam, 2003), pp. 120–2. For false teeth generally, see J. Woodforde, *The Strange Story of False Teeth* (London, 1968), esp. chs. 7, 8, 9 (based almost entirely on Dagen). Invaluable are Dubois's own writings, notably his *Dissertation sur les avantages des nouvelles dents et râteliers artificiels incorruptibles et sans odeur* (Paris, 1788). This was translated into English in supplemented editions: *A Dissertation on Artificial Teeth in General* (London, 1797; new edn, 1816). Fig. 5.6 is taken from the English language version. See the latter, p. 2, for the story of the origins of the idea of such teeth. For Fauchard, Pierre Fauchard, *Le Chirurgien-dentiste, ou traité des dents*, 2 vols. (Paris, 1728), esp. ii, chs. 13–19.

from the time of the pharaohs: see general histories of dentistry, plus Thierry Bardinet, 'Dentistes et soins dentaires à l'époque des pharaons', in DDAD.

138 **the first author in England to publish on the noble art of tooth-pulling**: Charles Allen, *The Operator for the Teeth*, ed. Robert A. Cohen (London, 1964 [1685]), p. 11. For Talma and his family, see Robert A. Cohen, 'The Talma Family', in Cohen, *Selected Papers* (London, 1997); and Baron, 'Dental Practice in Paris', pp. 143–4. For 'Waterloo Teeth', Stephanie Pain, 'The Great Tooth Robbery', *New Scientist*, 16 June 2001.

live teeth from the living poor to provide for the rich: Mark R. Blackwell, ' "Extraneous Bodies": The Contagion of Live-tooth Transplantation in Late-Eighteenth-century England', *Eighteenth-century Life*, 28 (2004); Thomas Rowlandson's print, 'Transplanting of Teeth' (1787); Dubois de Chémant, *A Dissertation on Artificial Teeth* (London, 1797), pp. 18, 20n. See John Hunter, *The Natural History of the Human Teeth* (London, 1778), pp. 126–8; John Hunter, *Treatise on the Venereal Disease* (London, 1786), p. 391.

139 **an unexpected compliment**: see the discussion of comfort, convenience, and health in advertising, pp. 105–10 herein.

as widespread among the population as wigs: Dubois-Foucou, *Exposé de nouveaux procédés pour la confection des dents dites de composition* (Paris, 1808), p. 39.

140–1 **'E'en helpless infants . . . our friend in need'**: I have taken the translation from the English 1816 translation of Dubois's puff, pp. 80–1.

Camille Desmoulins stood on a coffee-house table: René Farge, 'Une épisode de la journée du 12 juillet 1789: Camille Desmoulins au Jardin du Palais-Royal', *Annales révolutionnaires*, 7 (1914).

'the smile of the people is worth more than the favour of kings': cited in Mercier, *Tableau de Paris*, ii, p. 139. I have been unable to track down the quotation in Marmontel's works.

142 **'all eyes were wet with tears'**: the deputy Mounier, cited in William H. Sewell, Jr, 'Historical Events as Transformations of Structures: Inventing Revolution at the Bastille', *Theory and Society*, 25 (1996), p. 854. See too Antoine de Baecque, ' "Les Ris et les pleurs": spectacle des affections, 1790–1', in Beatrice de Andia and Valérie Noëlle Jouffre (eds.), *Fêtes et Révolution* (Dijon, 1989). (Note that I have translated '*ris*' as smile in this instance. See the discussion at p. 30 herein.)

a new politics grounded in the Rights of Man: for linkages between the Enlightenment project of human perfectibility and the Revolution's Rights of Man, see Lynn Hunt, *Inventing Human Rights: A History* (New York, 2007). For the relationship with the Declaration of Independence, see Stephan Rials, *La Déclaration des droits de l'homme et du citoyen* (Paris, 1988), esp. pp 360ff. For the quotation, see Lynn Hunt, *The French Revolution and Human Rights: A Brief Documentary History* (New York, 1996), p. 15. And for the American Revolution as less progressive, see David Armitage and Sanjay Subrahmanyam (eds.), *The Age of Revolutions in Global Context, c.1760–1840* (New York, 2010). The 'ardent revolutionary' was Antoine-Louis Saint-Just: see p. 146 herein.

A 'new man': see Mona Ozouf, 'Régénération' in Mona Ozouf and François Furet, *Dictionnaire critique de la Révolution française* (Paris, 1988).

143 **no laughter in its debates**: Antoine de Baecque, *Les Éclats du rire: la culture des rieurs au XVIIIe siècle* (Paris, 2000), 'Hilarités parlementaires', pp. 203–4; pp. 257 ff. for Gorsas's views; pp. 184ff for Cérutti's 'smiling [*réjouissante*] physiognomy'; and de Baecque, *Le Corps de l'histoire: métaphores et politique (1770–1800)* (Paris, 1993), p. 315.

Tennis-Court Oath: Philippe Bordes, *Le Serment du Jeu de Paume de David: le peintre, son milieu et son temps de 1789 à 1792* (Paris, 1983). See p. 140 herein.

144 **'This nation, so gay, so witty, so ready to laugh'**: de Baecque, *Les Éclats du rire*, p. 207.

'moderation' was becoming a dirty word: Henriette Walter, *Des mots sans-culottes* (Paris, 1989), pp. 160–1.

'France isn't laughing any more': de Baecque, *Les Éclats du rire*, p. 136. See p. 226 ('laughter wars'); pp. 136ff. (for the *Actes des apôtres*); p. 141 ('sign of counter-revolution'). See also Georges Minois, *Histoire du rire et de la déraison* (Paris, 2000), ch. 12, pp. 427ff.

war was declared: Jones, *The Great Nation*, ch. 10, for the entry into warfare and its impact on revolutionary culture, including during the Terror. For the Terror generally, see David Andress, *The Terror: Civil War in the French Revolution* (London, 2005); and Keith Baker, *The French Revolution and the Creation of Modern Political Culture*, IV: *The Terror* (Oxford, 1987).

145 **full-throated plebeian humour**: de Baecque, *Les Éclats du rire*, esp. pp. 226ff. for anti-aristocratic laughter. See Minois, *Histoire du rire*, pp. 428ff. Curiously, Hébert's Père Duchesne (or Duchêne) has not spawned a lively scholarship. See though, Gérard Walter, *Hébert et 'Le Père Duchesne'* (Paris, 1946). For denunciation as a political virtue,

Jacques Guilhaumou, 'Fragments of a Discourse of Denunciation (1789–94)', in Baker, *The Terror*.

146 **managed a faint smile**: de Baecque, *Les Éclats du rire*, citing Hébert, pp. 284–7.

'Face too jolly to be accounted a true republican': cited in Lise Andries, 'État des recherches', *Dix-huitième siècle: numéro spécial, Le Rire*, 32 (2000), p. 18.

Saint-Just: 'La dissimulation sourit; l'innocence s'afflige'. Saint-Just, *Oeuvres* (Paris, 2004), p. 606. For smiles at the royal court, see pp. 120–1 herein. For Couthon's remark, Jon Cowans, *To Speak for the People: Public Opinions and the Problem of Legitimacy in the French Revolution* (London, 2001), p. 135. And for the prohibition on carnival masks, see Antoine de Baecque, *Le Corps de l'histoire: métaphores et politique (1770–1800)* (Paris, 1993), p. 329.

147 **the tumbril journey**: an excellent source for the conduct of prisoners and the executed under the Terror is the account of the public executioner Charles-Henri Sanson: *La Révolution française vue par son bourreau*, ed. Monique Lebailly (Paris, 1988), esp. pp. 106–9 (Madame de Barry); p. 188 (Paris parlementaires); p. 201 (Malesherbes); p. 128 (prisoners in the gaols); and pp. 134–5 (wine-quaffing).

148 **They treated misfortune like a naughty child . . . you will never stop us being loveable**: *Mémoires du comte Beugnot*, ed. A. Beugnot, 2 vols. (Paris, 1866), p. 203 (inc. Mme Roland's execution). More generally, see Paul Friedland, *Seeing Justice Done: The Age of Spectacular Capital Punishment in France* (Oxford, 2012).

her 'Nouvelle Héloise' moment: Manon Phlipon, *Mémoires de Madame Roland*, ed. Paul de Roux (Paris 1986), p. 302. See too Sian Reynolds, *Marriage and Revolution: Monsieur and Madame Roland* (Oxford, 2012), esp. pp. 56, 70, 277. Sanson, *La Révolution française vue par son bourreau*, pp. 82–4. The smile on the way to the scaffold is corroborated by an eye-witness: see *Mémoires de Madame Roland*, p. 28.

149 **a generation of Rousseau-lovers**: Sanson, *La Révolution française vue par son bourreau*, pp. 62–5 (Charlotte Corday); pp. 166 and 182 (the Desmoulins couple); and p. 204 (Madame Elisabeth). There are numerous other eye-witness accounts of these events, which are largely corroboratory. Some are covered in H. Fleischmann, *La Guillotine en 1793* (Paris, 1908).

'weapon of the weak': the phrase has become familiarized through James C. Scott, *Weapons of the Weak: Everyday Forms of Peasant Resistance* (New Haven, CT, 1985).

official festivities: Mona Ozouf, *La Fête révolutionnaire, 1789–99* (Paris, 1976); de Baecque, 'Ris et pleurs' (for 14 July 1790).

150 **Jacques-Louis David became official pageant-master**: David L. Dowd, *Pageant-master of the Republic: Jacques-Louis David and the French Revolution* (Lincoln, Nebraska, 1948).

David's political mentor, Maximilien Robespierre: David was an ardent follower of Robespierre. The best recent biographies of the latter are Ruth Scurr, *Fatal Purity: Robespierre and the French Revolution* (New York, 2006) and Peter McPhee, *Robespierre: A Revolutionary Life* (New Haven and London, 2012). Robespierre's smile is evoked in the memoirs of his sister, Charlotte: *Mémoires de Charlotte Robespierre sur ses deux frères*, 2nd edn (Paris, 1835), p. 68. On this theme too, see Colin Jones, 'French Crossings III: The Smile of the Tiger', *Transactions of the Royal Historical Society*, 21 (2012). For the (possibly) smiling portrait, see Anne-Marie Passez, *Adelaïde Labille-Guiard, 1749–1803: biographie et catalogue raisonné de son oeuvre* (Paris, 1973), pp. 248–9.

a tumour around his lip: for David's facial tumour, see T. J. Clark, 'Gross David with the Swoln Cheek: An Essay in Self-Portraiture', in *Rediscovering History: Culture, Politics and the Psyche*, ed. Michael Roth (Stanford, 1994); and Hutan Ashrafian, 'Jacques-Louis

David and his Post-traumatic Facial Pathology', *Journal of the Royal Society of Medicine*, 100 (2007).

he possessed a toothbrush: the Barras incident is recounted in Barras, *Mémoires*, ed. Georges Duruy, 4 vols. (Paris, 1895), i, p. 149.

151 **'like the weediest of little women'**: Fleischmann, *La Guillotine en 1793*, p. 182. For Saint-Just on Hérault de Séchelles, see Marisa Linton, '"The Tartuffes of Patriotism": Fears of Conspiracy in the Political Language of Revolutionary Government, France 1793–4', in Barry Coward and Julian Swann (eds.), *Conspiracies and Conspiracy in Early Modern Europe from the Waldensians to the French Revolution* (London, 2004), p. 250; and also Philippe Buchez and Pierre Roux, *Histoire parlementaire de la Révolution française*, 40 vols. (Paris, 1833–8): xxxii, esp. pp. 220 (Desmoulins) and pp. 210, 214 (Danton).

The overthrow of Robespierre's Committee of Public Safety: see Jones, *The Great Nation*, pp. 494 and, for the Thermidorian and Directorial period, ch. 11; and Martin Lyons, *France under the Directory* (Cambridge, 1975).

152 **as Couthon, Saint-Just and Robespierre had all urged**: see pp. 146–7 and 151 herein.

Physiognomy was in the process of resurrection: for 'physionomie' in the Enlightenment, see p. 71 herein. Lavater's work in English and French has tended to become better known in recent years through works focused on the impact of his writings on nineteenth-century culture. See esp. in this vein Melissa Percival and Graeme Tytler (eds.), *Physiognomy in Profile: Lavater's Impact on European Culture* (Newark, Delaware, 2005); Sibylle Erle, *Blake, Lavater, and Physiognomy* (London, 2010); Lucy Hartley, *Physiognomy and the Meaning of Expression in Nineteenth-century Culture* (Cambridge, 2001); and Sharrona Pearl, *About Faces: Physiognomy in Nineteenth-century Britain* (London, 2010). Buffon is cited in Percival, *The Appearance of Character*, p. 30. See also Guédron, *L'Art de la grimace*. Lavater's works started to appear in German in the early 1770s: see esp. his *Physiognomische Fragmente*, 4 vols. (Leipzig, 1775–8). Later editions were added to progressively. The first French edition of his work was *Essai sur la physiognomonie destiné à faire connaître l'homme et à le faire aimer*, 4 vols. (The Hague, 1781–1803). What became the standard work was published by Louis-Jacques Moreau de la Sarthe after Lavater's death as *L'Art de connaître les hommes par la physiognomonie*, 10 vols. (Paris, 1806). The *Lavater portatif* was published in Paris in 1806 and went into numerous editions. The references to Lavater's *Essai sur la physiognomonie* are as follows: i, p. 99 ('the extract of creation'); on pathognomy, see 'De la physiognomonie et de la pathognomonique': i, pp 231ff; for 'physiognomical frenzy', see Melissa Percival, *The Appearance of Character: Physiognomy and Facial Expression in Eighteenth-century France* (London, 1999) p. 13.

153 **teeth had more to say about character than smiles**: *L'Art de connaître les hommes*, ii, pp. 244–5 ('Clean, white and well-arranged teeth'); i, p. 177 ('mirror of the courtier'); v, pp. 319–21 ('one of the elements of scorn'); ii, p. 29 ('form of predestination').

154 **more like a still life than a *tableau vivant* of the passions**: rather than invent new technologies of measurement, Lavater adapted existing ones. See the overview of Barbara Maria Stafford, *Body Criticism. Imaging the Unseen in Enlightenment Art and Medicine* (Cambridge, MA, 1993), esp. pp. 84–129.

'Death stops the agitations to which the body is prey while it is united to the soul': *L'Art de connaître les hommes*, v, p. 24. For craniometry, see Marc Renneville, *Le Langage des crânes: une histoire de la phrénologie* (Paris, 2000). See the story of the physionotrace, as described in Halliday, *Facing the Public*, pp. 43–7. Bichat is cited in Laurent Baridon and Martial Guedron, *Corps et arts: physiognomonie et physiologie dans les arts visuels* (Paris, 1999), p. 85.

156 **racial science**: see esp. Pierre Camper, *Dissertation sur les variétés naturelles qui ont pour object l'histoire naturelle, la physiologie et l'anatomie comparée* (Paris, 1791). Blumenbach's ideas can be sampled in English in *The Anthropological Treatises of Johann Friedrich Blumenbach*, ed. Thomas Bendyshe (London, 1865). See David Bindman, *Ape to Apollo: Aesthetics and the Idea of Race in the Eighteenth Century* (Ithaca, NY, 2002).

mystified by women: *Essai sur la physiognomonie*, vii, p. 1. See the discussion in Martine Dumont, 'Le Succès mondain d'une fausse science: la physiognomonie de Johann Kaspar Lavater', *Actes de la recherche en sciences sociales*, 54 (1994), pp. 19–22.

the disciples of alienist Phillippe Pinel within the emergent science of psychiatry: see Sander Gilman, *Seeing the Insane* (New York, 1982); and see Richard T. Gray, *About Face: German Physiognomic Thought from Lavater to Auschwitz* (Detroit, 2004).

an inherent politics in Lavaterian theory: *Essai sur la physiognomonie*, iii, p. 191 ('free like a bird in a cage').

CHAPTER 6

157 **'Monsieur de Charmant from Paris . . . He also distils'**: For Dubois de Chémant's revolutionary trajectory, see Colin Jones, 'French Dentists and English Teeth in the Long Eighteenth Century: A Tale of Two Cities and One Dentist', in Roberta Bivins and John V. Pickstone (eds.), *Medicine, Madness and Social History: Essays in Honour of Roy Porter* (Basingstoke, 2007), esp. pp. 77–9, 88–9. See also Georges Dagen, 'Dubois de Chémant' in Dagen, *Documents pour servir à l'histoire de l'art dentaire en France, principalement à Paris* (Paris, 1925). A legal wrangle in the 1820s saw Dubois justifying his career: see notably *Réfutation des assertions fausses et calomnieuses connues dans un libelle dirigé par M. Audibran, dentiste, contre M. Dubois de Chémant . . .* (no place or date) and *Mémoires pour M. Dubois de Chémant, . . . contre le Lord Egerton, comte de Bridgewater . . .* (no place or date). These pamphlets throw up additional biographical information on his later life. For the estimated price of the dentures, see *Réfutation des assertions*, p. 21 (without fitting costs).

158 **'odourless dentures made of incorruptible paste'**: the patent was registered at the national patent office. See dossier Dubois, September 1791, Institut national de la propriété industrielle (INPI).

individuals eschewed dressing up and flaunting their fidelity to fashion: see esp. Richard Wrigley, *The Politics of Appearances: Representations of Dress in Revolutionary France* (Oxford, 2002), esp. chs. 5, 6.

159 **One-fifth of the community of emigrants**: Kirsty Carpenter, *Refugees of the French Revolution: The Émigrés in London, 1789–1802* (London, 1999), p. 197 and esp. ch 4, 'Soho'.

aristocratic archbishop of Narbonne: Phillip A. Emery and Kevin Wooldridge, *St Pancras Burial Ground: Excavations for St Pancras International, the London Terminus of High Speed 1, 2002–3* (London, 2011), esp. pp. 103–5; and N. Powers, 'Archaeological Evidence for Dental Innovation: An Eighteenth-century Porcelain Dental Prosthesis Belonging to Archbishop Arthur Richard Dillon', *British Dental Journal*, 201 (2006).

160 **the finest-quality pastes**: Robert A. Cohen, 'Messrs Wedgwood and Porcelain Dentures: Correspondence, 1800–15', *British Dental Journal*, 139 (1975).

as widespread as wigs: see pp. 116 and 140 herein. Dubois-Foucou, *Exposé de nouveaux procédés pour la confection des dents dites de composition* (Paris, 1808), p. 39. For the decline in wig-wearing, see Michael Kwass, 'Big Hair: A Wig History of Consumption in Eighteenth-century France', *American Historical Review*, 111 (2006). The evidence about Dubois's sales come from different versions of his publicity brochure, cited herein, note to page 136 herein. For 'dents de Paris', see Louis Laforgue, *Théorie et pratique de l'art du dentiste*, 2 vols. (Paris, 1810), ii, p. 101.

Dubois de Chémant's originality . . . was generally acknowledged: besides Edward Jenner, the discoverer of smallpox vaccination, other endorsements came from, *inter alios*, John Hunter in England, and medical luminaries Vicq d'Azyr, Dessault and Geoffroy in Paris. For da Fonzi, Pierre Baron, 'Dental Practice in Paris', in Christine Hillam, *Dental Practice in Europe at the End of the Eighteenth Century* (London, 2003), pp. 125–6. For denture sales, see Christine Hillam, *Brass Plate and Brazen Impudence: Dental Practice in the Provinces, 1755–1855* (Liverpool, 1991), p. 142.

Joseph Murphy in 1811: Joseph Murphy, *Natural History of the Human Teeth, with a Treatise on their Diseases* (London, 1811), p. 133.

161 **criticisms soon built up**: Joseph Fox, *The History and Treatment of Diseases of the Teeth, the Gums and the Alveolar Processes* (London, 1806), pp. 127, 130; and John Gray, *Preservation of the Teeth, Indispensable to Comfort, Appearance, Health and Longevity* (London, 1838), p. 37, n. 6.

the Rabelaisian humour of the early modern period: see pp. 23–8 herein.

162 **Rowlandson who was in Paris in 1787**: see John Hayes, 'Thomas Rowlandson', *Oxford Dictionary of National Biography*, ⟨http://oxforddnb,com/view/aticle/24221m⟩.

163 **she left France in disgust**: see the sources cited herein, note for p. 134, for Vigée Le Brun's Revolutionary trajectory.

'light and lively gaiety . . . now it is in general sly, grimacing, cruel or stupid': Félicité de Genlis, *Dictionnaire critique et raisonné des étiquettes de la cour ou l'esprit des étiquettes et des usages anciens* (Paris, 1818), p. 238.

'I seasoned [them] . . . as people then used to say', he noted: Jacques-Louis David, cited in Percival, *The Appearance of Character*, p. 109. For David's facial tumour, see T. J. Clark, 'Gross David with the Swoln Cheek: An Essay in Self-Portraiture', in *Rediscovering History: Culture, Politics and the Psyche*, ed. Michael Roth (Stanford, 1994).

164 **the Gothic style**: the best introduction to the theme is now Catriona Seth (ed.), *Imaginaires gothiques: aux sources du roman noir* (Paris, 2010). Other works which provide the English angle include David Punter, *The Gothic* (London, 2006); and Emma J. Clery, *The Rise of Supernatural Fiction* (Cambridge, 1995).

a new and different sensibility as regards the smile: I am drawing here again on the Frantext-ARTFL data-base: see p. 185 and note for p. 62 herein.

The notorious marquis de Sade: Sade is cited from his *Idée sur les romans*, ed. O. Uzanne (Paris, 1878), pp. 32–3. Nodier is cited in Alexandre Minski, *Le Préromantisme* (Paris, 1998), p. 53.

165 **the first modern melodrama in France**: Peter Brooks, *The Melodramatic Imagination: Balzac, James, Melodrama and the Mode of Excess* (London, 1976); and Sarah Hibberd (ed.), *Melodramatic Voices Understanding Music Drama* (Aldershot, 2011), esp. Kate Astbury, 'Music in Pixérécourt's Early Dramas'.

166 **Honoré-Jean Riouffe's highly popular *Mémoires d'un détenu***: Henri-Jean Riouffe, *Mémoire d'un détenu, pour servir à l'histoire de la tyrannie de Robespierre* (Paris, 1794). This not only went into numerous editions but was also anthologized in collections of writings about prison life under the Terror. For *Dolbeuse*, see p. 164 herein.

the severed head of Charlotte Corday: Daniel Arasse, *The Guillotine and the Terror* (London, 1989), p. 37. See p. 42 for the experiment, which was recounted in 1797. See

H. Fleischmann, *La Guillotine en 1793* (Paris, 1908), pp. 53–8: 'Le tête coupée souffra-t-elle?'

an image captured by the artist Anne-Louis Girodet: Girodet's sketch is shown alongside similar drawings of decapitated heads by Jacques-Louis David in Thomas Crow, *Emulation: Making Artists for Revolutionary France* (London, 1994), p. 120.

some of Madame Vigée Le Brun's sitters: see the discussion of these, a number of whom are shown smiling, pp. 135–6. A number of these have the 'Vigée Le Brun smile', but they were not exhibited at the Salon.

167 **The fate of the princesse de Lamballe**: Mercier's account is in his *Le Nouveau Paris*, ed. Jean-Claude Bonnet (Paris, 1994), pp. 98–9. See Antoine de Baecque's account in his *La Gloire et l'effroi: sept morts sous la Terreur* (Paris, 1997): 'La Princesse de Lamballe, ou le sexe massacré', pp. 77ff. De Baecque shows how Michelet in particular was responsible for the legend's durability across the century.

the death of Robespierre: Jones, 'The Smile of the Tiger', pp. 32–5.

168 **Revolutionary assemblies set out to improve . . . medical education and training**: the major reforms in medical education and institutions are outlined (though with little reference to dentistry) in Mathew Ramsey, *Professional and Popular Medicine in France, 1770–1830: The Social World of Medical Practice* (Cambridge, 1988), esp. pp. 71ff.; Mathew Ramsey, 'The Politics of Professional Monopoly in Nineteenth-century Medicine: The French Model and its Rivals', in Gerald L. Geison (ed.), *Professions and the French State, 1700–1900* (Philadelphia, PA, 1984); Toby Gelfand, *Professionalizing Modern Medicine: Paris Surgeons and Medical Science and Institutions in the Eighteenth Century* (Westport, CT, 1980); Dora B. Weiner, *The Citizen-patient in Revolutionary and Imperial Paris* (Baltimore, MD, 1993); and Caroline Hannaway and Ann La Berge (eds.), *Constructing Paris Medicine* (Amsterdam, 1998). On issues of specialization, George Weisz, 'The Development of Medical Specialisation in Nineteenth-century Paris', in Ann La Berge and Mordechai Feingold (eds.), *French Medical Culture in the Nineteenth Century* (Amsterdam, 1994). For the impact of the Revolution on dentistry, see Pierre Baron, 'Dental Practioners in France at the End of the Eighteenth Century', in Christine Hillam (ed.), *Dental Practice in Europe at the End of the Eighteenth Century* (Amsterdam, 2003). For the 'birth of the clinic', see the classic Michel Foucault, *La Naissance de la clinique: un archéologie du regard médical* (Paris, 1963).

169 **'with the abolition of the communities of surgeons . . . dentists will have no future existence'**: François Vidal and Philippe Caron, *Histoire d'un diplôme: de l'expert pour les dents au docteur en chirurgie dentaire, 1699–1892*, 10 fascicules (Paris, 1994), p. 133.

'the apanage of the empiric . . . who can garner the confidence of the sick': Louis Laforgue, *Dix-sept articles, relatifs aux maladies des dents* (Paris, Year VIII = 1800]), p. 22. There is a sizeable ministerial dossier covering Laforgue's efforts to attain legitimacy between 1806 and 1815 in AN F8 158. For similar efforts by Delabarre in 1816, see AN AJ16 6998, and AN F8 150).

170 **'the everyday and commonplace'**: cited in Gelfand, *Professionalizing Modern Medicine*, p. 170.

in the manner of the old *chirurgiens-dentistes* of the *Ancien Régime*: see the dossier at AN F8 161. For the following quotation, AN AJ 16 6701 (dossier Delabarre). The medical faculties when consulted on this were always utterly recalcitrant to concessions to the dentists. (See AN F 8, *passim* and AN AJ16 6998; and for the Montpellier faculty AN F8 155). For the 1820s and 1840s and beyond (besides the general histories of dentistry cited herein, note to page 21 herein), see Thomas Davis, *De la réglementation de l'art dentaire en France* (Paris, n.d.), pp. 10ff.; François Vidal, *Histoire d'un diplôme*; and François Vidal,

'Regards sur l'histoire de l'art dentaire, de l'époque romaine à nos jours', available at ⟨http://www.academiedentaire.fr/attachments/0000/0095/CH_VIDAL.pdf⟩.

171 **the paraphernalia of daily mouth care**: the archives of the French national patent office INPI (Institut national de la propriété industrielle) are useful here. The INPI dossiers are arranged by date and name, and can often be cross-referred to dossiers from the Ministry of the Interior in the Archives Nationales. Some representative and informative dossiers include: INPI Audibran Year VII—denture glue (also AN F12 1022A); INPI Ricci 1807—denture glue (also AN F12 1010); INPI Cambon 1815—toothache remedy (also AN F12 1024B); INPI Brousson 1816—sea-shell dentures (also AN F12 1026B); INPI Naudin 1819—toothbrush; INPI Arman 1820—dentifrice. For toothbrushes see too Sacha Bogopolsky, *Itinéraire culturel et technologique de la brosse à dents* (Paris, 1999).

Dubois-Foucou, Louis XVI's dentist: Baron, 'Dental Practice in Paris', p. 123. The nineteenth-century story of French dentistry can be followed in Caron and Vidal, *Histoire d'un diplôme*. See too Carlo Gysel, *Histoire de l'orthodontie: ses origines, son archéologie et ses précurseurs* (Antwerp, 1997), esp. 532–9.

Philadelphia-trained Thomas Evans: Anthony D. Branch, 'Thomas W. Evans, American Dentist in Paris, 1847–97', PhD thesis, University of California Santa Barbara, 1981; *The Memoirs of Dr. Thomas W. Evans: Recollections of the Second French Empire*, ed. Edward A. Crane (London, 1905); Gerald Carson, *The Dentist and the Empress: The Adventures of Dr. Tom Evans in Gas-lit Paris* (Boston, 1983).

the new product champion of dental science: the emergence of US dentistry as world leader is covered in all the general histories of dentistry.

173 *classes dangereuses*: see the classic treatment of this theme by Louis Chevalier, *Classes laborieuses, classes dangereuses à Paris au XIXe siècle* (Paris, 1958). See too Priscilla Parkhurst Ferguson, *Paris as Revolution: Writing the Nineteenth-century City* (Berkeley, CA, 1994); and Chris Prendergast, *Paris and the Nineteenth Century* (Oxford, 1994).

'affecting and beautiful': 'caressant et beau': Chateaubriand, *Mémoires d'outre-tombe*, ed. Maurice Levaillant and Georges Moulinier, 2 vols. (Paris, 1951), i, p. 490. See generally Xavier Riaud, 'Napoleon and his Teeth', *International Napoleonic Society* (no place or date), available at <http://www.napoleonicsociety.com/english/denta.htm>.

174 **'the great masculine renunciation'**: John Carl Flugel, 'The Great Masculine Renunciation', in Flugel, *The Psychology of Clothes* (London 1966).

'separate spheres' . . . a world of family, domesticity, and private virtues: from a large bibliography, see esp. Joan Landes, *Women and the Public Sphere in the Age of the French Revolution* (Ithaca, NY, 1988).

175 **it is striking how rarely that freedom was taken up**: David Sonstroem's excellent survey, 'Teeth in Victorian Art', *Victorian Literature and Culture*, 29 (2001) confirms that the long-established negative conventions about the open mouth were still largely in place in Victorian Britain. It would be instructive to compare this against the situation in France—which seems quite similar in fact.

POSTSCRIPT

177 **the twentieth-century Smile Revolution**: the subject awaits its historian. The general overview by Angus Trumble, *A Brief History of the Smile* (New York, 2004) provides a good overview of present as well as past.

very much a minority taste: this is an impressionistic judgement. On the Pre-Raphaelites, one only has to browse the exhibition catalogue, *Pre-Raphaelites: Victorian Avant-Garde*, ed. Tim Barrington et al. (London, 2012). Despite the exhibition title, the show failed to notice the avant-garde acceptance of the display of teeth by the movement's practitioners. See David Sonstroem, 'Teeth in Victorian Art', *Victorian Literature and Culture*, 29 (2001).

linked to the grimace: see Martial Guédron, *L'Art de la grimace: cinq siècles d'excès de visage* (Paris, 2011).

178 **Queen Victoria was famously 'not amused'**: the images may be seen in Richard Ormond and Carol Blackett-Ord, *Franz Xaver Winterhalter and the Courts of Europe, 1830–70*, Exh. cat. National Portrait Gallery (London, 1987). The full listing of his work in *Franz-Xaver Winterhalter (1805–83)* (Gouesnou, 2011) shows he completed over a dozen portraits of Victoria either singly or with family members.

179 **Darwin's image of a 'smiling ape'**: Charles Darwin, *The Expression of the Emotions in Man and Animals*, ed. Paul Ekman (London, 1999), p. 135. See p. 6 herein.

improved camera technology: I am drawing in this section on the excellent and comprehensive treatment in Robin Lenman (ed.), *The Oxford Companion to the Photograph* (Oxford, 2005). See too E. A. McCauley, *Likenesses: Portrait Photography in Europe, 1850–70* (Albuquerque, NM, 1981); Audrey Linkman, *The Victorians: Photographic Portraits* (London, 1992); and Graham Clarke (ed.), *The Portrait in Photography* (London, 1992). For the links between technology and popular culture, see too F. E. H. Schroeder, 'Say Cheese! The Revolution in the Aesthetics of the Smile', *Journal of Popular Culture*, 32 (1998).

180 **Jacques-Henri Lartigue**: see esp. Kevin Moore, *Jacques-Henri Lartigue: The Invention of an Artist* (London, 2004) and *Lartigue: album d'une vie (1894–1986)*, ed. Martine d'Astier (Paris, 2012).

forensic photography: Alphonse Bertillon, *La Photographie judiciaire* (Paris, 1890); Matt Matsuda, *The Memory of the Modern* (Oxford, 1996); Jane Caplan and John Torpey (eds.), *Documenting Individual Identity: The Development of State Practices in the Modern Era* (London, 2001): esp. Martine Kaluszinski, 'Republican Identity: Bertillonage as Government Technique'; and Peter Hamilton and Roger Hargreaves, *The Beautiful and the Damned: The Creation of Identity in Nineteenth-century Photography* (London, 2001).

film and the associated medium of studio photography: John Kobal, *The Art of the Great Hollywood Portrait Photographers* (London, 1920); and Joel W. Finler, *Hollywood Movie Stills: The Golden Age* (London, 1995).

182 **enormously influential *How to Win Friends and Influence People***: The work has allegedly sold 15 million copies worldwide.

Charles de Gaulle: thanks to Julian Jackson on this point.

the USA led the way: besides all general histories of dentistry, see now Alyssa Picard, *Making the American Mouth: Dentists and Public Health in the Twentieth Century* (Brunswick, NJ, 2009).

Marilyn Monroe dyptych, also in 1962: see the discussion in Richard Brilliant, *Portraiture* (London, 2002), pp. 49, 134–7.

183 **the emergence of some social practices**: some guidelines are offered in the exhibition catalogue, *Signes du corps* (Paris, 2004) This is the kind of development, however, that may well best be followed on the worldwide web and on social media.

Picture Acknowledgements

0.1 © RMN-Grand Palais (musée du Louvre) / Franck Raux

0.2 Wellcome Library, London

0.3 Wellcome Library, London

0.4 National Library of Medicine (NLM)

0.5 *Un Petit Souper à la Parisienne, or A Family of Sans-Culottes Refreshing after the Fatigues of the Day*, published by Hannah Humphrey in 1792 (hand-coloured etching), Gillray, James (1757–1815) / © Courtesy of the Warden and Scholars of New College, Oxford / The Bridgeman Art Library

1.1 *Louis XIV in Royal Costume*, 1701 (oil on canvas), Rigaud, Hyacinthe (1659–1743) / Louvre, Paris, France / Giraudon / The Bridgeman Art Library

1.2 Bibliothèque nationale de France

1.3 Theatre scene, title page from collection of works, by Tabarin (1584–1626), 1858 edition / De Agostini Picture Library / G. Dagli Orti / The Bridgeman Art Library

2.1 © RMN-Grand Palais (musée du Louvre) / Thierry Le Mage

2.2 *Marie-Adelaide, daughter of Louis XV, as Flora*, 1742 (oil on canvas), Nattier, Jean-Marc (1685–1766) / Galleria degli Uffizi, Florence, Italy / The Bridgeman Art Library

2.3 *Madame de Pompadour at her Toilette*, c.1760 (oil on canvas), Boucher, François (1703–70) / Fogg Art Museum, Harvard University Art Museums, USA / The Bridgeman Art Library

2.4 © RMN-Grand Palais (musée du Louvre) / Madeleine Coursaget

2.5 © RMN-Grand Palais (musée du Louvre) / Michèle Bellot

2.6 © RMN-Grand Palais (musée du Louvre) / image RMN-GP

2.7 © RMN-Grand Palais (musée du Louvre) / Madeleine Coursaget

2.8 *The Club Foot*, 1642 (oil on canvas), Ribera, Jusepe de (lo Spagnoletto) (c.1590–1652) / Louvre, Paris, France / Giraudon / The Bridgeman Art Library

2.9 *The Beggars' Brawl*, c.1625–30 (oil on canvas), Tour, Georges de la (1593–1652) / J. Paul Getty Museum, Los Angeles, USA / The Bridgeman Art Library

2.10 *The Buffoon Calabacillas*, mistakenly called *The Idiot of Coria*, 1639 (oil on canvas), Velázquez, Diego Rodriguez de Silva y (1599–1660) / Prado, Madrid, Spain / Giraudon / The Bridgeman Art Library

2.11 *The Shrimp Girl*, *c*.1745 (oil on canvas), Hogarth, William (1697–1764) / National Gallery, London, UK / The Bridgeman Art Library

2.12 Bibliothèque nationale de France

2.13 Julie and Saint-Preux, illustration from 'La Nouvelle Héloise' by Jean-Jacques Rousseau (1712–78) (engraving), Monsiau, Nicolas Andre (1754–1837) (after) / Bibliotheque des Arts Décoratifs, Paris, France / Archives Charmet / The Bridgeman Art Library

2.14 *The well-beloved mother*, *c*.1770 (brush & grey ink wash with black chalk), Greuze, Jean Baptiste (1725–1805) / Art Gallery of New South Wales, Sydney, Australia / The Bridgeman Art Library

3.1 Bibliothèque nationale de France

3.2 Bibliothèque nationale de France

3.3 Wellcome Library, London

4.1 The British Library

4.2 Wellcome Library, London

4.3 © RMN-Grand Palais (musée du Louvre) / Michèle Bellot

4.4 Wellcome Library, London

5.1 Self-Portrait, 1737 (oil on canvas), La Tour, Quentin de (1704–88) / Private Collection / Photo © Christie's Images / The Bridgeman Art Library

5.2 © RMN-Grand Palais (musée du Louvre) / Gérard Blot

5.3 Portrait bust of Madame Houdon, the wife of the artist, 1786 (plaster), Houdon, Jean-Antoine (1741–1828) / Louvre, Paris, France / Peter Willi / The Bridgeman Art Library

5.4 Madame Pierre Sériziat (née Émilie Pecoul) with her Son, Émile (b.1793) 1795 (oil on panel), David, Jacques Louis (1748–1825) / Louvre, Paris, France / Giraudon / The Bridgeman Art Library

5.5 Wellcome Library, London

5.6 Wellcome Library, London

5.7 © The Trustees of the British Museum

5.8 Wellcome Library, London

5.9 Wellcome Library, London

6.1 Wellcome Library, London

6.2 Getty Images

6.3 bpk | Hamburger Kunsthalle | Christoph Irrgang

6.4 Bibliothèque nationale de France

6.5 Science Museum London/Wellcome Images

7.1 Queen Victoria, 1843 (oil on canvas), Winterhalter, Franz Xaver (1805–73) / The Royal Collection © 2014 Her Majesty Queen Elizabeth II / The Bridgeman Art Library

7.2 Wellcome Library, London

7.3 Marilyn, left hand side, 1964 (silk screen), Warhol, Andy (1928–87) / Private Collection / The Bridgeman Art Library © 2014 The Andy Warhol Foundation for the Visual Arts, Inc. / Artists's Rights Society (ARS), New York and DACS, London

Index